THE HANDBOOK
For Relationship Selling

Acquire the Selling Focus

Dr. David Lill and Jennifer Lill

Sundog, Ltd. • Nashville, TN 37206

The Handbook for Relationship Selling:
Acquire the Selling Focus.

Dr. David J. Lill
Jennifer K. Lill

 Published by Sundog, Ltd., Nashville, TN 37206

This book may be purchased for educational, business, or sales promotional use. For information or to order, please contact Sundog, Ltd., or Express Media Corporation, Inc., 1419 Donelson Pike, Nashville, TN 37217. Phone: 800-336-2631; email: fulfillment@expressmedia.com

FIRST EDITION

The Library of Congress Cataloging-in-Publication data

Lill, David

Lill, Jennifer

The Handbook for Relationship Selling: Acquire the Selling Focus / Dr. David J. Lill / Jennifer K. Lill. – 1st ed.

ISBN 1-932203-95-8 (paper)

1. Business 2. Sales training 3. Career development 4. Self help

I.Title.

Library of Congress Control Number: 2004110396

Special Thanks to:

Chris Cunningham - Cover Design
The Warehouse Multimedia Studios
Phone: 615-851-9179
www.thewrhse.com

Jolene Reynolds - Layout Design
Express Media, Inc.
Phone: 615-360-6400
www.expressmedia.com

BRIEF CONTENTS

TABLE OF CONTENTS

TABLE OF CONTENTS

PART III Gaining Knowledge, Preparing, and Planning for the Presentation

PART IV The Face-to-Face Relationship Model of Selling

TABLE OF CONTENTS

Preface

INTRODUCTION

The Handbook for Relationship Selling is your guide for success in today's modern selling environment. Becoming a great salesperson involves no less a commitment to your profession than does becoming a great physician, lawyer, or teacher. Read this book cover to cover, and then read it periodically to refresh in your mind the principles of "relationship selling". Before you know it, applying the principles will be natural and become a part of who you are as a sales professional. Success begins by taking a single step. It begins by learning the correct principles and gaining the proper knowledge to lead you down the right path to success. We believe that path to your success begins here.

Your ability to develop and maintain long-term customer relationships is the foundation for your success as a salesperson. For your customer, a buying decision usually means a decision to enter into a long-term relationship with you and your company. It is very much like a "business marriage." *The Handbook for Relationship Selling* shows you how to bring about that union.

Because of the complexity of most products and services today, the relationship can be more important than the product being sold. Customers don't always know the ingredients or components of your product, how your company functions, or how they will be treated after money changes hands, but they can make an assessment about you and about the relationship that has occurred over the course of the selling process. Ultimately, customers' decisions are based on the

Relationship Selling

- The traditional role of selling has evolved from the art of persuasion to the psychology of relationship selling.

- The relationship cycle of selling begins with approaching the prospect, discovering needs, presenting your product or service as the solution, overcoming objections, and gaining commitment. Service after the sale completes the cycle.

- The purpose of the relationship approach to selling is to discover the needs or problems of the prospect. You become a solutions provider! It is customer-oriented and requires extensive knowledge of the prospect.

- Build relationships through customer-oriented continuous quality improvement. This is an outside-in approach, encouraging the mind-set that every one inside and outside the company is a customer.

- Team selling fosters relationships through encouraging a sharing of ideas, resources, capabilities, and responsibilities.

Part II

Cultivating an Ethical Climate and Developing Communication Skills

"IT'S OK, KID, EVERYBODY DOES IT"

by Jack Griffin

When Johnny was six years old, he was with his father when they were caught speeding. His father handed the officer a twenty-dollar bill with his driver's license. "It's OK, son," his father said as they drove off. "Everybody does it."

When he was eight, he was present at a family council presided over by Uncle George, on the surest means to shave points off the income tax return. "It's OK, kid," his uncle said. "Everybody does it."

When he was nine, his mother took him to his first theater production. The box office man couldn't find any seats until his mother discovered an extra $5 in her purse. "It's OK, son," she said. "Everybody does it."

When he was 12, he broke his glasses on the way to school. His Aunt Francine persuaded the insurance company that they had been stolen and they collected $75. "It's OK, son," she said. "Everybody does it."

When he was 15, he made right guard on the high school football team. His coach showed him how to block and at the same time grab the opposing end by the shirt so the official couldn't see it. "It's OK, son," the coach said. "Everybody does it."

When he was 16, he took his first summer job at the supermarket. His assignment was to put the overripe strawberries in the bottom of the boxes and the good ones on top where they would show. "It's OK, son," the manager said. "Everybody does it."

When he was 18, Johnny and a neighbor applied for a college scholarship. Johnny was a marginal student. His neighbor was in the top three percent of his class, but couldn't play right guard. Johnny got the scholarship. "It's OK, son," his parents said. "Everybody does it."

When he was 19, he was approached by an upperclassman who offered him the test answers for $50. "It's OK, kid," he said. "Everybody does it."

Johnny was caught and sent home in disgrace. "How could you do this to your mother and me?" his father said. "You never learned anything like this at home." His aunt and uncle were also shocked.

If there's one thing the adult world can't stand, it's a kid who cheats.

Chapter 3

Ethical Issues in Selling

- Develop principles for ethical behavior
- Recognize influences on ethical behavior
- Your role in your company's behavior toward customers
- How to handle questionable ethical behavior

THE ETHICAL DILEMMA

Katherine Lewis feels as though she is being torn apart. The pharmaceutical company she works for is pressuring her to meet a sales quota twenty percent higher than last year's. She is a single parent with two children to support, and she sees an opportunity to meet her sales quota if she can beat out a competitor for a large order from a drugstore chain. She is tempted to plant some carefully worded negative comments about the competitor in the ear of the store chain's purchasing agent. What should she do? What would you do?

Katherine Lewis is facing a situation that falls in the category of ethical considerations. Because salespeople are relatively free and independent operators, they may encounter more ethical dilemmas than many other business people. For this reason, you must be clear on your own ethical standards before getting caught up in something that escalates beyond your control.

Today's renewed interest in ethics can be used by sales professionals to their advantage. We have this heightened interest in ethical issues due to the shocking, unethical, and immoral activities of a variety of business and government leaders and other public figures. It is not companies, institutions and political organizations, however, that are unethical; individual people are unethical. Ethics is a personal matter. The ethics of a business, government, or other organizations is merely a reflection of the combined value systems of its members.

Some say that business ethics is an *oxymoron*, a contradiction in terms. They suggest that business has no ethics or that ethics is something that people worry about on Sunday and not when they are out selling in the real world. This thinking is ludicrous! The notion that honest salespeople finish last is poisonous; in addition, it is untrue. Unethical behavior is ultimately self-destructive; it generates more unethical conduct until a person hits rock bottom financially, spiritually, and morally.

The Origin of Ethics

A legal standard is enforced by laws and statutes, but an ethical standard is an outgrowth of the customs and attitudes of a society. Most of us have a shared concept of what we mean by

Ken Blanchard and Norman Vincent Peale

One of the significant books published in the field of business ethics is *The Power of Ethical Management*. This small book by Dr. Kenneth Blanchard and Dr. Norman Vincent Peale is especially significant for salespeople, who are on the firing line of relations between companies and their customers and clients.

Few individuals have had as great an impact on company management as has Kenneth Blanchard, co-author of *The One Minute Manager* and *The One Minute Manager Library*. Dr. Norman Vincent Peale has written thirty-four books, including *The Power of Positive Thinking*, one of the most widely circulated books ever published. He was also the founder of the monthly magazine *Guideposts*, which has a circulation of sixteen million.

The basic message of *The Power of Ethical Management* is simple: You don't have to cheat to win! Blanchard and Peale tell us that many people demand immediate tangible evidence that ethical conduct works, but such evidence is often not available. In fact, you may actually get farther in the short run by cheating. But in the long run, where it really counts, you never gain by unethical conduct. They remind us that "nice guys may appear to finish last, but usually they are running in a different race." Unethical behavior occurs in sales because people forget the real purpose of professional selling — to fill the needs of others.

Salespeople sometimes say near the end of the day, "I ought to make one more sales call before I go home. I wonder who I might be able to see this late?" Blanchard and Peale suggest that the better question might be, "I wonder if there is someone else I can help before I go home?" When you focus on your purpose—solving the problems of clients and helping customers be more successful and more profitable—you understand the need for ethical behavior. Cheating, lying, and short-changing the customer on service may bring a satisfactory profit today, but is a sure way to court failure for the future.

ethics, but defining it in a way that everyone would accept is hard. Essentially, ethics is a systematic effort to judge human behavior as right or wrong in terms of two major criteria: truth and justice.

The root of the word ethics derives from the Greek word *ethos*, which means the character or sentiment of the community. A society cannot exist unless people agree fundamentally on what is right and wrong, just and unjust. The three most important value-forming institutions in America are family, religious institutions, and school. Many people believe that the decreasing strength and changing roles of these three institutions have produced a society with lower ethical standards than those of its earlier history.

Why Behave Ethically? Guidelines for Ethical Behavior

Today, no matter which specific method of ethical decision making is followed, most Americans embrace three basic guidelines: universal nature, truth telling, and responsibility for one's actions. Without them, the free enterprise system itself would be threatened and any kind of business exchange would be difficult. Our society would disintegrate into a "dog-eat-dog" environment.

Universal Nature. The universal nature guideline is a derivation of the Golden Rule. We want others to play by the same basic rules by which we would play in a similar situation. This guideline sets up a basic level of trust between people and makes life predictable.

Truth Telling. A salesperson needs to believe that what others say is true. The idea of honesty may originate in a set of rules we have been taught, but truth telling makes sense on purely logical grounds as well. Trust facilitates cooperation, buyer commitment, and the development and maintenance of long-term client-salesperson relationships.

Responsibility for Your Actions. President Harry S. Truman kept a sign on his desk stating, "The buck stops here." He reminded himself that he had no one to blame when things went wrong. Individuals may choose to live by this attitude and accept personal responsibility for their actions, or they may attempt to follow the impulse of the moment and blame someone else for the consequences. If we and our society demonstrated a higher level of trust and credibility based on universal willingness to accept responsibility for personal actions, our system would work more efficiently and in a less suspicious atmosphere.

Personal Accountability

INFLUENCES ON A SALESPERSON'S ETHICS

Although individual salespeople each have a basic value system and may know what is right and wrong, they encounter many new influences and experience many new pressures on the job. Nothing creates more direction for employee's decision-making, or a better balance for judgment than ethical guidelines. Knowing in advance what can be expected and having a feel for how to balance and integrate them into a personal code of ethics make handling ethical decisions easier.

Company Code of Ethics

Many companies have codes of ethics and adhere strictly to the code as part of corporate culture. Companies may also have ethics training for new employees, as well as an ethics committee to rule on ethical dilemmas.

The government has also increased its role in ethical issues. Federal sentencing guidelines have been established that help reduce the penalties for companies, based in part on what a company has done to prevent ethical problems in the past. Driven by these government actions and fear of retribution, companies are paying more attention than ever to the behavior of their employees. Ethics is a monetary issue as well! A survey conducted by the Center for Business Ethics at Bentley College reports that of 279 top U.S. companies responding to their survey, 208 had written codes of conduct and 99 had formal training programs in ethics for their employees. Seventeen have telephone "hot lines" to assist employees with ethical problems. Typical issues covered in these ethics programs include:

1. Using expense accounts.
2. Handling the decision about the appropriateness of gift giving.
3. Dealing with a prospect's unethical demands.
4. Keeping product performance or delivery promises.
5. Ensuring that you do not push unnecessary products onto a customer.

Implementing a code of conduct statement communicates to your customers that you and your company have high moral standards. The findings by the Ethics Resource Center and the Society for Human Resources Management show widespread usage of ethics statements: 84 percent of surveyed companies have codes of conduct, and 45 percent have ethics offices. These guidelines can only be effective if sales managers are reinforcing them on a daily basis — traveling with reps, guiding them through the sales process, and engaging them in open, honest dialogue.

Executives as Role Models

The likelihood that unacceptable selling practices will occur is affected by how executives behave. If a sales manager gives the impression that you must do anything possible to make more sales, you may assume that dealing unethically is acceptable in order to succeed. Often, an organization's culture influences how you behave toward your clients. Sales managers must emphasize ethical selling behavior in words and actions. The company's top executives must ensure that the managers do not put excessive pressure on their salespeople. If the CEO comes around once a year with a pep talk on moral behavior but proceeds the rest of the year to use underhanded methods of doing business, it is possible to get a mixed message.

> "As a manager the important thing is not what happens when you are there, but what happens when you are not there."
>
> — Dr. Kenneth Blanchard

Examples Set by Colleagues and Competitors

You may sometimes discover that colleagues and/or competitors are acting unethically. Imagine that you are riding in a cab one day, and a colleague asks the driver to provide a receipt for expense account purposes and to indicate a figure higher than the actual fare. As an observer, do you join in the activity, rebuke the colleague, report the colleague (commonly called *blowing the whistle*) or ignore it? A customer reports that a competitor has said you have an alcohol problem and are therefore undependable. Do you simply deny the charge, or do you retaliate by making detrimental remarks about your competitor?

The Bottom Line

Bottom line profit is one of the most powerful influences on your own income and that of your company. Saul Gellerman, in explaining why good people can make poor ethical choices, says that "contrary to popular mythology, maximizing profits is a company's second priority — not its first. The first is ensuring its survival." Its survival will surely be compromised if salespeople take casual views of the legal and ethical implications of their behavior. The company's short-term profits may be maximized by unethical behavior, but the company's very existence could be threatened if it were hit with huge fines or unwanted exposure in the media. Although short-term profits are important for both the company and its salespeople, the long-term success and good name of the company must always be the first priority.

Groupthink and Gamesmanship

Groupthink refers to the pressure exerted on salespeople to be part of the group and not to buck the system — to be team players, no matter what. Being a team player is good if the team has ethical goals and plays by ethical rules, but if the group's thinking contradicts your own personal code of ethics, you must weigh your options carefully.

Gamesmanship is becoming totally caught up in winning simply for the sheer joy of victory and a dislike of losing. Much of our culture nurtures this type of competitive spirit — from winning the high school football game to beating a friend at chess or golf. The typical gamesman in selling looks for shortcuts and is willing to use any technique to sell a product or service. To the gamesman, winning means doing whatever is necessary to make the sale. The danger of gamesmanship becomes quite clear — the temptation to cross over the line into unethical or illegal behavior.

DEVELOPING A PERSONAL CODE OF ETHICS

Clearly many competing forces that influence your decisions have an ethical dimension. Situations often arise in which a clear right or wrong is not readily apparent and discretion in behavior is up to the individual. Because the influences that come to bear upon you do not always agree and because conflicting demands are numerous, you must develop a personal code of ethics.

Responsibility to Self

In the final analysis, the still, small voice of conscience is the arbiter of conflicting ethical claims. It provides the ability to say that you have made the best decision under the circumstances and take full responsibility for it. If you have personal integrity, then you cannot be dishonest with others — company, competitors, or customers.

Responsibility to the Company

Salespeople sometimes rationalize that cheating here or there in dealing with the company would not hurt. After all, the company makes lots of money and what you do would never be noticed. Several areas particularly lend themselves to temptations to be less than ethical.

Accuracy in Expense Accounts. Often padding expense accounts is relatively easy. A salesperson can add extra mileage, submit charges for a meal that was actually eaten at a friend's house, or take friends out to dinner and report the charge as entertaining customers. As a practical matter, it unnecessarily increases the costs to the company and may put it at a competitive disadvantage.

Honesty in Using Time and Resources. The temptation to do some shopping between sales calls, to linger over a third cup of coffee in a restaurant, and to sleep late in a hotel room are examples of ways a salesperson may misuse time. No time card is punched, and slipping in personal time may be relatively easy. This ultimately hurts both the salesperson and the company because fewer sales calls are made.

It is estimated that losses of goods and cash to worker theft have reached $120 billion a year. Misusing resources such as automobiles and selling samples for one's own profit hurt the company. These kinds of dishonest activities decrease the company's profits.

Accuracy in Filling Out Order Forms. Certain kinds of compensation plans, particularly contests, may tempt salespeople to withhold or delay orders or to oversell some items. This practice ultimately hurts the company because it results in unhappy customers. It also takes unfair advantage of co-workers who compete fairly to win contests.

Representing the Company. You are the spokesperson for the company and for that reason must accurately represent products and services and deliver the kind of follow-up service that the company promises. Exaggerating the capabilities of a product or failing to point out any problems that might be associated with its use is unethical and can be disastrous to a long-term relationship with a customer. In some instances it is also illegal, with the potential for causing both you and the company serious legal consequences.

Responsibility to Competitors

Being honest and refraining from taking unfair advantage are the basic guidelines when dealing with competitors. Making untrue, derogatory comments about competitors or their products is poor business. At the very least, the legal implications of this behavior simply make the risks too great. In the same sense, pressing a competitor's salesperson for information at a trade show in order to steal the competitor's customers is not ethical.

Some salespeople go so far as to use sabotage, espionage, and dirty tricks to gain unfair advantage over a competitor. These tactics include hiding the competitor's products on a display shelf and planting "spies" in a business to hear a competitor's sales presentation. Persuading a customer to put out a fake request for bids to see what bids competitors would submit is another unfair tactic sometimes practiced. Instead, the company should want to gain customers fairly by providing quality products and superior service.

Responsibility to Customers

Behaving honestly and providing quality information and services are the ingredients for establishing mutually satisfying relationships with customers. Fortunately, the stereotype of the silver-tongued, flattering, deceptive salesperson is disappearing. Still, many opportunities for unethical tactics exist.

Overselling and Misrepresenting Products. Some salespeople persuade customers to buy more than they need because the salesperson needs to meet a quota or wants to win a trip to the Caribbean. Overselling eventually catches up with the salesperson because customers realize that they have more than they need. In addition, repeat sales probably won't be possible for a very long time.

Keeping Confidences. Because of the relationship between you and the customer, you may be privy to valuable information about the customer. That information could be very useful to other customers, and providing it might ingratiate you to them. Failing to keep confidences is, of course, unethical, and eventually it results in a reputation for you as an untrustworthy gossip.

Giving Gifts. Although giving a customer a token gift as a thank-you or as a reminder of you and your company is customary, the intent with which a gift is given usually reveals its ethical or unethical nature. If a gift is a way to get business or a bribe, then it is unethical and may well be illegal. The value of the gift in comparison to the sale is also something to consider. According to *Business & Incentives* magazine, approximately $3.5 billion is spent on business gifts yearly. Ultimately, gift giving should be practiced only when you feel that gratitude in a specific situation should be genuinely and ethically expressed.

Entertaining Clients. Policies regarding entertainment are similar to those that cover gift giving. In some industries entertaining a client with a meal, an excursion, or tickets to the theater or a football game is customary. If the intent is as a means of saying thank you to a customer or of developing a more personal relationship, entertainment may be acceptable and even expected. Finding out the rules of behavior in a particular industry and within an individual company is important in determining what is and is not an ethical entertainment policy.

ETHICS AND JOB TENURE

When is it time to look for a new job? Of course, you want to be affiliated with a company of which you can be proud. Disagreements or issues of unethical behavior on the part of the company may, however, emerge during your employment. Deciding how to handle conflicts involving ethics can be stressful because your decision may mean either your termination or resignation. Weigh the options carefully and determine who is being helped and who is being hurt. Are there any alternative, creative options that minimize risk and allow career and conscience to be reconciled?

Whistle-Blowing

According to Nancy R. Hauserman, "In the pursuit of the goals of productivity and consumption, we have failed to preserve individual and community values. The individual has been reduced to a cog in the corporate wheel, a capital investment, a corporate property." This attitude can make salespeople feel unimportant and fear that their ideas, suggestions, or revelations are not valid. This reaction is particularly true if they attempt to pass on valuable information to superiors and are rebuffed.

Consider the following scenario:

> *Six months ago Jim Hollis started a job with an industrial supplier selling valves for acid lines. A safety engineer at a chemical company has noticed that the secondary lining on the valve is not strong enough to keep acid from splattering in the event that the internal seal fails. Jim informed the appropriate people at his company that a major safety problem has been revealed to him, but they told him to keep selling the valves with no modifications.*

What should someone like Jim Hollis do? A number of options could be considered:

- Negotiate consensus for a change in management's views.
- File a memo that explains that he was overruled by his superiors when he brought up the problem.
- Blow the whistle on the company.
- Ignore the whole situation and continue selling.
- Look for another job.

As careful as you may be when joining a company, an ethical dilemma such as this may arise eventually. In the best of all possible worlds, the violation should be exposed and those responsible punished, but what if pointing a finger at someone would cause the whistle-blower to be fired and put yourself and your family in financial difficulties?

On the surface, the wiser course appears to be to keep quiet and let the problem resolve itself. Sometimes the best policy is to keep quiet until solid evidence can be accumulated or until the co-conspirators are identified, but silence as a long-term strategy is indefensible. "The greatest good to the greatest number" is often a sound rule to go by in business. Therefore, in the scenario involving the valve linings, the value of human safety must be given higher priority than saving the company and some of its sales in the short term.

The correct course of action may not be as black-and-white as the one described. In all but the most extreme cases, trying to negotiate a consensus probably makes good sense. If that is not an option, a wise move could be to go public. Recent rulings encourage whistle-blowers to follow their ethical urges. Settlements under the Federal False Claims Act are becoming larger. The act says a whistle-blower may receive 15 percent to 30 percent of any financial settlement won by the government.

Treatment of the Salesperson as a Resource, Not Rubbish

A company may treat its salespeople as partners joined with it in a common mission or simply regard them as cannon fodder out in the field. You are an extremely valuable resource to your company and deserve to be treated fairly, informed of decisions affecting you, and protected from situations in which you might be under pressure to make unethical decisions. Here are some measures that companies can take to prevent unethical behavior among salespeople.

- Avoid setting up management-incentive systems in a way that makes fudging the data tempting.
- Be accessible to salespeople in order to get early warnings on troublesome developments.
- Set up appropriate controls not only on financial accounts but also in customer complaints, salesperson dissatisfaction, and expense accounts.
- Set sales goals that are motivating but not impossible to achieve.

If you know that your ideas are important and your judgment valued, you feel ownership in the organization and want to do a better job overall. Companies like Southwest Airlines and Levi Strauss have adapted to this new reality that workers need to feel valuable, so they are treating their employees not as forces to be controlled but as individuals to be empowered, in order to unshackle their skills, talents, and potential. At Levi Strauss, for example, the predominant vision is that customer value comes from the values of its employees. That's why one-third of managers' raises can depend on how well they live up to the company's value-based philosophy.

One of the most excruciating decisions you face is that concerning territories. You may have spent years cultivating customers in a territory and then have it divided by management or even taken away. A key account that is your bread-and-butter may be made a house account so that you no longer get those commissions. Companies must also be sensitive to their sales force's territorial issues. One of the common e-commerce blunders is that companies do not consider the impact of their Web strategies on sales force compensation. The most important thing is to involve your sales reps in the decision and treat them in a straightforward manner.

SEXUAL HARASSMENT

A number of prominent sexual harassment cases have made the news in recent years. Perhaps the most famous was the case involving Anita Hill and Supreme Court Justice Clarence Thomas. In today's legal environment, any institution's failure to recognize the consequences of workplace sexual harassment can be a capital blunder. For employees in organizations lacking sound policy practices, the negative impact from sexual harassment — including liability, embarrassment and lost productivity — can be extensive. Title VII of The Civil Rights Act of 1964 strictly prohibits sexual harassment. The Equal Employment Opportunity Commission (EEOC) defines sexual harassment this way:

> "Unwelcome sexual advances, requests for sexual favors, and other verbal or physical conduct of a sexual nature constitutes sexual harassment when submission to or rejection of the conduct explicitly or implicitly affects an individual's employment, unreasonably interferes with an individual's work performance or creates an intimidating, hostile or offensive work environment."

Sexual Harassment in Action

Read the following true-life situation on the next page (in disguised form) and imagine what you would do if you were in Sue's position. The situation described here is one of 36 authentic workplace incidents on sexual harassment documented by Dr. N. Elizabeth Fried in her book, *Sex, Laws and Stereotypes*. How would you handle such a situation if it were reported to you? Several options exist today for victims of sexual harassment. Should Sue decide to pursue legal action, she has hard evidence against Mike that he would be hard-pressed to explain away. If you truly feel that you have been the victim of sexual harrasment, the best course of action is to immediately report it to your boss or the superior of the offender.

"Yes sir, I'll schedule that with our driver for a Tuesday delivery," Sue said to the customer on the line, making a note of the request on her pad. "You're welcome," she responded to the customer's appreciative "Thank you."

But before she could put the phone down, another line began flashing. "Customer service, Sue speaking," her voice sang out into the receiver. "How can I help you?" While Sue was busy listening to the customer's request, Mike, her boss, came up behind her. He dropped a piece of paper on her desk and quickly left. He was bending over with laughter. Sue sensed Mike's presence and turned around to respond when the customer put her on hold. But Mike was already gone; however, the one page of paper lay on the top of her desk.

Sue recognized the paper as the company's standard performance appraisal. The scale ran from one-to-five, with one representing "unacceptable" and five saying "exceeds expectations." In the section where Mike was to fill in the key duties of her job and rank them, he had written the following:

1. Face = 3; 2. Breasts = 1; 3. Butt = 5; and 4. Legs = 3

Sue's face turned red and her teeth clenched in anger as she tried to maintain her composure. When the customer came back on the line, she strained to keep a smile in her voice.

Sexual harrassment charges filed with the EEOC have gone up 230 percent over the past decade. With the increasing incidents of sexual harrassment in the workplace, it is important for companies to institute effective policies in order to avoid liability. National surveys of more than 1000 organizations found that sexual harrassment had become one of the hottest topics in formal training programs. In the past several years sexual harrassment consultant Maria Gottlieb says she has seen training requests on the issue rise by 75 percent, particularly in sales. When considering employment with a particular company, make sure there is a clearly defined sexual harrassment policy firmly in place.

With a clear stand on sexual harassment, a business can avoid liability and legal costs, retain talented people, and preserve the goodwill and trust of its customers. AT&T is an excellent example of a company whose sexual harrassment policy has achieved these things. An AT&T employee once sued the company for hostile-environment sexual harrassment. When taken to court, AT&T was held not liable because they handled the situation promptly and took appropriate remedial action. It is increasingly important for businesses to develop and put into practice sound sexual harassment policies.

Checkpoints in Ethical Decision Making

When faced with an ethical conflict, a standard set of questions to ask yourself is helpful. Use the five questions suggested below to guide your thinking.

A Five-Question Ethics Checklist

1. Is it legal? Look at the law and other standards.

2. Is it fair to all concerned?

3. Would I want someone else to act this way toward me?

4. How would I explain my actions to someone else?

5. How will it make me feel about myself?

These questions first require careful evaluation regarding existing standards and personal liability. Next, the questions are designed to activate your sense of fairness and rationality. Last, realize that your personal feelings are important because negative feelings adversely affect positive performance. If your truthful answer to any one of these questions damages your self-image or causes you to be troubled by your conscience, then you should probably avoid the action in question.

There Is No Pillow As Soft As A Clear Conscience.

THE HANDBOOK FOR RELATIONSHIP SELLING

Ethical Issues in Selling

- It is essential that you develop your own personal code of ethics, but you should also be aware of the ethical obligations your company sets forth.

- Salespeople who find themselves in situations in which company violations are evident must make difficult choices about whether to blow the whistle on the company or settle on another strategy that could include finding another job.

- Ethics is a smart business decision because salespeople who are honest in relationships with employers, customers, and competitors become trusted and respected business professionals.

- When faced with an ethical conflict, use a standard checklist of principled questions to guide your thinking.

Figure 4.1

THE GETTYSBURG ADDRESS

Four score and seven years ago our fathers brought forth on this continent, a new nation, conceived in Liberty, and dedicated to the proposition that all men are created equal.

Now we are engaged in a great civil war, testing whether that nation, or any nation, so conceived, and so dedicated, can long endure. We are met here on a great battlefield of that war. We have come to dedicate a portion of it as a final resting place for those who here gave their lives that that nation might live. It is altogether fitting and proper that we should do this.

But in a larger sense we cannot dedicate — we cannot consecrate — we cannot hallow this ground. The brave men, living and dead, who struggled here, have consecrated it far above our poor power to add or detract. The world will little note, nor long remember, what we say here, but can never forget what they did here. It is for us, the living, rather to be dedicated here to the unfinished work which they have, thus far, so nobly carried on. It is rather for us to be here dedicated to the great task remaining before us — that from these honored dead we take increased devotion to that cause for which they here gave the last full measure of devotion — that we here highly resolve that these dead shall not have died in vain; that this nation shall have a new birth of freedom and that government of the people, by the people, for the people, shall not perish from the earth.

— The famous speech delivered by President Abraham Lincoln
at the dedication of the Gettysburg National Cemetery
November 19, 1863

Chapter 4

Purchase Behavior and Communication

- **Why people buy**
- **Influences on the purchase decision process**
- **Organizational buying versus consumer buying**
- **Developing your communication agenda**
- **Using your voice as a selling tool**
- **Selling without words**
- **Overcoming communication barriers**

CAUTION: SMALL WORDS AT WORK

Figure 4.1 on the previous page is the famous Gettysburg Address by President Abraham Lincoln. The entire speech lasted about two minutes. It has a total of 266 words: 198 are one-syllable words; 49 are two-syllable words; and just 19 are words of more than two syllables. Today, the Gettysburg Address is recognized as a classic model of the noblest kind of oratory.

When asked to explain Britain's wartime policy to Parliament, Prime Minister Winston Churchill said, "It is to wage war, by sea, land and air, with all our might and with all the strength that God can give us." As Neil Armstrong first set foot on the moon he said simply, "That's one small step for [a] man, one giant leap for mankind."

You don't have to be a great author or statesman to tap the energy and power of small words, so use them wherever you can. Not only are small words more understandable and exact than large words, they also add elegance to your speaking and writing. Realize and appreciate the persuasive power of a well-written sales proposal. Just think how much more you could sell if you could talk and write equally well. If you must choose between a large word and a small word, pick the small word every time. Take a lesson from your local highway department. Place a sign at the boundaries of your speech that reads: *Caution—Small Words at Work*.

WHY PEOPLE BUY

Consumer behavior is the set of actions that make up an individual's consideration, purchase, and use of products and services. The term *consumer behavior* includes both the purchase and the consumption of products or services. Your role is vital in this process of matching the company's product offerings to the needs of the prospective buyer. However, this process does not end with the sale. You must be equally concerned with consumer satisfaction after the sale.

Understanding the Purchase Decision Process

The model presented in Figure 4.2 provides a useful tool for examining the buying process. It presents a view of the buyer as someone observed not in a single act, but in a complex problem-solving process.

To understand why a person makes a particular purchase decision, look at events before and after the purchase act itself. A buyer generally passes through five stages: (1) problem recognition, (2) search for alternatives, (3) evaluation of alternatives, (4) the actual purchase decision, and (5) post-purchase evaluation.

Figure 4.2

The Purchase Decision Process

Problem Recognition (Motive Arousal)

⬇

The Search for Alternatives

⬇   ⬇

Internal Search
- Habitual
- Routine

External Search
- Extensive
- Limited

⬇   ⬇

Evaluation of Alternatives

⬇

The Purchase Decision

⬇

Post-Purchase Evaluation

Problem Recognition. The purchasing process begins with conscious recognition that a problem or need exists and must be satisfied. A need may be something regarded as necessary, or simply something the buyer wants or desires and therefore perceives as a need. No one takes action until motivated to do so, and motivation arises from awareness of need. Therefore, you must recognize needs that are already active or to find a way to create, or stimulate recognition of, a need of which the prospective buyer has not yet become aware. All kinds of needs affect buying decisions. Abraham Maslow defined five levels of needs as physiological, safety, social, esteem, and self-actualization. Regardless of the kind of need, some buyers will not be aware of the nature of their needs until you bring them out into the open.

Search for Alternatives. After recognizing an unsatisfied need, the buyer begins to search for information concerning the available alternatives. The search may involve both internal and external sources. The internal search makes use of the buyer's previous experience, learning, and attitudes, and occurs largely without conscious effort. Even in the organizational markets, much purchasing is routine: A great deal of it can be done through catalogs, list prices, or simply a phone call to a regular supplier. The external search process adds dynamics. It may require an extensive information search or a more limited search for alternatives.

Evaluation of Alternatives. The search process provides the buyer with knowledge of several alternative products. All individual consumers have specific criteria for making a decision—that is, personal mental rules for matching alternatives with motives. These criteria are learned by actual experience with the product or derived from information obtained from commercial or social sources.

The implications for the relationship salesperson are important here. If you can determine the buyer's choice criteria, you can tailor the presentation to focus on specific product or service benefits that differentiate your product from the competition's. Once you have matched the prospect's buying motives with what you have to offer, the determinant attributes come into play: Price, reputation, service capabilities, and design components. Identifying the dominant buying motives that determine a particular buyer's behavior in the actual decision-making process is vital to closing the sale.

Purchase Decision. After evaluating all the alternatives discovered during the search process, the buyer is ready to make the purchase decision—actually, a whole set of decisions. Buyers want to minimize the risk and simplify the decision-making process as much as possible. The professional salesperson knows this and assists the buyer in making decisions. Your role in assisting prospects to reach a satisfactory purchasing decision is what makes professional relationship selling so rewarding and fulfilling.

Post-purchase Evaluation. The purchase decision process continues after the product or service choice has been made. The buyer evaluates the purchase in terms of pre-purchase expectations and decides whether it has been satisfactory. Sometimes the buyer experiences postpurchase anxiety or *cognitive dissonance*, also commonly known as buyer's remorse. The magnitude of the anxiety or tension depends on the importance of the decision and the attractiveness of the rejected alternatives. You can help lessen this feeling by providing exceptional customer service and follow-up after the sale (as discussed in Chapter 14).

INFLUENCES ON THE PURCHASE DECISION PROCESS

Buying motives cannot be observed directly, but can be inferred from observed behavior. Figure 4.3 illustrates some of the many psychological and sociocultural factors that influence a buyer's purchase decision process. You must understand the significance and impact of these factors at the various stages of the decision-making process.

1. Behavioral concepts, such as perception and self-image, affect *problem recognition.*

2. Sociocultural factors, such as culture, physical enviroment, and social class, all influence the nature and scope of the *information search.*

3. Psychological factors, such as the mood of the moment, attitudes, and perception of oneself, combine with sociocultural factors to influence *purchase decisions.*

You can make positive use of these factors by becoming proficient in the art of communication — the sending and receiving of messages in a manner that results in understanding and productive discussion.

Figure 4.3

Influences on the Buyer's Purchase Decision Process

Psychological Influences
- Perception
- Mood of the moment
- Attitudes
- Self-image

Sociocultural Influences
- Culture
- Physical environment
- Social class

Buyer
(Psyche)

Psychological Influences: It's All in Your Head

Several psychological factors affect a prospect's buying decision. You must be aware of these factors and understand the role they play in the process.

Perception. Individual behavior is an organized, meaningful response to the world as that particular person sees it. We perceive situations according to our own personal needs, values, expectations, past experience, and training. Figure 4.4 illustrates the difference in individual perceptions. How many squares do you see? *There are 40 squares.* Can you find them? If you didn't see that many, you may be exercising selective perception. What prospects perceive as important to themselves is often not what you think is most important.

Mood of the Moment. Perception is also influenced by an individual's psychological state or mood of the moment. On some days a minor mishap may be laughed off, but if nothing has gone right all day, the very same situation may infuriate you.

Attitude. Attitudes are merely habits of thought and habitual patterns of response to experiences. Because they have been used so often, to save the time that would be required to think about a situation and make a decision, they have become automatic. For example, some prospects operate from the concept that what has been done in the past is the best way to do things in the future. Their basic attitude is that change is bad. Any attitude of a prospect that makes the purchase decision more difficult creates a barrier that must be overcome before a sale can be made.

Figure 4.4

How many squares do you see in the figure?

You may not see what others see.

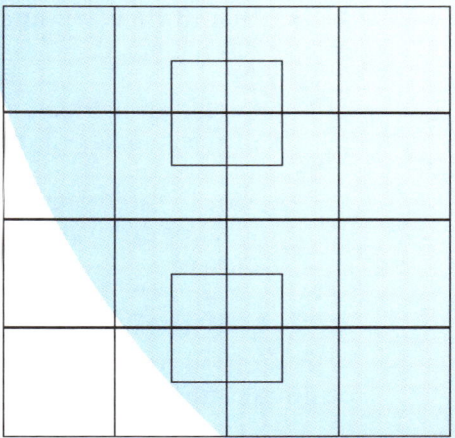

Self-Image. Self-image is an individual's unique and personal self-appraisal at a given moment in time. It affects what is perceived as reality and, as a result, how communication proceeds. In choosing how to communicate, even more important than what is true is what the person believes is true.

Every behavior can be explained if the individual's self-image is understood. In one sense we are all self-centered, and we act in keeping with what we consider best for us at the moment. If you wish to communicate effectively, you must learn to recognize these important dimensions of the prospect's self-image:

1. **Physical**. People picture themselves as tall or short, weak or strong, attractive or unattractive, lean or fat. They buy products that fit their self-image or that promise to change it to fit a desired goal.

2. **Social**. Individuals see themselves as liked or disliked, accepted or rejected, loved or unwanted, successful or failing.

3. **Moral**. Internalized values give people a picture of themselves as loyal or disloyal, honest or dishonest, straightforward or devious.

Sociocultural Influences

In addition to psychological influences, it is essential to understand how sociocultural influences operate to determine people's communication.

Culture. Individuals' values develop as a result of their reactions to the environment in which they live. The cultural environment exerts a powerful influence on how messages are both sent and received. For example, a large percentage of Americans attach a positive connotation to concepts such as success, competition, efficiency, freedom, and material wealth. The positive reception to these words is not, however, universal. Even within the United States, subcultures of many kinds exist, each with its own set of values, priorities, and concepts.

From a Global Perspective. Foreign cultures adhere to business customs, protocols, and body language for basic communication that differ from those in America. If you want to sell to international customers, whether here or overseas, you must establish rapport. Insensitivity to other people's customs and ways of communicating could derail your best selling efforts.

Those who sell to international customers may get by on a wink, a blink, and a "see ya later," but only if they know how their language and gestures will be interpreted; body talk does not have a universal language. According to Diane Ackerman's book *A Natural History of the Senses*, "Members of a tribe in New Guinea say good-bye by putting a hand in each other's armpit, withdrawing it, and stroking it over themselves, thus becoming coated with the friend's scent." Thank goodness that when we say goodbye to a client, we can just shake hands — or can we?

In France, the traditional American handshake is considered much too rough; a quick handshake with just slight pressure is preferred. Throughout Latin America, however, the greeting is often more exuberant. A hearty embrace is common among both men and women. They often follow it with a slap on the back. In Ecuador, though, greeting a person without shaking hands is a sign of special respect. Throughout India, it is considered quite rude to touch women, so never offer to shake their hands. Figure 4.5 illustrates several cross-cultural considerations when conducting business globally.

Physical Environment. Americans usually keep their houses and offices at a cozy 72 to 78 degrees; the British prefer a cozy 60 to 65 degrees. Other elements of the environment, such as sound level, are also important. Most people of middle age

Figure 4.5

Cultural Differences from a Global Perspective

- Avoid slang or sports metaphors, such as "That proposal is way out in left field!" or "Are we in the ballpark on price?" They may mean nothing to other cultures.

- Always use your last name when answering the telephone in Germany; for example, "Bond speaking." When you are calling a customer, say your last name first: "This is Bond, James Bond."

- Americans and Canadians will take a business card and pocket it without reviewing the information on it. In France and Japan, the business card is an extension of the person who gives it, so cards should be treated with much respect.

- After introductions, Americans and Canadians may tend to move quickly to business matters. In Latin America and China, especially in meetings where large transactions will be taking place, business can proceed only after a relationship has been built.

- In Japan, you can never be too polite, too humble, or too apologetic. Make apologizing routine. Always appear to be less informed and less skilled in the negotiation process than you really are. To the Japanese, there is no such thing as a quick deal.

and older like a quiet, restful environment; younger people tend to be stimulated by loud music and object less strenuously to machine noise. The perceptive salesperson won't attempt to make a presentation to a 60-year-old prospect over dinner in a restaurant that features live rock music. The physical environment must be conducive to communication.

Social class. Almost every society has some class structure. In the United States, social structure is much less rigid than in some other nations, in which it may be tied to religion, kinship, or inherited ownership of land. Americans often climb into new social classes by earning higher educations and filling prestigious jobs. Social class groupings are based largely on source of wealth, occupation, education, type of house, and location. It is important to be aware that people tend to adopt buying behaviors, tastes, and ways of communicating that are in keeping with the social class of which they consider themselves members.

ORGANIZATIONAL BUYING VERSUS CONSUMER BUYING

Organizational buyers include all organizations (profit and nonprofit) that buy products or services for their own use, or that resell to other organizations, or that sell to the ultimate consumer. Individual consumers, with their relatively small transactions, are not considered here. The five-stage purchase decision process fits the ultimate consumer buyer adequately, and the two processes are generally similar, but the organizational buyer follows a more complex purchase decision process. The following are the four main areas where fundamental differences exist between consumer purchasing and organizational buying:

Decision maker. The ultimate consumer is the decision maker in a purchase. In an organizational setting, decisions are often made by a team, commonly referred to as a buying center.

Buying criteria. Individual consumers have a limited set of factors to weigh in making a buying decision, whereas business markets often require products that are complex, expensive, and purchased in larger quantities. Because of this, buyers operate under purchasing constraints imposed by the company.

Length of relationship. Organizational buyers desire to stay with suppliers longer, to reduce the need for frequent negotiation. This interdependence underlies the need to build a long-term relationship. As a result, many business buyers and sellers have formed what are referred to as strategic business alliances.

Buying motives. Every buying decision made — consumer or organizational — is based on a dominant motive. Buying motives may be either rational or emotional. Individual consumers often buy based on emotion and later attempt to rationalize their decisions. For organizational buyers, however, rational motives are usually dominant, though they must take emotional motives into account as well. Table 4.1 lists the basic motives that lead to both consumer and organizational purchases.

Table 4.1

Consumer and Organizational Buying Motives

Individual Consumer Buying Motives	Organizational Buying Motives
• Gain profit	• Wealth or income
• Alleviate fear	• Economy
• Secure social approval	• Flexibility
• Satisfy bodily needs	• Uniformity of output
• Experience happiness or pleasure	• Salability
• Gain an advantage	• Protection
• Imitate	• Utility
• Dominate others	• Guarantees
• Enjoy recreation	• Delivery
• Improve health	• Quality

Purchase Policies. Organizational buyers operate under the constraints of purchase policies established by the company. Such policies range from strict specifications to general standards of performance. They may include guidelines for installation, warranty and repair agreements, the availability of technical assistance, and product performance standards. Product quality, delivery guarantees, and durability are additional policy items often considered.

Multiple Buying Influence: Who Do I Need to Talk to?

The responsibility for organizational buying decisions may lie with more than a single individual. Many organizations set dollar limits beyond which purchase decisions must involve additional executives. Buying committees or teams drawn from various departments become involved in decision making. The members of this team, called a *buying center*, share common goals and knowledge relevant to the purchase decision. A major reason for working with the buying center is to discover the key person or persons who actually make or strongly influence the final decision. Researchers have identified five specific roles played by the people who constitute a buying center:

1. **Users**. Those who will actually use the product or service purchased; for example, a telemarketing sales force whose members will be the primary users of a proposed new telephone system.

2. **Buyers**. Those who have formal authority to make the purchase, such as the purchasing agent.

3. **Influencers**. The individuals who provide information, directly or indirectly, throughout the buying process to members of the buying center. For example, the supervisor for the telemarketing division may suggest certain features needed in a telephone system to make the calling process more efficient.

4. **Deciders**. Those who have the power and authority to choose from among the various suppliers. They make the final decision.

5. **Gatekeepers**. Those who control the flow of information into the buying center. Gatekeepers are invaluable to the group's decision-making process. A purchasing agent acting as a gatekeeper may control which suppliers are notified and how much pertinent data these potential suppliers are given access to.

DEVELOPING YOUR COMMUNICATION AGENDA

Success in relationship selling depends on accurate communication—the useful exchange of information between you and the prospect. Communication can be viewed as the verbal and nonverbal passing of information between you, the *sender*, and your prospect, the *receiver*. However, for effective communication to take place, you each must understand the intended message. Thus, the goal of communication is a mutual understanding.

Figure 4.6 shows the channel through which communication must flow in a selling situation. At each intersection the potential exists for both problems and opportunities. Although the model considers communication from the salesperson's perspective, in any successful relationship both parties participate meaningfully in an active two-way process.

Figure 4.6

The Communication Model for Verbal and Nonverbal Messages

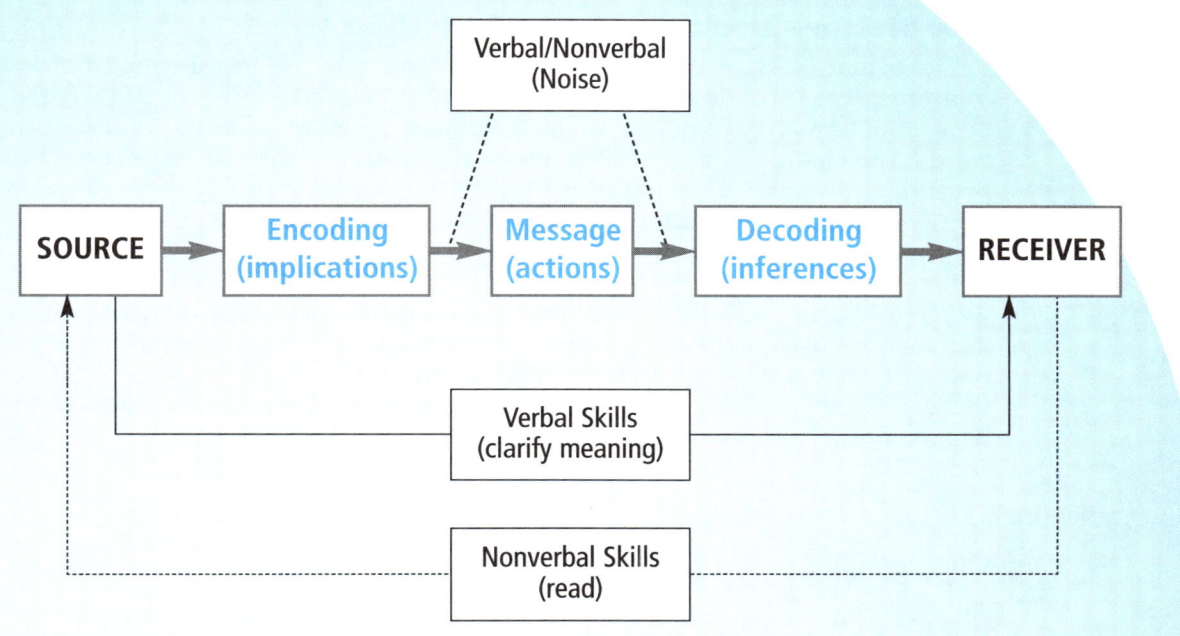

Encoding the Message: How to Get Your Point Across

Encoding is the process in which you convert an idea or concept into symbols the buyer can clearly understand. You know what you are trying to say; the real challenge is getting your point across. This requires the proper mix of symbols to express your meaning correctly. The most common symbols used in delivering a message are words, pictures, numbers, sounds, physical touch, smell, body movement, and taste. You, as the source, must encode your message, organize it, and put it into a presentation format the prospect will understand, accept, and believe. Effective encoding of the message is based on your knowledge of the prospect's needs.

Communication is successful if the symbols you choose make it possible for the listener to understand you. The real challenge in communication is to transfer your thoughts, ideas, and intentions without distortion or omission. Because communication is affected by the assumptions and needs of both parties — as well as by outside factors such as time pressures, interruptions, and the environment — communication is often far from perfect.

The Message Itself: So Much More than Words

The actual message is a blend of symbols that you use to influence a change in a prospect's attitude or behavior. The message itself involves both verbal and nonverbal elements. In his book *Silent Messages*, Albert Mehrabian points out that words convey only 7 percent of feelings and emotions, tone of voice conveys 38 percent, and visual communication conveys the remaining 55 percent. Nonverbal elements in the presentation make up the majority of the total impact.

If verbal and nonverbal messages conflict, the listener relies on the nonverbal message. Figure 4.7 illustrates the contribution of various factors to the messages we deliver to others and the amount of control we maintain over each one. The factors most easily controlled are those that have the least effect, and those with the biggest impact are the most difficult to control because they happen automatically.

Figure 4.7

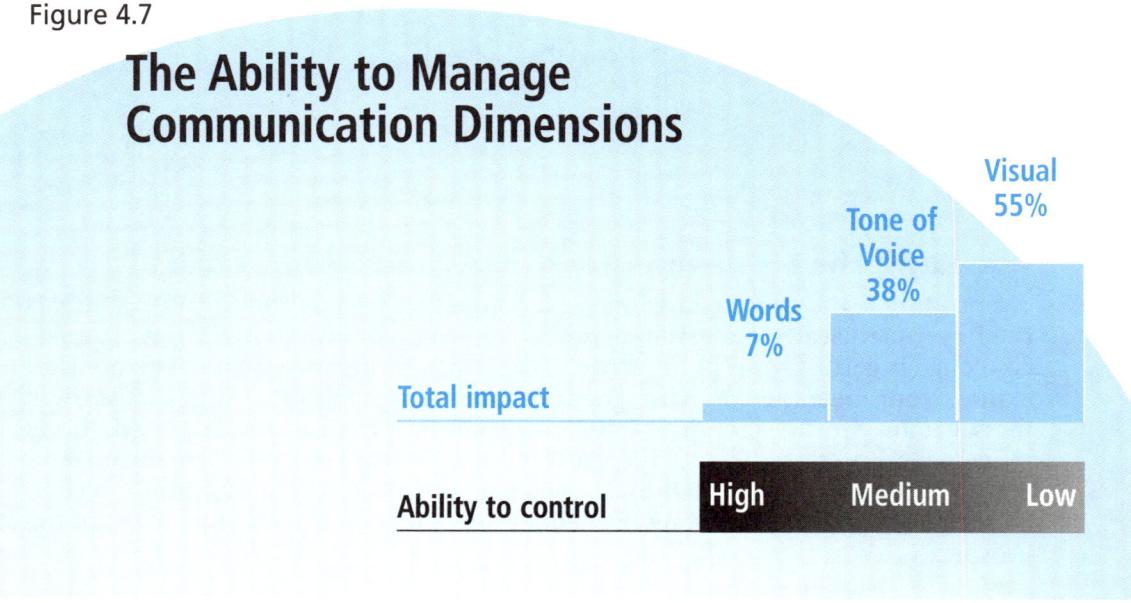

The Ability to Manage Communication Dimensions

Visual 55%

Tone of Voice 38%

Words 7%

Total impact

Ability to control

| High | Medium | Low |

Research suggests that if the first thirty seconds of a communication result in a negative impression, you have to spend the next four minutes overcoming that impression before any real communication can begin.

Evaluating the Prospect's Decoding: Did They Get It?

Decoding is the mental process by which a prospect figures out the meaning of your message. It is the way in which your prospect attempts to translate the symbols used in your presentation into something that relates to his or her needs. If the message was obviously both understood as intended and also accepted, there is no problem. At this step in the process, though, either real communication or misunderstanding can occur. Your prospects listen to your message, then make their own conclusions. If the prospect fails to understand the message, the result is called noise, which means that a breakdown in communication has occurred. This happens when there are barriers to effective communicaton, as discussed in the following section.

Overcoming Communication Barriers

Seldom does the buyer interpret exactly the same meaning that you intended. As mentioned earlier, when the result of decoding is different from what you encoded, noise exists. Anything that interferes with or distorts understanding of the intended message is called *noise*. Noise can take many forms and may affect any or all parts of the communication process. There are logical reasons why your sales message may not be understood or accepted. Some reasons for such miscommunication are the following:

Words. All language is a code. Even if you and your prospect use the same words, you are probably putting out different meanings. Words only represent ideas. Noise is created when words are inappropriate: For example, casual profanity that may offend the listener, language implying that the listener is poorly informed, language that assumes too much knowledge on the listener's part, or language that obscures the real meaning.

Distractions. Any element that may focus the prospect's attention on something other than the message is a distraction. Some typical distractions are inappropriate dress, uncomfortable room temperature, loud noise that makes concentration difficult, or a nagging personal problem occupying the prospect's mind.

Timing. If a prospect has some reason for not wanting to listen, no amount of communication skill on your part is enough. The prospect may be feeling under the weather, may be preoccupied with an unpleasant disciplinary task, or may be facing a pressing deadline. Some prospects need time to warm up before getting down to business; others want to get right to your proposal and skip the small talk.

Interruptions. Phone calls, people walking in to ask questions, and emergencies typify the kinds of interruptions that reduce or distort the impact of the message.

Technical Erudition. Information overload often complicates a message. An unconscious desire to appear personally knowledgeable often results in the salesperson talking too much, poorly organizing the presentation of features and benefits, or wrongly assuming that the prospect has adequate knowledge. As a result, the prospect fails to see a need for the product or service. Avoid using technical terms or jargon without clarification.

Poor Listening Habits. If the prospect is a poor listener, you are faced with a monumental challenge in designing a message and delivering it in an effective and successful manner. The other end of the spectrum is the salesperson who is a poor listener, who never picks up the prospect's cues that are the keys to molding the message for quick acceptance.

Making Use of Feedback

The buyer will draw conclusions from the messages received and react accordingly. This feedback is crucial to your success. During face-to-face communication, verbal and nonverbal feedback is immediate and quite revealing. Become skilled in receiving feedback so that you can adapt your sales presentation to fit each individual buyer's requirements. Use the feedback loop from the prospect to you to bring you closer to an exact understanding of what is being said by each participant. This filters out the noise and results in clear communication.

USING YOUR VOICE AS A SELLING TOOL

The first impression you make is often based on your voice. When you call for an appointment, your voice is all you have for communicating. A voice that is pleasing and confident is a great asset. Your voice and how you use it play an important part in your success in selling. Several basic components of verbal communication deserve your attention.

Clarity or Articulation. Do you recall the device Professor Higgins used in *My Fair Lady* to help Eliza Doolittle improve her speech? He had her talk with marbles in her mouth. To be understood at all, she was forced to form her words very carefully. As a result, her articulation improved. When you speak, do people hear separate words and syllables, or *doyourwordsallruntogether?* A salesperson with poor articulation leaves prospects confused and bewildered.

Volume. The normal volume of the speaking voice varies during conversation. The same is true of a sales presentation. Stressing a benefit may call for increased volume. Lowering your voice, sometimes almost to a whisper, may produce quite a dramatic effect; it causes the prospect to lean forward (a body position that signals agreement or approval) to avoid missing your words. Variation in volume enhances the message if it is not overdone.

Silence. Silence is a powerful selling tool. Use it to give the prospect time to absorb the full impact of what you have said. Slight pauses between major points in the presentation suggest that you are thoughtful, intelligent, and analytical. Pauses also give the prospect an opportunity to comment, ask a question, or think about how the idea you have presented can be applied to an existing need or problem. Avoid becoming so enamored with the sound of your own voice that you talk all the time.

Rhythm. The rhythmic pattern of your speech comes from your basic personality style and your emotions of the moment. Some voices seem to flow in long, continuous sentences, whereas others come in short, choppy chunks. Just as the rhythm in music changes to indicate that something new is happening, the same happens in speech patterns. Be alert to any changes in your own or the prospect's speech patterns. Changes are even more revealing than initial patterns. If the prospect suddenly shifts to a more drawn-out rhythm, for example, the message may be "Let me think more about that" or "I don't believe what you're saying."

Rate of Speech. The tempo of your delivery should be comfortable for you as a speaker and for your listener. Speaking too rapidly may cause you to lose a prospect who customarily speaks more slowly and feels that your fast pace is pushing for a decision without allowing time for thought. Speaking too slowly may make the prospect want to push your fast-forward button. A moderate pace allows you to enunciate clearly, establish natural rhythmic patterns, and speed up or slow down for proper emphasis of some point.

SELLING WITHOUT WORDS

Different people have different levels of competence in nonverbal communication skills, and some professions require more skill than others. The success of a professional gambler depends on the ability to exercise strict control over nonverbal messages to disguise a bluff. A mime depends exclusively on nonverbal skills to deliver a message. However, to achieve excellence in the sales profession, you must be skilled in both verbal and nonverbal communication. Two particularly important components of nonverbal communication are *body language* and *proxemics* (use of space).

Body Language

Body language can be conceived of as messages sent without using words. The essential elements of body language include shifts in posture or stance (body angle), facial expressions, eye movements, and arm, hand, and leg movements. It includes every movement and gesture, from the subtle raising of an eyebrow to the obvious leaning forward of an interested listener.

Through body language, prospects express their emotions, desires, and attitudes. As a result, body language is a valuable tool for discovering what the prospect is really saying. When you can read the prospect's body language and, in addition, control your own body signals to add impact to your words, you are likely to be understood.

Understanding the Language of Gestures. Important signals involve body angle; position of hands, arms, legs, and the face — especially the eyes and lips. All of these should be observed as a cluster of gestures that together state a message. A prospect sitting with arms crossed may be communicating doubt or rejection — or may simply be sitting comfortably. In this case, you must also observe whether the legs are crossed, the body withdrawn, the eyes glancing sideways, and an eyebrow raised. All these signs, taken together, surely suggest doubt or rejection, but one of them in isolation is inconclusive.

Body Signals. A hunched figure, rigid posture, restless stance, or nervous pacing may contradict what a person says verbally. Prospects allow you to sit closer if they feel comfortable and lean toward you if they like what you are saying and are intent on listening. John Molloy used videotape to study the behavior of successful and unsuccessful salespeople. One mannerism difference noted was the relative calmness of professional salespeople in comparison to those who were less successful. Their body movements were smooth and unhurried; there were no jerky motions, particularly when handing a contract or a pen across the table. Every movement was gradual. Less successful salespeople exhibited jumpy, nervous movements that were picked up — perhaps unconsciously — by prospects.

Look for changes in the prospect's body posture and gestures. For example, one who is ready to buy shows signs of relaxation: Nodding in agreement, mirroring your movements, moving to the front of the chair, extending the palm of the hand outward toward you, and uncrossing legs. Your posture and gestures also communicate your feelings to the prospect. If you sit in an open, relaxed position, you are likely to be more persuasive and better accepted than if you sit in a tight, closed posture.

Hand Movements. Rubbing the back of the neck may indicate frustration, but it can also indicate that the prospect has a sore or stiff neck from painting the bathroom ceiling over the weekend. Next time you are speaking with a client, notice his hand movements and read his hands as indicators of what he is really feeling. People can say so much with simple, unthinking hand motions. If you begin to notice that you are also making involuntary hand gestures during a meeting, focus your hand gestures toward your presentation or notes rather than letting them give away what you are feeling!

Evaluate the following hand gestures in the context of other nonverbal clues.

1. **Other gestures of hand and head**. Tugging at the ear suggests the desire to interrupt. Pinching the bridge of the nose and closing the eyes says that a matter is being given serious thought.

2. **Posture**. Leaning back in the chair with both hands behind the head communicates a sense of superiority.

3. **Involuntary gestures**. Involuntary hand gestures that contradict a facial expression are likely to reveal the true feelings. Tightly clasped hands or fists indicate tenseness.

4. **Steepling of the hands**. Fingertips together, forming what looks like a church steeple, often indicate smugness, self-confidence, or feelings of superiority.

Facial Expressions. Eyebrows, eyelids, eyes, lips, jaw, mouth, and facial muscles all work together to communicate feelings and emotions. Research attributes as much as 70 percent of nonverbal message sending to the muscles of the face.

The face is a highly reliable indicator of attitude. A person may avoid eye contact when trying to cover up true feelings. Increased eye contact signals honesty and interest. Be sure to maintain eye contact at critical moments of the presentation. For example, when describing technical characteristics of the product, direct the prospect's eyes to the product itself, the brochure, or the specification sheet. In contrast, when stressing the benefits of using the product, maintain eye contact. Lack of eye contact sends a negative message that neutralizes the impact of the intended benefit. Proper eye contact makes a positive statement that words alone cannot.

Suspicion and anger are shown by tightness around the cheeks or along the jaw line. Muscle movement at the back of the jaw line just below the ears indicates an angry gritting of the teeth. A sudden flush of facial redness may warn that the situation has taken a bad turn; embarrassment or hostility may be radiating under an apparently calm exterior.

An isolated gesture or posture is seldom a reliable indicator of attitude or feelings. Obviously, you have to take a look at the buyer in the context of the whole situation. The buyer may fold her arms just to be more comfortable. Generally, if there is an objection, the whole body will become more rigid. You will see other signals as well: Skin texture will tighten up; voice tone will change. The prospect may even have a frustrated look on her face. When a cluster of gestures is consistent with the verbal messages, it is relatively safe to accept their validity.

Proxemics

Proxemics is the distance individuals prefer to maintain between themselves and others. Most people seem to consider the observation of desired distance a matter of courtesy. Violations of distance comfort risk closing down the communication process. Highly successful salespeople tend to move closer to clients when closing a sale. Their skill in reading the individual prospect allows them to move as close as possible without causing discomfort for the prospect. The difference between how successful and unsuccessful salespeople use physical closeness can be observed in the prospect's reaction. Carefully test for the existence of comfort barriers; then place yourself just outside those barriers.

Figure 4.8 shows the four basic zones or ranges that apply in the typical sales situation. Generally speaking, the intimate zone is about two feet (hence the expression, "to keep someone at arm's length"). Enter this range only if invited. Moving inside the intimate zone, except for a handshake, is not a good idea. Beyond that, we all have a personal zone, which is an envelope around us extending from two to four feet. Move into the buyer's personal zone only after invitation, which typically occurs after a satisfying professional relationship has been established. The outer shell is the social zone, which extends up to 12 feet.

Figure 4.8

How to Use Space

	Intimate Range	Personal Range	Social Range	Public Range
	up to 2 feet	2 to 4 feet	4 to 12 feet	12 or more feet
	Back off. Too close for business situation.	Use only if prospect is comfortable.	Allows prospects plenty of room for gestures, without invading their space.	Good for group presentation or giving a speech.

A customer is not a transaction, a customer is a relationship!

THE HANDBOOK FOR RELATIONSHIP SELLING

Purchase Behavior and Communication

- The consumer's purchase decision process involves five stages:

  1. Problem recognition
  2. Search for alternatives
  3. Evaluation of alternatives
  4. The purchase decision
  5. Post-purchase evaluation

- Organizational buyers must abide by specific restrictions and buying procedures, often consult with other executives, and must deal with budget constraints. Purchases of this nature often involve a purchasing team, sometimes referred to as a buying center.

- Salespeople are successful in closing sales when they discover the buying motives of the prospect, present benefits of the product that relate to those motives, and are sensitive to both psychological and sociocultural influences.

- Communication is the vehicle for delivering your message in a manner that the buyer comprehends, accepts, and believes.

- Understanding body language and how prospects use their space adds to your ability to communicate with the prospect.

- We send the majority of our messages in daily communication through nonverbal means. We cannot **not** communicate!

Understanding the strengths and liabilities of your communicating style and learning to be versatile in your style can help you sell to more prospects more often.

Chapter 5

Finding Your Selling Style

- Recognizing the various behavioral styles
- Recognizing your own favorite style
- Dealing with people from each of the styles
- Versatility and your ability to relate to all styles
- Gender issues in selling
- Neurolinguistic programming

A DIFFERENCE IN SOCIAL STYLE

Six weeks into his job as a sales and marketing executive in a high-technology manufacturing company, Charlie Kromer realized that something was very wrong. Not the work itself — Kromer loved digging for the facts, arranging timetables, charting the development of new products. The job was fine. It was the boss he couldn't stand.

Recently Kromer had approached his boss with a new product development plan. Everything was detailed precisely: Target dates, costs, sales approaches, presentation data, the works. Halfway through the presentation, the boss leaped to her feet and began tossing out ideas right and left. Some were impractical; all would throw the carefully thought-out plan completely out of whack. When Kromer pointed this out, his boss got miffed and charged out of the room, bellowing over her shoulder, "Now you've got the concept. Go to it."

"Go to what?" Kromer pondered. "All I've got to work with is a blast of hot air."

Some call such an incident a personality conflict. Others would say they are not on the same wavelength. They're not seeing eye to eye. Let's call it what it really is—a difference in social style. Conflict or miscommunication will exist not simply because of work pressures, but because of social style differences. Charlie, as you will learn in this chapter, has an *analytical social style*, while his boss has an *expressive style*. Unknowingly, they communicate disrespect to one another. This lack of understanding and knowledge concerning behavioral styles can cause lost sales, frustration, resentment, or resignation.

Communication broke down in the situation because Charlie did not recognize that his ideas got his boss thinking, and she did not stick around to clarify her suggestions. Charlie stopped listening and took her brainstorming personally, seeing it as criticism rather than as development of his original thoughts. They were like the two old-timers who sat on the front porch in their rocking chairs reminiscing about days gone by. Both were so hard of hearing that neither ever knew for sure what the other was saying. They just took turns talking, each lost in his own memories, but content that there was someone nearby. For the salesperson who wants to succeed in a selling career, however, "being nearby" isn't enough.

Success and Behavioral Styles

Because of the importance of communication in the selling process, successful salespeople constantly search for new ways to make their communication more effective. They are eager to learn how they may better anticipate and avoid conflict situations. A selling transaction, whether it involves products, services, or ideas, is a communication exchange in which two individuals develop a mutually desirable solution to a problem about which both are concerned. The best sales relationships are long-term ones based on mutual trust and credibility. The pertinent question then becomes, "How can I sell so that I demonstrate respect for the customer, build credibility for myself and my product, and set up a win-win situation for both of us?"

Of tremendous importance for salespeople is the concept of behavioral styles, first developed by the Swiss psychologist Carl Jung. Jung built upon the knowledge of the adult ego state developed by Sigmund Freud. Jung's work on behavioral functions resulted in a theory of personality that included four functions: Intuition, thinking, feeling, and sensing. Several behavioral style models of interest to salespeople have been developed by various authors. David Merrill and Roger Reid began the development of their Social Styles Model in the early 1960s. Dr. Paul Mok, developed what he calls the Communicating Styles Technology Model. More recently the Wilson Learning Corporation and Dr. Tony

Alessandra and Associates Inc. have expanded and added their own research. The material presented in this chapter has been gleaned from these four related approaches.

THE SOCIAL STYLES MODEL

Everyone learns as a child that family members and friends have different personalities. Perhaps you could always elicit sympathy from your mother but found that your father considered each situation and evaluated the circumstances prior to sympathizing or reprimanding you. You may have had a sibling who had a totally different personality from everyone else in the household. In your family, you had time to learn the ways you can best persuade or get along with various relatives. In a business or social situation, you have less time to evaluate and adjust your persuasive skills. The prospect's manner and social style are often deceptive and you may miss what is happening. The most common mistake is not understanding how prospects think and make decisions. The social styles model provides a useful tool for making such an evaluation in the shortest possible time. The better you understand personality types, the more successful you will be in communicating with the various people you meet.

The Four Distinct Social Styles

Each person has a primary communicating style that is blended or fine-tuned by a secondary style. These primary and secondary styles shape others' perceptions of you and filter your perceptions of other people. A second dimension to this model comes into play when you are under stress. At such times, you may shift to a different style of behavior. You may be aware of the shift yet feel unable to prevent it.

We use four basic styles to deal with the world. Each is based upon one of four basic functions of human personality.

- The **driver** or **sensing** function of taking in here-and-now sensory information and reacting to it.

- The **expressive** or **intuitive** function of imagination and abstract thought.

- The **amiable** or **feeling** function of both personal and emotional reactions to experience.

- The **analytical** or **thinking** function of organizing and analyzing information in a logical fashion.

Everyone uses each of the four functions, but the frequency of use differs among individuals. These styles can be observed even in young children. Behavior patterns, psychologist Carl Jung claimed, are genetically determined and are seen in infants during their first days of life. Like adults, young children process experience according to their own individual styles.

Basic Concepts

Four basic concepts underlie the behavioral styles communication model presented in this chapter:

1. Everyone uses a blend of the driver, expressive, amiable, and analytical styles, although each person has a favorite style that is used more often than others. A style is an overall approach used to receive and send messages. It consists of verbal, nonverbal, and behavioral elements.

2. Every person operates the majority of the time from a favorite style. This is the primary style. Everyone also has a secondary or backup style that may replace or modify the primary style.

3. Because style is reflected in behavior, you can identify someone else's primary style by observing behavioral clues. These clues include use of time, manner of speech, typical reaction to other people, and approach to job performance.

4. People respond favorably to a style that is similar or complementary to their own primary and backup styles. When a salesperson's style is too different from that of the prospect, the resulting style conflict can be disastrous to the outcome of the transaction. What is said is often much less important than how it is said.

Behavioral Styles in Selling

Your choice of style affects what you do and say. It also affects what prospects hear and believe during your presentation. Understanding the strengths and liabilities of your primary communicating style and learning to be versatile in your style can help you sell to more prospects more often. The objective of this chapter then is to help you learn how to manage your daily interactions with customers and prospects more productively.

Figure 5.1 illustrates that your most damaging weaknesses (-) are merely exaggerations or over-extensions of your strengths (+). Your behavior responds to circumstances like the volume dial of a radio. When the volume is just right, the music is pleasing. Similarly, when a behavioral style is used in moderation it is seen as a strength; when overused (that is, when the volume is too high), it becomes a weakness and leads to ineffective communication. Professional selling is all about managing relationships. Remember that a customer is not a transaction, a customer is a relationship! Most of us don't even think about working on relationships in our daily lives. On the other hand, relationship salespeople take time to think about and understand those around them.

Figure 5.1

Social Style Strengths and Weaknesses

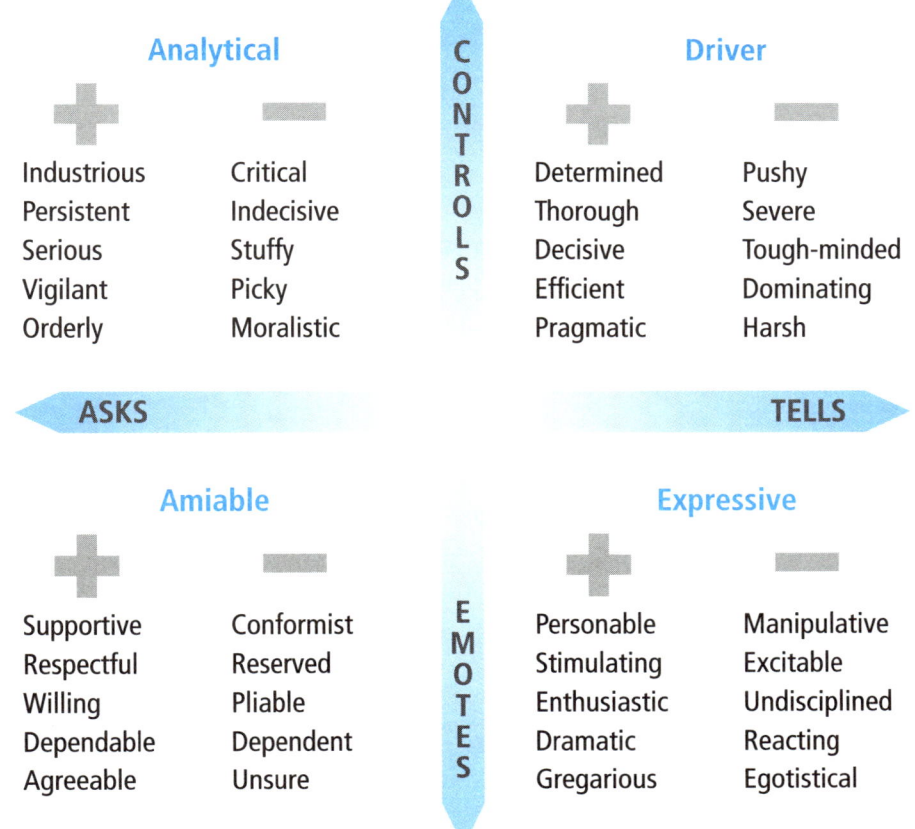

Remember that the emphasis in studying behavioral style characteristics is on surface behavior, not on an in-depth personality analysis. Human behavior is predictable because ninety percent of our actions are controlled by habits and attitudes. Social styles do not reveal a person's complete personality, but rather, they describe three basic attributes or characteristics of behavior: assertiveness, responsiveness, and versatility.

Attributes of Behavior

When you meet someone for the first time, your mind subconsciously reacts to two main characteristics: assertiveness and responsiveness. *Assertiveness* represents the effort a person makes to influence or control the thoughts and actions of others. *Responsiveness* is the willingness with which a person outwardly shares feelings or emotions and develops relationships.

Assertiveness and responsiveness levels vary from one individual to another. Several basic terms provide a thumbnail sketch of the characteristics of each dimension:

Low in Responsiveness
- formal and proper
- fact-oriented
- guarded, cool, and aloof
- disciplined about time
- seldom makes gestures
- controlled body language

High in Responsiveness
- relaxed and warm
- open and approachable
- dramatic and animated
- flexible about time
- oriented toward relationships and feelings

Low in Assertiveness
- introverted
- supportive, a team player
- easygoing
- avoids taking risks
- good listener
- reserved in their opinions

High in Assertiveness
- risk-taker
- swift in decision-making
- willing to confront others
- very competitive
- take-charge attitude
- readily expresses opinions

Recognizing Social Styles

Combining the assertiveness and responsiveness characteristics makes it possible to develop a map of what others are doing or saying. Figure 5.2 shows the relationships among the four social styles. The horizontal axis is the range from the least to most assertive. Assertive people take a stand and make their position clear to others. Because they are ambitious, competitive, and quick to take action and express strong opinions, they are located on the telling end of the social style axis. Nonassertive individuals are seen as cooperative, silent, and slow to act, and they are located at the asking end of the axis. The least assertive individuals are in quartile D, and the most assertive in quartile A, with quartiles B and C representing intermediate levels of assertiveness.

Figure 5.2

The Social Styles Profile

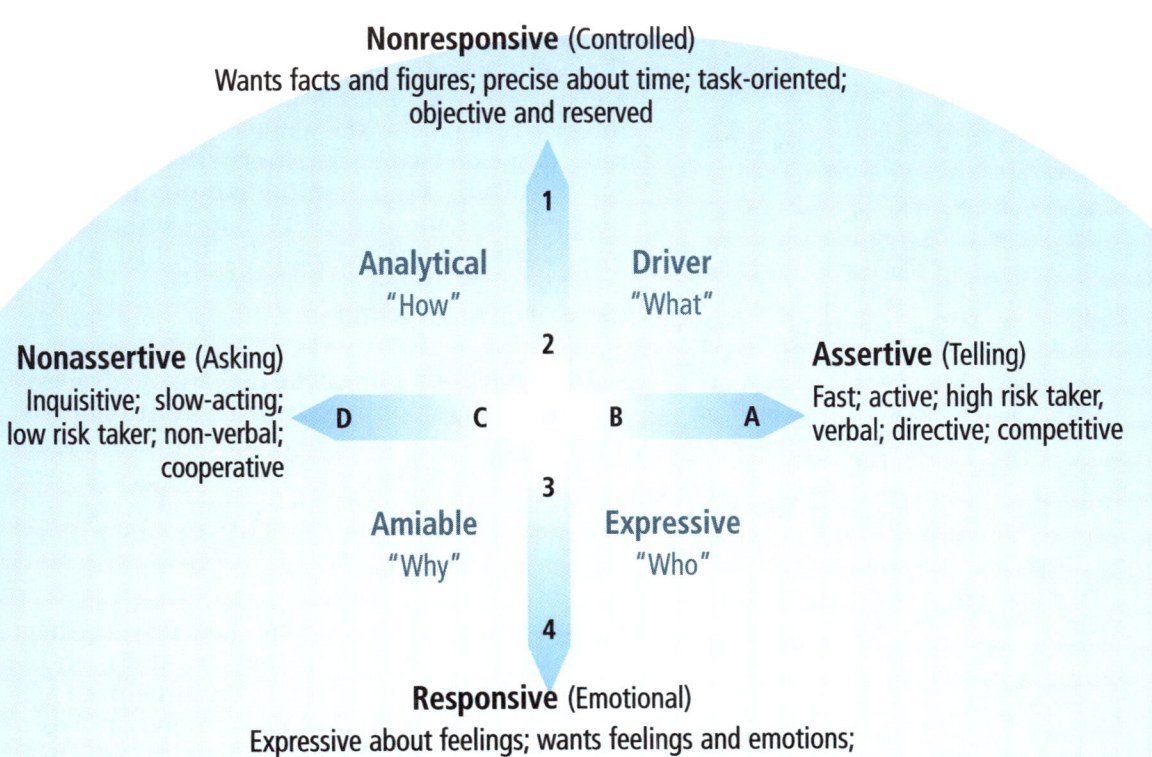

Nonresponsive (Controlled)
Wants facts and figures; precise about time; task-oriented; objective and reserved

1

Analytical   **Driver**
"How"   "What"

2

Nonassertive (Asking)   **Assertive** (Telling)
Inquisitive; slow-acting;   D   C   B   A   Fast; active; high risk taker,
low risk taker; non-verbal;   verbal; directive; competitive
cooperative

3

Amiable   **Expressive**
"Why"   "Who"

4

Responsive (Emotional)
Expressive about feelings; wants feelings and emotions; imprecise about time; people-oriented; subjective

The vertical axis indicates the range from least to most responsive. Nonresponsive individuals, those in quartile 1, are largely indifferent to the feelings of others, reserved, and no-nonsense in attitude. The responsive individuals found in quartile 4 are strongly people-oriented, concerned about relationships, and subjective. Those in quartiles 2 and 3 display intermediate levels of responsiveness.

Identifying the Four Behavioral Styles

Identifying the levels of assertiveness and responsiveness a person demonstrates is not a precise method of complete personality evaluation. With study and practice, however, you can become seventy to eighty percent effective in using your observations to predict habitual behavioral patterns and be prepared to use your knowledge to improve the communication environment. The four styles are linked to distinctive and unique habits of interactive behavior. The name given to each style reflects general characteristics rather than full, specific details. Keep in mind that no one style is preferred over another. Each has its own strengths and weaknesses, and successful individuals as well as failures are found in each style group, as are those of different ethnic groups, ages, and gender.

- **Drivers** tell and control, are high in assertiveness, and low in responsiveness. They control others by telling them what to do and control themselves by remaining objective. They are task-oriented and combine personal power and emotional control in relationships with others. *They are control specialists.*

- **Expressives** tell and emote. Like drivers, they are highly assertive, but they are also high in emotional responsiveness. They attempt to tell people what to do, but place more emphasis on their relationships with people than they do on the task itself. *They are social specialists.*

- **Amiables** ask and emote, are low in assertiveness, and high in responsiveness. They rely on a personal feeling approach to get things done. *They are support specialists*, combining personal reserve and emotional expression.

- **Analyticals** ask and control, and are low in both assertiveness and responsiveness. They are highly task-oriented but soften that style with low assertiveness. They ask rather than direct. *They are technical specialists*, combining personal reserve and emotional control.

VERSATILITY AS A COMMUNICATION TOOL

When people of different styles meet and behave strictly according to the characteristics of their own personal styles, conflict often results. A salesperson who is an amiable and a prospect who is a driver can quickly arrive at cross-purposes. A driver client wants to get facts and to accomplish the task at hand; the amiable salesperson wants to cultivate a personal relationship.

When such a situation occurs, the only way to avoid an escalation in miscommunication or a conflict is for one of the two people involved to engage in some style flexibility. In an ideal situation, both are willing to move part way, but you must be capable of making most or all of any necessary temporary adjustment. This willingness to try behaviors not necessarily characteristic of your style is called *behavioral flexibility* or *versatility*.

You must learn to assess prospects' "comfort zone," but this is only half the battle. You must also practice the *versatility* which will allow you to move into their comfort zone, even though it is not your natural social style. Studies show that some salespeople fall into the category of *drivers*, one which may interact badly with *amiables*, unless the style is modified to suit the prospect, which is why the concept of versatility is a crucial one for you to master.

Versatility is your willingness to control personal behavior patterns and adapt to other people as a means of reducing the possibility of ineffective communication. Your own personal style does not change, but rather techniques are applied that work in that particular situation. For example, when meeting with an analytical, the expressive salesperson can incorporate versatility by talking less, listening more, and focusing on facts. Versatility should never be equated with either insincerity or mere imitation of the prospect's style. Versatile salespeople seek a reasonable compromise. Do not become so changeable that your pace and priority needs are constantly set aside for those of clients.

The prospect's preferences in pace and priorities must be recognized and given the importance that seems right to the prospect. Strive for *Psychological Reciprocity*. That is, you make the initial attempt to get into the client's world. The person is then challenged to move toward you; to reciprocate. You connect! Rapport is established with the client much quicker than if each of you had stayed firmly entrenched in your own particular social style.

The Interaction of Styles

The dimensions of assertiveness and responsiveness operate in people's pace and their priorities. *Pace* is the speed at which a person prefers to move. Those who are low in assertiveness (analyticals and amiables) prefer a slow pace; those high in assertiveness (drivers and expressives) prefer a fast pace in conversation, deliberation, and problem solving.

Priorities are what a person considers important and tend to be related to the dimension of responsiveness. Those who are low in responsiveness put tasks at the top of their priority list, and those who are high in responsiveness put relationships in first place. These conflicts may be summarized as follows:

The Interaction of Styles

Style	Shared Dimension	Source of Conflict	Area of Agreement
Analytical — Amiable	Low Assertiveness	Priorities	Pace
Driver — Expressive	High Assertiveness	Priorities	Pace
Analytical — Driver	Low Responsiveness	Pace	Priorities
Amiable — Expressive	High Responsiveness	Pace	Priorities
Analytical — Expressive	None	Both	None
Amiable — Driver	None	Both	None

Conflicts that involve only priorities or only pace can be handled with relative ease; real trouble results when the styles of two people conflict in both pace and priorities. If you deal with every client in the same way, you will close a small percentage of all your contacts, because you will only close one personality style. But if you learn how to effectively work with all four personality styles, you can significantly increase your closing ratio.

Salespeople who do not adjust their behavior to meet the style needs of clients face deteriorating situations. For example, an expressive salesperson's questions may be interpreted as a personal challenge or attack by an analytical prospect. If the analytical prospect responds to the questions merely to save face, the expressive salesperson then tends to talk more, move faster, and push the analytical into still greater conflict.

In any situation, conflict is finally relieved in a manner typical of the individual style. The expressive usually attacks verbally. The driver tends to become overbearing, pushy, and dictatorial. The amiable generally submits in order to avoid conflict at all costs but experiences resentment and distrust. The analytical withdraws — flight rather than fight. In a conflict situation, most people tend to move to the extreme dimensions of their favorite style.

To avoid distrust and ultimately a breakdown in communication, you must meet the needs of your prospects, especially their behavioral style needs. Treat them as they want to be treated, and move according to their pace and priority.

Identifying Pace and Priority

How do you go about determining someone's pace and priorities? Ask yourself these three questions and observe the answers:

1. How fast does the person make decisions and get things done?

2. How competitive is the person? Not primarily in sports, but:
   • Is the person competitive in a conversation?
   • Does the person fight for air time in a meeting?

3. How much feeling is displayed in verbal and nonverbal communication?
   • How often does the person smile?
   • Do they gesture broadly?

Your goal is to identify pace and priorities accurately and respond in an appropriate manner. How can you find out your prospect's information preferences? Use one of these statements to assist you:

1. *"Ordinarily I have an organized presentation and get right to it, but today maybe I should get to know you better. What would you like me to do?"*

2. *"I am prepared to get right into my presentation or if you prefer we can chat a bit so that I can learn more about you and your organization. Which do you prefer?"*

3. *"There are a lot of ways I can start explaining exactly how this process would work based on the concerns you were kind enough to share with me at our meeting last week. Would you prefer I start with the end in mind and then work backwards, or would you like to go over the step-by-step details first?"*

The expressive and amiable styles would respond to these statements indicating a desire to chat and get to know one another. While the driver and analytical styles would want you to begin your presentation.

GENDER STYLE DIFFERENCES

While it is essential to recognize and adjust to different social styles, it is also necessary to recognize the contribution that gender makes to our communication in the business world. The issue of proxemics, the distance that individuals prefer to keep between themselves and others, also becomes more recognizable when speaking to someone of the opposite sex.

That is why we must be sensitive to gender issues and adjust to them just as we do for social style differences. If not handled correctly, these seemingly insignificant differences can break down communication lines and damage relationships, and this ultimately hurts your company and your income!

One way to ensure effective cross-gender communication is to emphasize and encourage male and female distinctions in management processes and interpersonal relationships. By emphasizing the differences in a positive manner, the different viewpoints can be highly productive. Both men and women bring to the selling table different perspectives, experiences, and communication skills, and they interpret language in very distinct ways. Ultimately, however, they use these distinctly different styles and patterns of speech to deliver roughly the same message.

Relating to the Opposite Sex. Whether or not you have experienced how gender differences hinder relationships in selling when handled improperly, it is clear that the unequal treatment of employees by management hinders the success of any business. A research study by Russ & McNeilly concluded that managers who treat male and female sales reps the same miss the potential benefits that different gender styles provide.

A key question to ask is whether gender differences, in and of themselves, create diverse ways of thinking or different behavioral relationships. If so, what are some things to be aware of when you're selling to someone of the opposite sex? When men and women find themselves sitting across from one another at the bargaining table, they must learn to adjust their styles. During the sales interview they should use the strengths unique to their gender.

While it is true that men and women both bring unique talents to selling that deserve appreciation and respect, it is still impossible to deny the feeling of discomfort or tension when meeting someone for the first time of either gender. Yes, some salespeople are so experienced that they have learned how to ignore this feeling, but it is still a natural human reaction. When meeting someone of the opposite sex, this can appear as sexual tension, while between the same sex, the feeling may emerge as competitive tension. Some view this as stressful or distracting, but it does not have to be so if you see the initial discomfort for what it really is.

This seemingly unproductive tension actually indicates a subconscious desire to further the relationship, not in an improper way, but in a way that will open the lines of communication and establish trust. Ultimately, you must be aware of this feeling and recognize it as a sign of progress in the sale. You are connecting with that person, whether male or female. Once you recognize this, communication will immediately become less tension-filled and more productive. Just remember that nothing can kill a sale more quickly than acting on stereotypes or generalities, regardless of gender.

Exhibit 5.1 provides some suggestions for dealing with gender differences. You must be prepared to communicate effectively with your male and female sales managers, fellow sales reps, as well as the men and women decision-makers you call on. No one can make a sweeping statement about how all women or all men like to sell or be sold. In any selling situation it's vital to communicate in a way that substantiates what's meaningful to that individual, and gender may help determine what a client feels is important. Subtle, gender-based changes to your presentation may give you the edge you're looking for to boost sales.

Exhibit 5.1

How Can Men and Women Better Understand Each Other?

Report talk vs. rapport talk

Bonding through storytelling and anecdotes is fine and often helpful to connect with clients, but be sure to choose good gender gap crossing stories. Acceptable topics include family, school, vacation, pets, or hobbies.

Stop interrupting

Tension or nervousness caused by gender differences can often cause people to interrupt each other. This is a good way to lose a sale. Learn to listen. Then answer in a confident and clear manner.

Feel the sale

There is more to selling than numbers. Read your prospects. Sometimes they need emotional satisfaction as well as bottom line results.

Control the language

Never use terms such as "honey", "dear", or "sweetie" in a professional situation. This is simply not acceptable.

Practice your humor

Being funny at the right moment is very important to almost any presentation. However, think about your jokes and make sure they are not offensive or rude.

Watch your language

Avoid "guy" or "girl" talk when presenting to mixed genders. For example, women should avoid using descriptive words such as "cute" or "adorable" and men should keep away from the use of overtly masculine phrases and terms.

READING THE PROSPECT'S ENVIRONMENT

Important clues to a client's style appear in the environment as well as in verbal and nonverbal actions. Observe how the office is decorated and arranged, how objects are displayed, and what seating arrangements are available. Suppose that upon entering a prospect's office, you notice family pictures on the desk, nature posters, a round desk, and a separate seating area with four comfortable chairs. What would be your first impression of that client's behavioral style? Did you say *amiable*? If so, you are right. Next, you can confirm or adjust your initial impression by observing the prospect's actions and speech. If the prospect rises to greet you personally and sits in an easy chair your impression of amiable would tend to be confirmed.

Let's try another example. You enter the prospect's office and notice a diploma, an achievement plaque, and a poster on the wall that says "Why not?" The desk presents several jumbled stacks of paper and a generally chaotic appearance. Two overstuffed chairs by the open side of the desk provide seating. A bookcase with stacks of books and folders intermixed and a plant on the file cabinet complete the furnishings. The disorganization, the wall decorations emphasizing achievement, and the comfortable and accessible seating suggest that this office houses an *expressive*. But it is important to note here that you must confirm any initial environmental impression by noting the prospect's actions, tone of voice, speech patterns, and interpersonal behavior.

Use knowledge of these styles to characterize the observable behavior of most prospects. Although we all possess traits from each of the styles, you will find that one of the following four styles ordinarily dominates.

Drivers

Drivers exhibit minimum concern for the feelings of others. A vice-president of marketing for a major theme park in Ohio was heard to say, "My secretary used to drive me to distraction. I'd ask her how her weekend went and she'd actually tell me. In detail! All I wanted to hear was fine or not so hot." Now those are the words of a true driver. If you say something harsh, they don't even seem to notice. They consider yes-people to be weak. Stand up to drivers. Sell to them by showing them what your product can do. Drivers' feelings are not easily hurt because they do not take things personally.

Drivers tend to be intense, competitive, fast-paced, and goal-oriented. They pride themselves on the ability to get things done. They like to make things happen. Convince them that your proposed action works and that it will provide all the benefits you promise. They are more impressed by what they see and hear than by what others say about you or your offering.

At their best, drivers are human dynamos. Resourceful, organized, and pragmatic, they impose high standards on themselves and others. As a result, they may be seen as impatient or tireless. They push to perfect their own skills but also invest time and effort in coaching other people in skill development. At their worst, they appear to give inadequate consideration to the long-range consequences of their actions. They draw criticism for seeking to impose on others their expectations for drive, speed and zeal. Under stress, drivers can seem anti-intellectual and may defensively overreact to any opinions differing from their own, especially to those that seem to resist action. Drivers are likely to feel that any failure is evidence that others were not loyal enough or willing to work hard enough to make the project a success.

When selling to drivers, be prepared and organized, fast paced and to the point. Remain professional and businesslike. Study their goals and propose solutions that are clearly related to those goals. Suggest several options and allow them to choose.

Customize Your Selling Style to Hit a Hole-in-One with the Driver

Drivers do not care about developing a personal relationship with you. They are impatient and need to be in control. Therefore,

1. Spend little time attempting to relate to them on a personal level.
2. Move fast and isolate the most dollar-related product benefits that can be verified by producing concrete evidence.
3. Do not make a lengthy presentation citing all the benefits. Be brief and stress the bottom line.
4. The fewer visual aids you use, the better. Any visuals you choose must be absolutely relevant to the major points.
5. Ask questions to involve them, get them to talk, and allow them to lead. Asking questions helps you to maintain control of the presentation.
6. They will test you to see what you are made of; so be willing to joust with them. If you challenge them, challenge the concepts rather than the person.
7. Answer objections immediately, and never try to bluff.
8. Present several alternatives from which they may select their own solution. Avoid telling them what is best.
9. An action close stressing an immediate opportunity works well.

Expressives

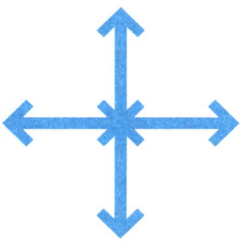

Expressives temper assertiveness with concern for the feelings of others. You must compliment them. They desire success, but are recognition motivated. Show them how to win. Let them talk and they often sell themselves. Tell them who else uses your product. Testimonials from well-known people or people they respect are important.

Expressives pride themselves on originality, foresight, and the ability to see the big picture. Reinforce their self-image as visionaries and idea people, and they will be receptive to your ideas. At their best, expressives often see new possibilities and present fresh ideas and approaches to problems. At their worst, they seem to base decisions on opinions, hunches, or intuition rather than on facts. They want to delegate the details of a project or deal to someone who has time for it while they are free to dream. They may be impatient when others demand some documentation before accepting the vision or ideas they offer. Under stress, expressives run the risk of seeming detached. They appear indifferent to problems and seem to be living in an ivory tower. They may spend time defending their ideas instead of trying to make them work in a practical manner.

The expressive's love of risk-taking makes it easier for them to take a chance on your product. Refer to the product as a "sure bet" or guarantee that you will "make this risk pay off big." Emphasize the importance of risk-taking to making progress and meeting goals, and show the expressive your product's payoff potential by sharing exactly what it can do and what that means to them. When you have a qualified expressive whose needs match your product's benefits, you should not have to do much persuading. Remember, expressives are intuition-driven.

Developing a Presentation Strategy for the Expressive

Expressives are visionaries and dreamers. Therefore,

1. Plan to show them how they can personally win and how their company can benefit.
2. Open with innovative ideas for them to grow and win with your offering.
3. Ask open-end questions that allow them to talk at length about "their" plans for growth. Then relate your product's benefits to their plans.
4. Present proposals and seek feedback, using them as sounding boards. Convey respect for their intelligence, foresight, and prominence. Be careful, however, to avoid patronizing them.
5. Use some showmanship. They like to see the yellow binder, but are not necessarily interested in the details of what it contains.
6. Never argue or back them into a corner.
7. Ask if they want you to respond to their stated concerns. Often they respond, "No, I just wanted you to know how I am thinking."
8. Use testimonials, especially from well-known people because they identify with who else uses the product.
9. Allow them to carry out their own game plan, not yours.

Amiables

Amiables are submissive and willing to go along with the crowd. They need time to get to know you personally, so allow plenty of warmup time. They are undisciplined in the use of time. Agreeable in nature, they are also easily hurt. They want to be liked.

Amiables tend to be perceptive and observant individuals who are concerned with whether they like you, trust you, and can picture a positive long-term relationship with you. They are people-oriented in their management style and resent doing business with anyone who makes them uncomfortable or is unresponsive to their feelings. Their business decisions are markedly influenced by how their various options might impact the people in the organization. Before they accept your proposal or idea, they must be convinced that you personally believe in it. They must also know what risks are involved — especially risks to personal relationships.

Amiables at their best are truly perceptive and aware, skilled in communication, and empathetic listeners. Their insight enables them to assess organizational politics accurately. At their worst, they seem more concerned with the process of interaction than with the content of the matter at hand. They appear to be flying by the seat of their pants instead of relying in any measure on logic and thought. They seem to regard their own emotions as facts and act on the basis of their feelings.

A Presentation Strategy for the Amiable

Amiables must be convinced that you are authentic and have their best interests at heart. They have a difficult time saying yes. Therefore,

1. Plan to approach with as much personal information as possible.
2. Avoid a rigid or canned approach and presentation.
3. Make an informal presentation with visuals and testimonial information.
4. Use empathy and show that you understand and accept their feelings.
5. Spend some time relating. Move to a first-name basis quickly.
6. Be open and candid. Develop a personal relationship with them.
7. Offer them money-back guarantees and personal assurances.
8. Avoid asking directly for their business. Instead, assume that they are favorably disposed to your proposition and suggest an easy next step.
9. Be prepared to use third-party references and case histories that link them to others.

THE HANDBOOK FOR RELATIONSHIP SELLING

To sell effectively to amiables, you have to show them you're a team player. Position yourself as their newest team member by first building rapport, then work side-by-side with them to accomplish the goals they have set. To minimize the amiable's insecurities, talk about the problems your product can solve and how solving them will help improve control and performance in the workplace, which will enhance management's image of them. It is the amiable's job to nurture the team, so don't forget to outline what your product will do for the people in the company.

Analyticals

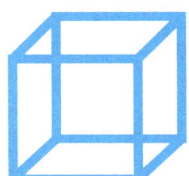

Analyticals are highly logical, organized, and unsentimental. They tend to be fact-oriented. Their contribution to the management team is their ability to solve difficult problems and make sound, rational business decisions based on evidence and intelligent inferences rather than on imagination or gut feelings. They take a logical, ordered approach to responsibilities.

The more supporting data you can provide for your ideas, the more likely you are to sell to them. They have little interest in your opinions and more in your ability to assemble and organize supportive data for use in weighing options and arriving at a systematic, well-thought-out solution to problems.

At their best, analyticals appear to be a consistent force for progress. They are top-flight planners and doers. They can cut through untested ideas and emotional fervor to find the core truth. They are effective organizers for research and planning. They are valuable in executing logical, painstaking, and profitable projects.

At their worst, they are overly cautious and conservative. They emphasize deliberation over action. They may become so involved in evaluating all the various details of a situation that others may regard them as indecisive stumbling blocks to innovative action. Under stress, analyticals can become rigid and insecure. They may fear taking risks. They seem more concerned with being right than with seizing opportunities.

In sales interviews with analyticals, be well prepared and equipped to answer all questions. Be cordial, but move quickly to the task. Study their needs logically. Ask lots of questions that show a clear direction and pay close attention to their answers. Support your logical proposal with full documentation.

NEUROLINGUISTIC PROGRAMMING

An entirely different approach to communicating effectively and understanding more about prospects is offered by neurolinguistic programming (NLP). When it first began to attract attention, many people considered NLP to be just another pop-psychology craze similar to the various communication approaches that have been offered as the ultimate answer for managers who wanted increased personal power and influence, for lawyers who wanted to sway judges and juries, and for salespeople who wanted to sell anything to anyone. Instead, NLP offers one more way to observe people and understand their needs. It is entirely different from the behavioral styles theory, but in no way contradicts it.

Indentifying Modes of Perception

NLP is based on recognizing and then appealing to the dominant modes of perception used by another person. We all use these forms to map reality and build a model of what the world is like that can guide us through our environment. NLP is the science of how the brain learns. All of us have a basic learning mode: Visual, auditory or kinesthetic. Each is used in various situations, yet most of us will favor one these types of perception.

1. Auditory

   Some people perceive the world largely by hearing. They learn more quickly by listening than by reading or seeing. Experiences presented through other senses are mentally translated into an auditory mode. These are the people who test ideas by how they sound. They often use responses like, "I hear what you're saying," "It sounds good to me," and "I'm hearing a lot of complaints about that situation."

2. Visual

   Other people perceive the world largely through sight. They learn and form opinions from what they see. They are the ones who originated the saying, "Seeing is believing." They form mental pictures of their experiences as a means of interpretation. They frequently use sentences like, "I see what you mean," "I'm in a fog about the whole concept," and "Do you get the picture?"

3. Kinesthetic

   A smaller number of people perceive the world through the sense of touch. They feel life. Everything has a texture that either attracts or repels them. Subsets of the kinesthetic mode are the taste and the smell modes that sometimes come into play for kinesthetic people. Those operating in the kinesthetic mode say things like, "This deal just feels right," "That was a smooth presentation," "That transaction left a bad taste in my mouth," and "I smell something rotten about this deal."

This information was first used to teach therapists how to recognize these representational modes, and then use them to build rapport with the patient, to establish a climate of trust, and to improve communication. It soon became clear that this powerful communication tool would work for people other than therapists, including salespeople.

Tapping Into Prospect's Perception

Some salespeople seem to have a natural or intuitive ability to identify a prospect's behavior and personality traits and to adapt to them. They seem to possess an automatic radar system that instantly and unobtrusively sends out test signals, interprets the feedback, and then chooses the best tactics for establishing rapport. Developing such skills is one of the most difficult parts of sales training. NLP is one technique you can use to develop this ability.

Learning Eye Cues

Our eyes are seldom still. The direction they move during a conversation reveals the system of perception that is active at the moment. Some left-handed people reverse the normal right and left eye cues; therefore, eye cues can be used only as clues to be confirmed by further observation. Figure 5.3 illustrates the various eye cues that help to identify the operative system. Eye movements in most people are similar and can be expected to show these processes:

Figure 5.3

Eye Cues Indicating Thought Processes

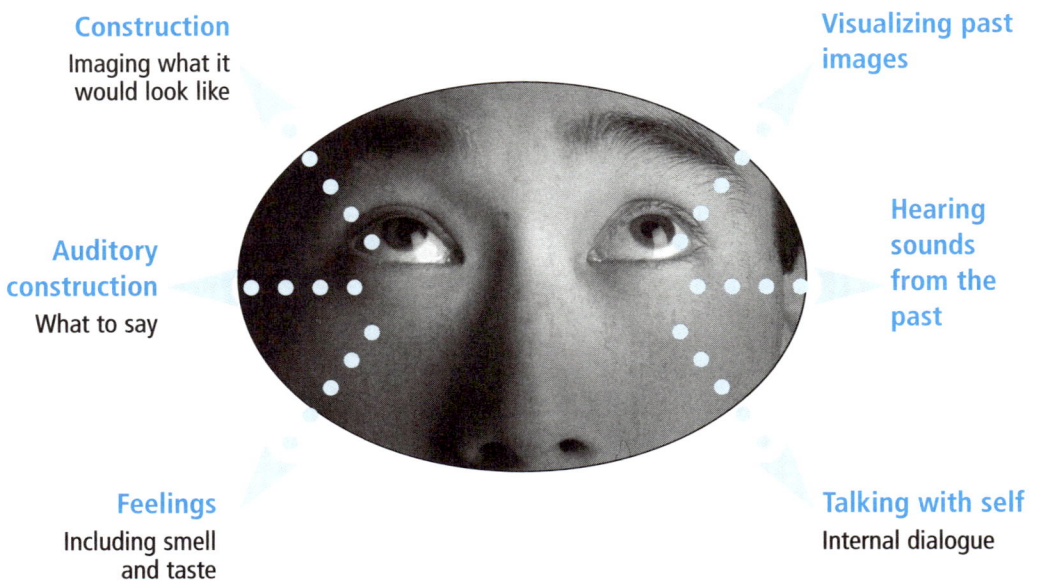

Construction
Imaging what it would look like

Visualizing past images

Auditory construction
What to say

Hearing sounds from the past

Feelings
Including smell and taste

Talking with self
Internal dialogue

Interpreting Predicate Words

Most people are fairly consistent in eye movements, body language, behavior style, and all the other ways anyone has devised to help you tune in on your prospects. NLP also teaches us to look at eye cues and test them against predicate words, that is, how people talk.

Table 5.1 provides a list of predicate words that provide important information to confirm what is observed from eye cues. These words tell you how the other person is processing information. When these words match eye cues, you are on fairly safe ground in deciding which mode of perception is operating for the prospect at that moment.

Table 5.1

Predicate Words — A Guide to the Modes of Perception

Visual		Auditory		Kinesthetic	
analyze	look	announce	noise	active	intuition
angle	notice	articulate	proclaim	affected	lukewarm
appear	obscure	audible	pronounce	bearable	motion
cognizant	observe	discuss	remark	concrete	panicky
conspicuous	perception	dissonant	report	emotional	pressure
dream	perspective	divulge	roar	feel	sensitive
examine	picture	earshot	rumor	firm	shallow
focus	scene	enunciate	shrill	flow	softly
foresee	sight	gossip	silence	foundation	solid
glance	sketchy	hear	sound	grasp	structured
hindsight	survey	hush	squeal	grip	tension
horizon	vague	inquire	talk	hanging	tied
idea		interview	tell	hassle	touch

To be a good builder of rapport, use a few initial questions to get the prospect to talk so you can discover which type of system is in use. You do not have to memorize a long list of specific questions to evoke the crucial responses needed to determine a prospect's system. The usual opening dialogue you use to get acquainted and put the prospect at ease serves admirably. Compare these examples of the type of responses you might receive to such opening questions and determine which system the answer seems to indicate:

Question: That's an impressive trophy. Do you play a lot of golf?

Answer A: I play in a club foursome almost every Saturday. I enjoy keeping active. It wards off some of the pressure. Sometimes when things get into an unbearable hassle, golf relieves some of the tension. Gripping the club, feeling the impact as I hit the ball, and getting into the swing of the physical motion seems to put me back on a concrete foundation and makes me ready to get back in touch with reality instead of lapsing into panicky emotions.

Answer B: I play on Wednesday afternoons and see it as an opportunity to get away from the work scene when the picture gets too crowded or blurred. On the golf course I have time to lose myself in a new perspective. I look down the fairway all the way to the horizon and dream of seeing my ball fly all the way to the hole in one shot. Of course, I've actually done that only once, but the dream lets me focus on what is most important, observe the obstacles, and picture a way to avoid them. Then when I get back to work, the whole view seems to have more clarity and the path around the obstacles becomes conspicuous where before it had been obscured because I was too close to the trees to see the forest.

How did you identify the systems used by these two different people? The first was **kinesthetic**. Did you note some of the key words?

active	tension	foundation	emotions
pressure	feeling	touch	concrete
hassle	motion	panicky	

The second answer was **visual**; note the key words:

see	blurred	dream	view
scene	look	focus	clarity
picture	horizon	picture	conspicuous

Be sure to take into account the eye cues, body language, and any other information you have about the prospect as you attempt to decide which system the prospect is using. Remember that we all use the different perceptual fields, often in quick succession, but most of us have one we use more often than the others. When eye cues fit the predicate words used, you have a fairly sound basis for deciding what is going on in the prospect's mind. Once you know the prospect's favorite system, you know how that person usually maps out the environment and plans a route to the solution of a problem or to the reaching of a goal. Then you can speak a language the auditory prospect can hear, draw a picture the visual prospect can see, or structure something concrete the kinesthetic prospect can grasp.

Reportedly, NLP has been used by people who have turned it into a powerful manipulative tool for their own benefit to the detriment of others. When used ethically, however, it is a great method for cutting down the time needed to build trust and rapport—a necessary process in relationship selling.

Its misuse does not discount its effectiveness; many kinds of knowledge gets twisted into tools for satisfying personal greed by those whose value systems allow such unethical action. If you look at NLP as an additional tool for interpreting the behavior, needs, and motivation of people, you can use it just as ethically and helpfully as you can use the information about behavioral styles, gender differences, and body language.

Social Style Summary

	Driver	**Expressive**	**Amiable**	**Analytical**
Backup style	Autocratic	Attacker	Acquiescer	Avoider
Measures personal value by	Results	Applause or approval	Security	Accuracy, "being right"
For growth, needs to	Listen	Check	Initiate	Decide
Needs climate that	Allows to build own structure	Inspires to reach goals	Suggests	Provides details
Takes time to be	Efficient	Stimulating	Agreeable	Accurate
Support their	Conclusions and actions	Dreams and intuitions	Relationships and feelings	Principles and thinking
Present benefits that tell	What	Who	Why	How
For decisions, give them	Options and probabilities	Testimonials and incentives	Guarantees & assurances	Evidence & service
Their specialty is	Controlling	Socializing	Supporting	Technical

THE HANDBOOK FOR RELATIONSHIP SELLING

Finding Your Selling Style

- Knowledge of behavioral styles is a useful tool for gaining insight into the thinking of buyers. The model uses the assertiveness and responsiveness dimensions of behavior to assess an individual's social style.

- Versatility is your ability to adjust your own personal pace and priorities to facilitate interaction with a person of another style.

- Recognizing typical behavioral cues makes it possible to classify people quickly into one of four basic personality styles: driver, expressive, amiable, or analytical.

- Gender differences require diverse ways of thinking and using our behavioral relationships. Adjust to different gender styles to enhance communication.

- A related tool for communication is neurolinguistic programming (NLP), which uses observation of eye cues and typical predicate words to discover the particular perceptual field a person is using at a given time.

- Never attempt to adopt a style that is an insincere imitation of the prospect. Take the lead in finding common ground with the prospect. Practice and use psychological reciprocity.

Part III

Gaining Knowledge, Preparing, and Planning for the Presentation

Goal-setting is the strongest human force for self-motivation.

Chapter 6

Preparation for Success in Selling

FOCAL POINTS

- **The product knowledge needed for success**

- **Sales technology tools. Use them to your advantage**

- **The concept of product positioning**

- **Fear, incentive, and attitude motivation**

- **Accepting responsibility for self-motivation**

- **Set and achieve goals for success**

PREPARING TO SELL

Success in sales involves a combination of the training provided by your company and your own active preparation in learning and personal commitment. The more help the company gives, the easier your job is. Because the company's success depends upon your success, your preparation is a major mutual concern. Adequate preparation for success in selling involves at least three areas that are considered in this chapter.

- Product knowledge

- Sales force automation

- Motivation and goal setting

Some elements in each of these three areas are the primary responsibility of the company; some are primarily your responsibility. No matter who bears the primary responsibility, both you and your company are active participants; neither can be passive because too much is at stake.

PRODUCT KNOWLEDGE

Newly hired salespeople may have general knowledge of their company or industry and may even have some knowledge of the specific products they will be marketing and selling. However, perhaps you were hired with little or no knowledge of the company and its products or even of the industry. Obtaining product knowledge is one of the first prerequisites of success. One of the most important activities you must do is to acquire sufficient product knowledge to feel comfortable on your sales calls.

What do you need to know about the product? One answer to that question is everything! Nevertheless, you cannot delay beginning sales activity until you have had time to learn everything, and you cannot cease to learn about the product or service once you begin to sell. Gaining product knowledge is an ongoing process.

The Product Itself

Product knowledge begins with the product itself: Its specific features, its benefits, and its acceptance in the marketplace. Product knowledge includes knowing all available options — how it can be adapted to the particular customer's needs, and how it performs under varying conditions. Detailed product knowledge prepares you to answer any question a customer might have and to offer whatever reassurance is necessary in the process of helping the customer reach a decision.

When you know the product backward and forward, you can answer detailed, technical questions from expert buyers or explain in simple terms to one who is considering a first purchase of a product of this kind. You seldom tell a prospect all the information you have, but having all the information gives you a whole library from which you can choose the best items for the current situation.

Performance

Performance information about the product is another vital area of product knowledge. How long will it last? What kind of wear and stress does it tolerate? How fast does it run? What is its output? How much training is necessary for an employee to operate or use it? How much fuel or power is needed to run it? Can it be repaired? How much maintenance is required? Who can perform needed maintenance? Are spare parts readily available? In the more technical industries, salespeople have access to company engineers and advisors who furnish engineering and technical information when it is required; sales knowledge in this case means knowing who to call on and when to ask for back up.

Manufacturing

Product knowledge includes thorough knowledge of the manufacturing process and methods that affect the quality, performance, or durability of the product. These vital ingredients of quality affect buying decisions. Knowledge of the manufacturing process also enables you to explain why the price that seems high to the prospect is actually reasonable or why delivery takes longer than the buyer had expected.

Distribution Channels

The company's distribution methods are an important area of product knowledge. What channels are used? Why? Are exclusive dealerships granted in certain areas? Is selective distribution used? Do discount houses and chains sell the product in competition with other types of retail outlets?

Another important element of distribution concerns pricing policies. How much the dealer pays, availability of quantity discounts, applicable credit terms, and whether the company will consider negotiating special deals are all elements of distribution about which customers are concerned.

Information About the Company

Product knowledge also involves gaining as much information as possible about the company you represent. You need to know something about the history of the company: Who founded it and when, how the present product line evolved, the company's position in the marketplace, its past and present performance and growth, and its primary customers or clients. Knowledge of the company also includes tactics and strategies that affect the customer — service, delivery options, and company policies.

Service Available

Once a product is sold, your responsibility has just begun. Service after the sale cements the client-salesperson relationship and ensures repeat orders. You must know the company's service policy: What repairs, replacements, or adaptations are considered the responsibility of the company? What charges are made for service? Who performs the service? Where? On what kind of time schedule? What kind of consulting service is available to adapt or adjust the product to the customer's needs?

Product Knowledge Application

Product knowledge is sterile and unproductive unless you can use it and apply it to the problems or needs of a particular client. Knowing the materials and specifications used in manufacturing enables you to advise a prospect to order your product and expect it to perform as desired. This knowledge also helps you suggest what custom changes might be made in the product to fit a particular need of the client.

Knowledge of the Competition

Knowledge of the competition is often overlooked as an element of product knowledge. You must know how to leverage information technology and assume the role of trusted advisor to the client's business. Learn about the products of your major competitors; know their credit terms, their prices, their delivery schedules, and their reputation for service. Most buyers — either personal consumers or company purchasing agents — are not weighing the advantages of buying against those of not buying; they are trying to decide which product to buy.

One of the advantages of studying your competition is that you are reminded of the good points of your own product or company. This will help refresh your own presentations, especially if you have been selling the same product for a period of time. Exhibit 6.1 provides an overview of the four possible areas of competitive advantage.

Exhibit 6.1

Differential Competitive Advantage

Product Superiority	Service Superiority	Source Superiority	People Superiority
Versatility	Delivery	Time established	Personal knowledge and skill
Efficiency	Inventory	Competitive standing	Knowledge and skill of support personnel
Storage	Credit	Community image	
Handling time	Training	Location	Integrity and character
Safety	Merchandising	Size	
Appearance	Installation	Financial soundness	Standing in community
Design	Maintenance	Policies and practices	
Mobility			Flexibility of call schedule
Packaging			Interpersonal skills
Life expectancy			Mutual friends
Adaptability			Cooperation

Product knowledge can be either a help or a hindrance, depending on how it is used. Exhibit 6.2 illustrates how salespeople can use their special knowledge to close — or to lose — a sale.

SALES FORCE AUTOMATION

Computers in Selling and Sales Training

To keep up with the increasing demands of the continually changing, competitive marketplace, salespeople are asked to become more productive at everything they do. They have to talk to more people, provide more value, and do a better job with each customer they call on. Technology relieves salespeople of many mundane administrative tasks and allows them more time for planning and selling.

Today the sales industry is experiencing an explosive trend toward automation. Salespeople can have a clear direction and the right incentive, but if they don't have the right tools, sales will suffer despite their best intentions. For example, Jim Hill, former director of sales for Sun Microsystem's Asia Pacific region, said, "I sent five managers into the field to talk to reps, and they all said the same thing. These guys were burning a lot of time sitting in front of their workstations trying to figure out all the administrative stuff." The sales reps just needed some tools that would help them reduce their administrative time so they could spend more time selling.

So Hill and his managers created the *One More Deal* program, which gave each of the 500 direct sales reps Web-based tools, such as standard proposal templates and better customer data so that they didn't have to "reinvent the wheel" every time they worked on a proposal for a prospect. As a result, the reps cut their administrative paperwork by over 50 percent, and sales in the region went up 45 percent.

Exhibit 6.2

Using Product Knowledge to Fit the Need

An automobile salesman was showing a new car to a husband and wife. They told him that the wife would be driving the car primarily for neighborhood errands. The salesman spent a lot of time explaining that the car had front-wheel drive and that the motor was mounted at a ninety-degree angle to the traditional position. He loaded his sales talk with terms like engine ratios, rpm's, and torque, and bragged about the car's ability to accelerate from zero to sixty faster than any of the competition. The woman's questions about what that meant for her needs produced even more complicated explanations that did not interest her or her husband. The couple bought a car demonstrated by the salesman from another dealer. He stressed styling, real leather upholstery, the comfort of adjustable seats, and the added visibility provided by the rear-window defroster, and then invited the wife to test-drive the car.

Web-Based Sales Training

Gone are the days when the only method of sales force training was to either rotate people through a program or close down once a year for an annual sales seminar. Web-based technology makes training easier and more affordable by maximizing flexibility and effectiveness for both the sales force and the sales managers. Selling time is a very valuable commodity. Any time spent out of the field is costly for your salespeople. The benefits of Web-based training include:

- 24-hour access — allows for fast and convenient training.

- Easier management of geographically dispersed teams.

- Instant new product information and current product updates — keeps sales force up to date on a daily or even hourly basis.

- Direct performance measurements — feedback can be immediate.

- Economical — reduces costs of airfare, hotel stays, and convention expenses.

- Sales reps can focus their attention on the specific training they need.

One such Internet-based sales training system is *RedHotSalesTV*. It is an Internet training system that allows sales reps to watch streaming videos of Paul Goldner's training seminars along with a synchronized PowerPoint presentation. There is also a workbook that can be downloaded by each participant.

E-learning is not where it needs to be when it comes to interpersonal sales training. Even the best Internet training cannot replace live sales training, role plays, and simulation exercises. The industry is really going toward *blended* training. You don't get rid of face-to-face training, and you don't get rid of *online* training. Together they form a mutually beneficial relationship.

THE IMPACT OF SALES TECHNOLOGY TOOLS

The companies that find ways of responding quickly to customer needs and making information easily available to their business partners will have a competitive edge. The implementation of an effective sales force automation program provides numerous company benefits which relate directly to improving the bottom-line profit picture. Sales force automation can help increase your sales efficiency in three functional areas:

Personal Productivity

a. Laptop Computers — provide you with desktop power wherever you go. Handheld computers and PDAs give you instant access to important contact information, sales scripts, and documents all in your pocket. Handhelds come with such built-in core applications as a calendar, contact book, memo pad, calculator, and expense report program.

b. Contact Management Software — no more paper mess and scribbled notes. In addition to providing the functionality of an electronic Rolodex listing all your customer contacts, these products offer you powerful tools for tracking detailed customer information; scheduling appointments, activities, and to-dos; and integrating a number of Web resources into a single sales force automation solution.

   Some of the better-known software programs available today are Surado Solutions' *SmartContactManager* and FrontRange's *Goldmine*, in addition to Interact Commerce Corporation's *ACT!*.

c. Mapping Programs and GPS technology — the road warrior will never be lost or late to an appointment with these new field guides and real-time location finders available in PDAs, handhelds, and in many new car models. With the information plotted on a map, the administration of territories becomes immeasurably more accurate.

Improved Communications

a. Internet and Videoconferencing — face-to-face interaction with clients globally without the travel costs. Also great for proposals and presentations. This may well be the personal selling medium of the future.

b. Telecommuting — no more fighting rush-hour traffic! Not only can you check e-mail, but you can update databases, product information, and appointments from the comfort of your home.

Transactional Processing

a. **Electronic Data Interchange (EDI) Technologies** — the entire company has up-to-date order, processing, and fulfillment information. When customers place an order they can have instant access to product information, just like e-mail. Automate the selling chain to include customers, distributors, and suppliers.

b. **Corporate Contact Management and Custom Reporting Programs** — shared contact information that is modified and updated by everyone in the sales office. You can customize reports to the specific needs for each of your individual customers and prospects.

c. **Internet Database Development Technologies** — providing online order and product information and order entry for salespeople or their customers. Utilizing Internet Web sites is an effective method of advancing information between a company, its sales channel members, and its customers.

PRODUCT POSITIONING

The level of competition today is just amazing. There are so many brands, and so many salespeople trying to get everybody else's business, and they're coming at you from all over the world. Just in the past 20 years, the number of new automobile models increased from 140 to 260 and the number of over-the-counter pain relievers went from 17 to 41. That makes positioning — the marketing strategy of differentiating a product or company in the mind of a prospect — more important than ever. Once a business identifies what makes it unique in the eyes of the consumer, the focus of its entire marketing and sales strategy. You must be given that differentiating idea. Exhibit 6.3 gives sales professionals five points that will enable them to go into an organization and say — "Allow me to explain to you how and why my company and its products are different."

Positioning was popularized by Jack Trout and Al Ries in their book *Positioning: The Battle for Your Mind*. The term "positioning" refers to developing a specific marketing mix to influence potential customers' overall perception of a brand, product line, or organization. *Positioning* is the place a product occupies in potential customers' minds relative to competing offerings. Once a position is selected, product, price, place, and promotion strategies and tactics are designed to reinforce the sought-after position. These marketing mix components represent a bundle of individual dimensions that are designed to work together to create a competitive advantage.

Exhibit 6.3

Key Points for Developing a Powerful Market Position

- **Find Out** what qualities of your products and services are most important to your customers. Then use the information to create a unique niche for yourself.

- **Put Together** a marketing strategy built around several features that are important to your customers and that will set you apart from the competition. And then develop an integrated marketing communication message that reinforces those attributes in the customer's mind.

- **Remember** the way you service your customers or sell to them can be a powerful difference. For example, if you are in an industry where the prevailing culture stresses face-to-face selling, the ability to buy directly online can be very attractive.

- **Recognize** that focusing on the few attributes that really set you apart means you can't be all things to all people. When you shout, "Hey, everybody," you end up satisfying nobody. Zero in on those customers that are a part of your specific target market.

- **Keep** an eye on how your competitors are positioning themselves. Be ready to respond to their claims and make sure you maintain a differential competitive advantage.

To illustrate this, the Otis Elevator Company has positioned itself as an innovator that offers tangible benefits for its customer base. For instance, their Remote Elevator Monitoring system (REM) allows Otis to monitor the performance of its elevators in their clients' buildings, so mechanics can fix minor problems before they cause a major shutdown. Otis has created an e-commerce plan that gives prospects and customers the opportunity to research and buy its elevators on the Web, and moves the REM system online, enabling existing customers to monitor the service of their elevators on the Web as well. Another competitive advantage is a display panel inside new elevators showing information from the Internet. These innovations have helped Otis expand its relationships with customers.

MOTIVATION AND GOAL SETTING

Salespeople often find that they have the needed product knowledge and sales and computer skills but have trouble getting around to using them, or else they work hard and long but find that what they accomplish fails to bring them lasting satisfaction. The missing ingredient is motivation.

Numerous definitions have been given for motivation. Perhaps the simplest is that motivation is the reason for taking action. This definition can be expanded slightly to say that motivation is the *impetus* to begin a task, the *incentive* to expend an amount of effort in accomplishing the task, and the *willingness* to sustain the effort until the task is completed.

The question most asked of business consultants is, "How can we motivate our sales force?" The answer most given by consultants is, "You can't." The reason for this answer is that the question typically implies that somewhere there are strategies, techniques, or gimmicks that, once discovered and implemented, will double or triple sales motivation and productivity. Consultants realize that genuine and lasting motivation is not something management does, but rather a process that management fosters and allows to happen.

The primary responsibility for developing and sustaining motivation rests with you; the company's role is to provide a supportive climate in which the development and sustaining of motivation is encouraged. Bob Nelson, author of *1001 Ways to Reward Employees*, says, "What motivates people the most takes just a little time and thoughtfulness." Recognize them as individuals and you're giving them what they most crave. Read **The Lighthouse Story** for an inspirational idea that cost just a few dollars but paid enormous dividends.

The Lighthouse Story

Jonathan Berger, director of strategic accounts for Square D/Schneider Electric, had a salesperson on his team close a very important account that put a fairly large bonus in the sales rep's pocket. So Berger decided to take the extra step that made this sale a truly memorable triumph. He knew the sales rep's wife had a passion for photographing lighthouses, so he sent her a small crystal lighthouse with a note that recognized her husband's achievements and thanked her for her support and the time she had invested. The wife wrote Berger back and said, "Never has anyone in any company ever acknowledged my existence or the contribution I make to my husband's career." This story is good enough to pass on. So relate the story to a sales manager friend of yours!

Practical Motivation for Salespeople

All motivation theories agree that motivation arises as a response to either an external or internal stimulus. Recognizing those stimuli that operate in your own experience can help you discover ways to control either the stimuli or your responses to them in a way that produces a positive, sustained motivational power and the success you desire. Motivation may arise in fear — the fear of punishment or withholding of acceptance if behavior does not conform to expectations. It may come from incentive—the promise of reward for desired behavior. But the most effective type of motivation is that arising in attitude — behavior chosen because it fits your internal values and standards.

Fear Motivation. Fear as a motivating force has some value. Fear is a natural emotion designed as protection from danger. Fear motivation has some advantages.

- It protects the individual from self-destruction or harm.

- It protects society from undesirable behavior.

- It is sometimes the quickest way to accomplish a desired reaction.

In spite of these advantages, fear motivation has serious disadvantages that more than offset its benefits.

- *Fear is external.* It is effective only as long as the enforcing power is stable. When the parent, teacher, or sales manager is out of sight, fear motivation is materially weakened.

- *Fear is temporary.* Threats or punishment may control behavior for a time, but people tune out warnings if they discover that threats are not always carried out.

- *Fear is negative.* It is directed largely toward not doing something or toward doing something unpleasant merely because it is an imposed duty rather than a chosen activity. A warning not to do something creates a void that may be filled by another equally undesirable behavior.

Incentive Motivation. The use of incentives for motivation is generally considered more enlightened than the use of fear. An incentive is the promise of a benefit or reward to be earned in return for certain behaviors. The attempt to produce motivated activity by offering incentives is common in sales organizations. Some common incentives used include the appeal to work harder to earn increased commissions; contests, certificates, and plaques for quotas reached; bonuses; the promise of an enlarged or better sales territory; and perks such as a reserved parking place, a private office, a personal secretary, or a company car. You have to understand what motivates each individual on your team and use that information. Like fear motivation, incentive motivation has advantages.

- Incentive motivation calls for extra effort. When a promised reward is highly desirable, salespeople put forth almost superhuman effort to win it.

- Incentive motivation is positive and promises something desirable. Salespeople are not frozen into inaction by fear of being punished or deprived.

It's All a Matter of Perspective

Two salesmen fell on hard times and ended up broke in a small town in Montana. They needed money to move on and learned that the town paid $20 each for wolf pelts. They sensed the opportunity. That night they set out with a couple of clubs and some borrowed supplies and made camp in the distant hills. They were no sooner asleep than one was startled by an eerie howl. He crawled outside the tent to find himself surrounded by hundreds of snarling wolves. Back into the tent he crawled and shook his buddy. "Wake up!" he cried. "Wake up! We're rich!"

It's all a matter of perspective.

Like fear motivation, however, incentive motivation carries built-in disadvantages.

- *Incentive motivation is external.* Behavior depends upon the initiative of the person who offers the reward rather than upon the salesperson who will earn it.

- *Incentive motivation is temporary.* A salesperson may put forth a great deal of effort to win a sales contest or to earn some desired reward but not continue that level of activity or effort once the contest is over.

- A promised reward that is *not perceived as desirable* provides no motivation for action.

- Incentives once earned often come to be regarded as *rights* instead of a special privilege for outstanding performance. For example, salespeople who qualify for a company car by high productivity and enjoy this reward for several years feel incensed if the requirements for having a company car are raised and they fail to meet the new quota, even though they improve their sales for the year.

Attitude Motivation. Attitude motivation operates on the concept that the only lasting and uniformly effective motivation is the personal motivation that comes from the internal structure of the individual. It is based on a strong self-image and a belief in the possibility of success. Attitude motivation is self-motivation. All great salespeople inherently possess this powerful, internal drive. Self-motivation can be shaped and molded, but it cannot be taught.

Self-motivation is the result of the choices made by individuals in response to conditioning influences. Fear and self-doubt are the habitual attitudes of some people, but others choose, instead, to respond to life positively. For example, some salespeople who are told they're too inexperienced decide that they are and always will be. Then they wait for someone to tell them what to do. However, others respond to the statement by choosing to believe that their condition is temporary. As a result, they are willing and eager to try different activities, stretch their imaginations, and attempt new goals. They do not wait for someone else to motivate them; they are always reaching out for new experiences. These salespeople are self-motivated. What you are, then, is not entirely a result of what happens to you. *What you are is a result of how you react to what happens to you, and your reactions are a matter of choice.*

The advantages of attitude motivation are the opposites of the disadvantages of fear and incentive motivation:

- *Attitude motivation is internal.* Because attitudes come from within, you do not need to wait for an outside stimulus to make appropriate choices and take action.

- *Attitude motivation is permanent.* An attitude, once thoroughly established, continues to operate on an automatic basis until you do something to alter it. Self-motivation is the only kind of motivation that can be sustained over a long period of time.

Attitude Motivation Through Goal Setting

The single most important tool for developing self-motivation is a program of personal goals. A personal goals program creates desire — one of the most powerful emotions operating in human experience. If you want to be able to choose where you will go with your sales effort, and how you will get there, you need clear goals and strategies. Only then will you have the power to direct your efforts.

Figure 6.1 is the Million Dollar Personal Success Plan that Paul J. Meyer, founder and chairman of the board of SMI International, developed for his own use at the age of nineteen. It provides a workable plan for achieving success in selling.

Crystallized Thinking. You must know what you want to achieve. If your goals are hazy and poorly defined, you cannot plan concrete action steps for their achievement. You must write down and date your goals. Monitoring your status keeps you focused. Without specific action plans, much of your time and effort is wasted. In Chapter 15, we will address action plans and effective time management techniques in much greater detail.

A Plan of Action with Deadlines. A written plan of action keeps you on track and headed toward the achievement of your goals. You know exactly what to do next. A written plan also reveals conflicts between various goals so that you can plan ahead and make a reasonable schedule for the time and resources needed to reach all your goals. Deadlines provide you with the needed time frame for achieving your goals. They give you something to aim for. Because most of us now use such a small percentage of our real potential, target dates serve the purpose of drawing out more potential and using it to bring desired goals into being. Deadlines help you maintain a positive attitude of expectancy toward goals achievement. They eliminate distractions and help you to think creatively.

Sincere Desire. A burning desire to achieve the goals you want often makes the difference between a wish and a goal. A *wish* is something you would like to have but are not willing to invest enough time or effort in order to achieve it; a *goal* is something you want so intensely that you will exert whatever effort is needed to reach it. The more goals you achieve, the more desire you develop. The greater your desire, the more you can achieve. Desire is an ascending spiral of success.

Supreme Confidence. Success demands supreme confidence in yourself and your ability. Self-confidence enables you to undertake challenging goals and believe you can succeed. Self-confidence lets you see problems as opportunities and obstacles as stepping-stones to success. Self-confidence builds your credibility so that the buyer

Figure 6.1

The Million Dollar Personal Success Plan
by Paul J. Meyer
founder and chairman of the board, SMI International, Waco, Texas.

I. Crystallize Your Thinking
Determine what specific goal you want to achieve. Then dedicate yourself to its attainment with unswerving singleness of purpose, the trenchant zeal of a crusader.

II. Develop a Plan for Achieving Your Goal, and a Deadline for its Attainment
Plan your progress carefully; hour-by-hour, day-by-day, month-by-month. Organized activity and maintained enthusiasm are the well-springs of your power.

III. Develop a Sincere Desire for the Things You Want in Life
A burning desire is the greatest motivator of every human action. The desire for success implants "success consciousness" which; in turn, creates a vigorous and ever-increasing "habit of success."

IV. Develop Supreme Confidence in Yourself and Your Own Abilities
Enter every activity without giving mental recognition to the possibility of defeat. Concentrate on your strengths, instead of your weaknesses . . . on your powers, instead of your problems.

V. Develop a Dogged Determination to Follow Through on Your Plan, Regardless of Obstacles, Criticism or Circumstances or What Other People Say, Think or Do.
Construct your Determination with Sustained Effort, Controlled Attention, and Concentrated Energy.
OPPORTUNITIES never come to those who wait . . . they are captured by those who dare to ATTACK.

is open to considering the solutions suggested. Self-confidence makes it easy to ask for the order — not once, but again and again until the sale is closed successfully.

The secret to developing this kind of confidence is a growing list of goals accomplished. Each time you succeed in reaching a goal you have set and worked toward, you gain added belief in your own capability to achieve. Confidence in your own personal ability is the greatest source of security you can possess.

Dogged Determination. Determination to stick to your plan of action until your goal is achieved is an outgrowth of desire and confidence. When you have a burning desire to achieve your goals, you are not easily swayed by others' thoughtless comments, by the disapproval of someone who does not understand your goals, or the active opposition of those who fear to be compared with you in either effort or results. Determination is the quality that enables you to continue calling on a difficult prospect until you close the sale. Determination gives you the creative freedom to discover new tactics for achieving your goal when your first effort fails and to think up more ideas until you discover a way that works.

All of these success elements are interdependent. Use of each increases your power to use the others. Success in any one intensifies your belief in the others. Self-motivation is the only real and lasting motivation. Its development is your responsibility. The company and sales manager can provide a climate in which self-motivation is easier, *but even the most negative climate cannot demotivate you without your permission.*

SUCCESS AND THE TOTAL PERSON

Organizations emphasize that sales forces are essential to corporate success. However, organizations seldom pay much attention to what constitutes success for an individual. Too often success for salespeople is measured only in terms of the amount of sales generated. This narrow view of success has been responsible for destroying the self-confidence of untold numbers of salespeople. An understanding of what success really means frees you to become all that your potential allows.

One of the most comprehensive definitions of success is this: *"Success is the progressive realization of worthwhile, predetermined, personal goals."* This definition is especially applicable to salespeople, who can begin their careers with relatively little training compared to that required of other professionals. Because success is *progressive*, you can be successful immediately just by choosing to pursue goals that are personally fulfilling and then beginning to work toward them. Obviously, such a beginning is not made at the level expected of a master salesperson with long experience but at a level consistent with present reality. When you learn this truth, you have the patience to study, learn the art of selling, and practice your skills.

Too many people fall into the same erroneous thinking that organizations often follow in measuring success. Those "worthwhile, predetermined goals" must involve more than money and position or the success that is achieved is likely to be hollow. Salespeople who concentrate only on career success and neglect other areas of life find their lives less than happy. Money and position are fairly low on the hierarchy of needs that all people experience. For this reason, *goals* must *be set in every area of life*: physical and health, mental and educational, family and home, spiritual and ethical, social and cultural, financial and career. Total personal growth in these areas is effectively pictured in Exhibit 6.4 as spokes on a wheel.

Exhibit 6.4

The Wheel of Life

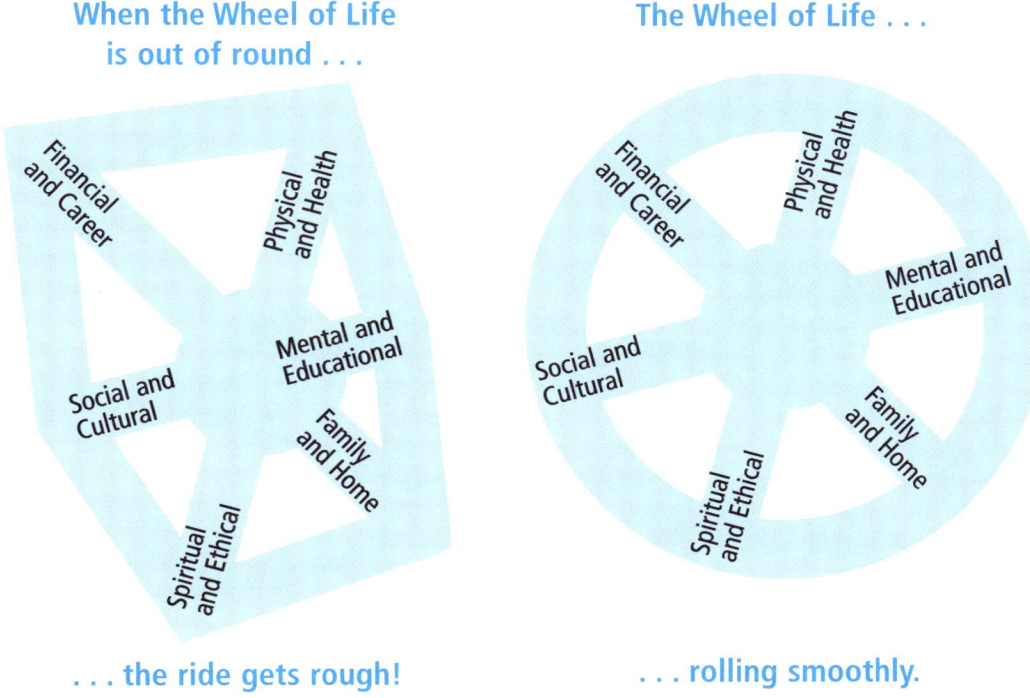

If some spokes are uneven, the wheel that represents total life achievement is not round. The ride is bumpy, and you feel dissatisfaction and a vague sense of uneasiness or unhappiness. Unmet needs prevent the enjoyment of achievements in other areas. Monetary success means little to the salesperson whose family life is shattered, health ruined, or the respect of friends lost. All areas of life must be included in your plan for becoming a "total person."

This definition of success also implies that success has different meanings for different people and that not every salesperson belongs in a particular organization selling a specific product or service. To succeed, market a product or service in which you personally believe. Selling a product that seems worthless or even damaging to the prospect prevents you from sincerely offering to help prospects solve their problems or fulfill their needs.

Once salespeople know what they want from a selling career and dedicate themselves to achieving those goals, the responsibility for reaching success is largely in their own hands. Too many people confuse *action with progress and effort with results*. Trying hard does not guarantee success. Success comes as a result of determining the desired goals, finding out what activity is required to reach those goals, and then completing those actions based on a personal commitment to oneself. *Real success never comes by accident.*

Preparation for Success in Selling

- Preparing for success in a sales career includes three areas of special importance: product knowledge, sales force automation, and motivation and goal setting.

- Product knowledge includes knowledge of the entire industry or field and specific knowledge about your product or service.

- Sales force automation and computer technology help increase your personal productivity, communications capabilities, and transaction-processing efficiency.

- Positioning refers to the place a product occupies in customers' minds relative to competing offerings. Once you select a position, design product, price, and promotion strategies to reinforce the desired position.

- All motivation comes primarily from one of three sources: Fear, incentive, and attitude. Fear and incentives used as motivating forces are limited in effectiveness because they depend on someone else as the source. Attitude motivation is internal and permanent.

- Successful goal setting begins with crystallized thinking about what is important to you, then developing a plan of action with deadlines for achievement.

What Causes Low Sales

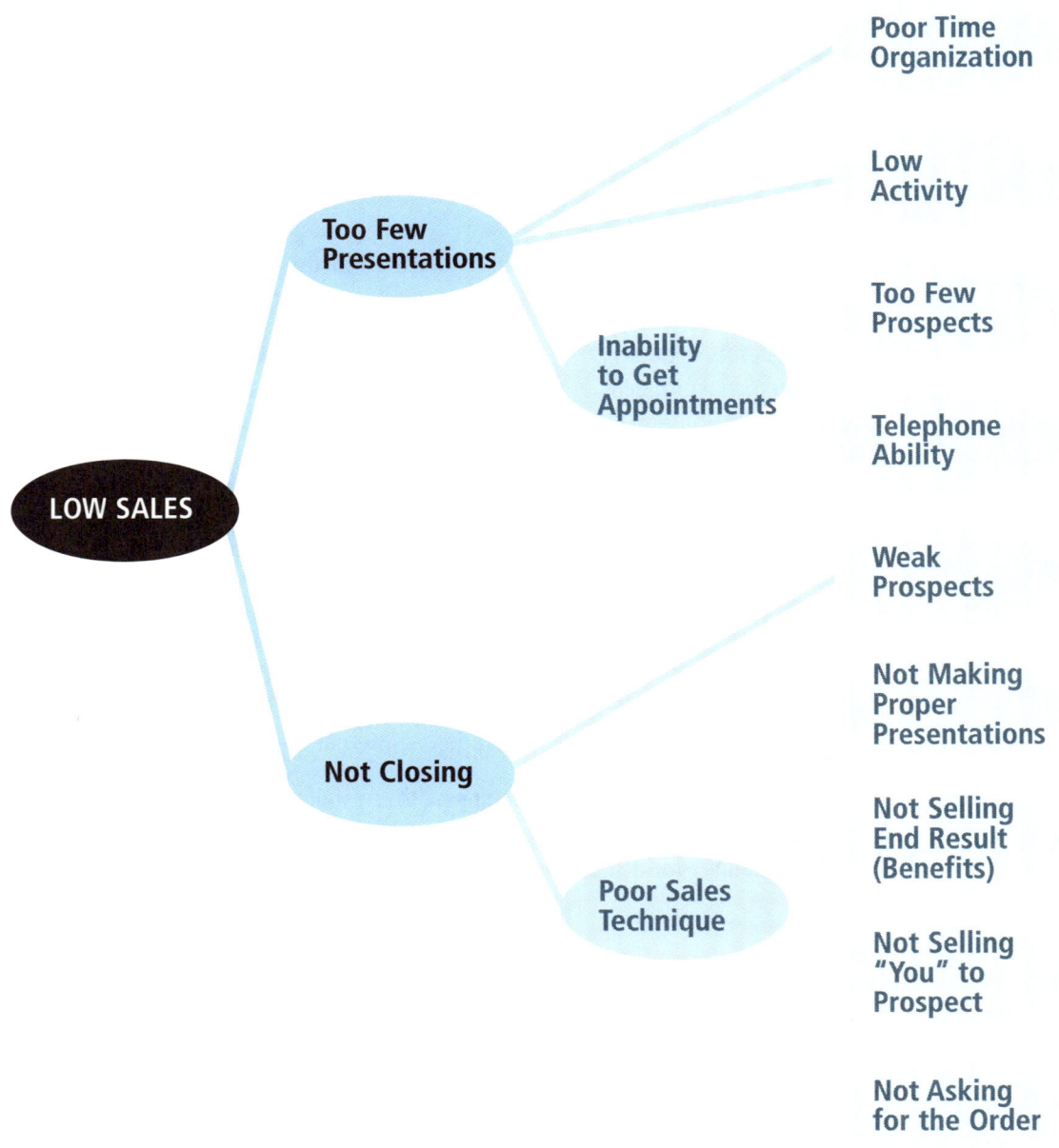

Poor Time
Organization

Low
Activity

Too Few
Prospects

Telephone
Ability

Too Few
Presentations

Inability
to Get
Appointments

LOW SALES

Weak
Prospects

Not Making
Proper
Presentations

Not Selling
End Result
(Benefits)

Not Closing

Not Selling
"You" to
Prospect

Poor Sales
Technique

Not Asking
for the Order

THE HANDBOOK FOR RELATIONSHIP SELLING

Chapter 7

Becoming a Master Prospector

- **The nature and importance of prospecting**
- **Who is a prospect**
- **Qualify prospects using the MADDEN test**
- **Different prospecting methods**
- **Managing prospect information accurately**
- **Computer technology in the management of prospect information**

THE CONCEPT OF PROSPECTING

Becoming a master salesperson begins with becoming a master prospector. A salesperson without prospects is as out of business as a surgeon without patients. Great salespeople ask smart questions, know how to close a deal, and have excellent follow-through. But the one trait they demonstrate more consistently than any other is constant prospecting enhanced by creative approaches that build value and relationships. They see opportunities everywhere and they know it's not just the numbers — but the numbers are what count. Mastering the basics of prospecting puts you at the top.

If your closing ratio is lower than you like, your major problem may be that you don't have enough good prospects and not that you are a poor closer. If you see enough people, sooner or later you sell to someone. Confucius taught, "Dig the well before you thirst." To succeed in professional selling, locate qualified prospects in advance — before you need them. Develop multiple sources from which names of prospects flow constantly. A fertile river valley quickly becomes a desert when the river dries up.

QUALIFYING THE PROSPECT

Establish a pattern for prospecting. You can waste a monumental amount of time calling on leads who are not prospects for your product or service. When all you have is a name and address, you have only a possibility of developing a prospect. Figure 7.1 illustrates the process of moving a name from the status of lead to that of a qualified prospect. Truly qualified prospects are those who are exactly right for you because they possess the necessary characteristics that make them logical buyers for your product or service. Applying a detailed screening process to each lead greatly increases your chances of successfully completing a sale. A good definition of the best prospect is this:

> "I'd rather be a master prospector than be a wizard of speech and have no one to tell my story to."
>
> — Paul J. Meyer

A Class 'A' qualified prospect is one to whom you have been referred by a person the prospect respects, one who has the ability to make a buying decision and to pay for the product or service, and one about whom you have all the personal information you need to make a good presentation.

To determine if you have a truly qualified Class 'A' prospect, use the **MADDEN** test to ensure that they: Have money, are approachable, have desire, have decision-making ability, are eligible, and have a need you can help satisfy.

Figure 7.1

Action of the Salesperson in Developing Leads into Qualified Prospects

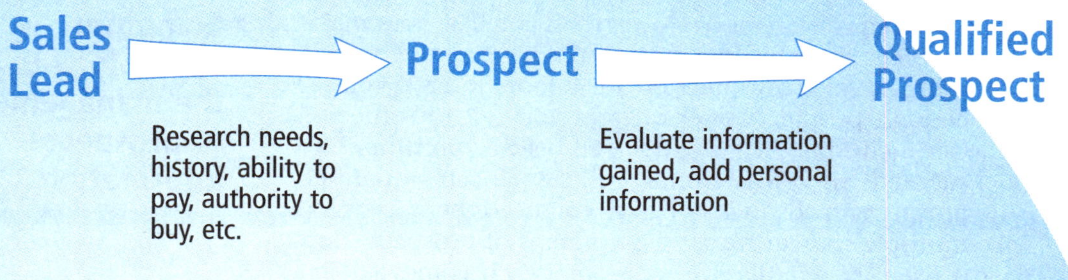

Sales Lead → **Prospect** → **Qualified Prospect**

Research needs, history, ability to pay, authority to buy, etc.

Evaluate information gained, add personal information

M Money

Separate the talkers from those who actually have the money to buy. You will save yourself and your company many headaches by determining a prospect's ability to pay before spending your time and energy gaining a client who may quickly become more of a liability than an asset.

A Approachable

Can you get an appointment? The president or CEO of a large company may grant an initial interview only to a senior level executive in your company. Do not hesitate to ask for such help when there is real possibility of gaining an important client. Individual prospects are often approachable only if you are willing to fit your time schedule into the unique time needs of their business or profession.

D Desire

The prospect may be quite satisfied with a present supplier and have no desire to change. You can sell such a prospect only if you create or discover a desire that will motivate the prospect to move from the present supplier to you. The prospect may desire to save money, to enjoy a wider variety of services, to receive more dependable service or quicker deliveries — all of which may have been the basis for selecting the present supplier in the first place.

D Decision Maker

Be sure the person you visit is the decision maker. If you are not sure who makes the decisions in a particular company, start the sales process with the head of the company. If you do reach the CEO or COO conducting business may be easier than you think. They earned the top spot by making tough calls and can appreciate the tough call you've just made. Let that executive tell you who to see.

E Eligible

Determine whether the prospect is eligible to buy from you. Some prospects are already committed to a competitor and cannot buy from you. Others need a product with greater or smaller capacity than you can offer or a service that is more or less extensive than yours.

N Need

Determine the need level for your product or service. To accomplish this you must ask questions and listen carefully to determine what the prospects' buying motives are in order to uncover their specific needs, and then decide if your company has the products that can effectively satisfy those needs. Ask yourself — will the business your company gains be worth the amount of time you must invest to get it?

METHODS OF PROSPECTING

Practice in prospecting invariably develops skill, provided the methods of practice are correct. Incorrect practice on a musical instrument produces only a greater ability to make errors. So it is with prospecting; aimless, hit-or-miss prospecting, no matter how much of it is done, generally leads only to failure. To streamline the job of prospecting and produce better results, master a number of different methods and use the ones that work best for your particular situation. The following is a list of eleven useful prospecting techniques discussed in this chapter.

- **Referrals** — Names given to you by a customer, friend, or someone else who feels good about you and your product.

- **Center of Influence** — A person who believes in what you are selling, influences others, and is willing to give you names and help to qualify them.

- **Group Prospecting** — Bringing a number of people together at the same time and place and capturing their names and other information about them. Some examples are trade shows, speaking engagements, meetings and luncheons.

- **Planned Cold Calling** — Calling on a lead without first making an appointment and knowing very little or perhaps nothing about the person.

- **Direct Mail** — Choosing a mailing list of individuals, businesses, or professional people who appear to be at least partially qualified and sending them a communication that requests a reply.

- **Observation** — Prospects are everywhere, so keep your eyes and ears open. Scan local newspapers, trade publications, and papers.

- **Civic Groups** — Membership in various civic groups such as the Chamber of Commerce gives you opportunities to meet people who can become prospects for membership.

- **Networking** — Salespeople from different businesses share information about the sales climate and exchange prospect information.

- **Directories** — Directories help identify possible prospects and provide information to determine whether they actually have the potential to become customers.

- **Company-initiated Prospecting** — A company may provide initial prospecting for salespeople. This frees them to have more face-to-face interviews with qualified prospects.

- **Web Sites** — A company can market its services and find customers utilizing the power of the Internet.

> **Develop a prospecting consciousness — a prospecting awareness; it is the key to success in professional selling. Prospecting is to successful selling what breathing is to living. There are prospects by the millions if you open your eyes and see them.**

Referrals

The use of referrals is one of the most powerful prospecting techniques. A referral is a name given to you as a lead by a customer, a friend, or even a prospect who did not buy but felt good about you and your product. The factor that makes this prospecting method so valuable is its *leverage*. Until the proper time to use that leverage arrives, a referral is just a lead like any other.

Referrals work because people are naturally fearful or skeptical of strangers, especially those who try to persuade them to make some kind of decision. People accept you and your product more readily if someone they know and respect has sent you to see them.

Gain More Referred Leads. Salespeople do not have more referrals because they don't ask or because they don't know how to ask. If you don't know how to ask for referrals, take the time and make the effort to develop this important skill. There are two reasons why people do not immediately give you referrals. The first is that they find it difficult to think of names to give you. Basically, they just do not want to exert the mental effort to decide who might be interested. The second reason is they consider themselves to be "conscientious objectors" — they say they just do not give referrals. Sales professionals estimate that 20 percent of clients won't give referrals no matter what you do. Another 20 percent of clients will give referrals no matter what you do. It's the other 60 percent where a plan of action is essential.

The Million-Dollar Referral

Michael Twining, sales rep for a large distributor of agricultural products, has a very clever way to secure more referrals. Whenever he gets a referral by an existing customer he quickly mails a handwritten thank-you note and includes a lottery ticket with the message — *Thanks a million for the referral. I hope you win a million!* It costs very little and always creates a lot of good will and laughs on his next visit with that customer. Michael says and, "it almost always gets me one more referral."

Exhibit 7.1 illustrates a step-by-step approach to use when asking for referrals. Practice and rehearse it with clients who think you are great or have given you referrals in the past. Customers think of themselves as professionals and they like to buy from professionals. Asking for referrals needs to become an automatic, habitual part of every presentation you make.

What to Ask For: The Issue of Control. The principal thing you are asking for in a referral is for your client to make it easy for you to contact the prospect. The big variable is how this contact should be made. What to ask for depends upon your client's need for control of the situation:

- Some customers want to handle the communication themselves.

- Others want minimal involvement. They prefer that you initiate the contact for them.

- Still others may have very specific instructions on what they want you to do or say with their referrals.

The best way to find out how much control your client wishes to have is to simply ask, using an alternate of choice type question: "Would you prefer that I call Mr. Singletary, or would you want to personally call and talk to him on my behalf?" Here is a sample statement that can be used to make the client feel comfortable about giving you names:

> "I'm not asking you to recommend me or my product. I am merely asking you to give me an introduction to some people you know. I will talk to them, as I have with you, in a professional manner and give them an opportunity to learn about me and my company."

When to Ask for a Referral. Make asking for referrals a part of the selling cycle. A logical time to ask for referrals is right after the close. A customer who buys is sold on you and likely to feel good about giving you names. Sometimes, however, a customer wants to use the product or service before giving any referrals. Salespeople are taught to go after referrals at the wrong time. They start asking for referrals before the ink on the contract is even dry. You can't ask for referrals; you must earn them. The best referrals come from satisfaction, not a signature on a contract.

Exhibit 7.1

A Seven-Step Approach for Gaining More Referred Leads

1. Ask for referrals with respect

Open the dialogue something like this, "I have an important question I want to ask you." It will capture your client's attention and indicate to them just how significant this is to you.

2. Ask for their help

Soften them up by saying, "I'm trying to build my business and I would value and appreciate your help."

3. Explain the course of action you are proposing in detail

Tell them what will happen if they give you a referral, and let them know that you will remain professional and report back to them.

4. Gain their permission to explore

You might give them another softening statement: "I can understand how you feel." Then go on to say, "I was wondering if we could agree on who you know who might also benefit from the types of products I have to offer. Are you comfortable with that?"

5. Narrow their focus by describing the prospect profile you are looking for

Once you have been given names, make a first step toward qualifying them. Ask your client, "if you were in my place, who would you see first?" Ask why. Then find out which one to contact next.

6. Report back to them

Whenever you receive referrals, be sure to report back to them on the result of your interviews with these prospects.

7. Be sure to thank the clients for giving you referrals regardless of whether they did or did not buy from you

Center of Influence

The best sales tool you can have is a person who believes in what you are selling, is influential with a number of people who are potential customers for you, and is willing to give you the names of these people and help you qualify them. Such a person is called a center of influence. When you have several centers of influence, you always have plenty of prospects. People respect the center of influence to the extent that an introduction from this source virtually assures you of a sympathetic hearing.

You can establish centers of influence among community leaders — social, political, business, cultural, or religious leaders. Cultivate their friendship, sell yourself to them, and ask them to help you. Centers of influence may or may not be actual customers of yours, but they must be sold on you and the value of the product or service you represent.

Centers of influence are one of the most valuable assets you can have as a salesperson. Follow up every lead they provide; then report your results to them and thank them for their help. Find a way you can show your gratitude by being of service to your centers of influence. A two-way relationship is rewarding to both parties.

> **The single most important ingredient in the formula for success is knowing how to deal with people.**

Group Prospecting

Some companies use group prospecting with great success. The idea is to bring together a number of people, from eight to twenty or even more. The group may meet in a home, a conference room in a hotel, or in an office. The purpose is to inform prospects about your product or service.

A number of direct sales companies use this method for finding prospective distributors or salespeople. Among the well-known organizations that use this approach are Tupperware, Amway, Shaklee, and PartyLite Inc. Companies that use party-plan selling not only expect to make sales at the parties but also hope to find prospects who will agree to host parties at which additional new prospective customers and party holders are likely to be present.

A variation of this method is to look for groups of potential prospects and offer to be a guest speaker. Members of civic clubs like the Toastmasters, Kiwanis, Lions, and Optimists may be ideal prospects for you, and they are always looking for speakers who have information that would make them more productive or successful. If you establish your credibility and sincerity, you may be able to close your speech with a brief presentation of your product or service. Be sure to meet as many members of the audience as possible before and after the meeting, ask for their business card, and give them yours. Because these people have heard you speak, they already feel they know you. If they were impressed enough to want you to call, you know you have a qualified prospect.

Planned Cold Calling

One prospecting method that is available to any salesperson is cold calling. Cold calling can become an enjoyable part of your day if you accept the reality of the situation. Each year 15 percent of all firms become dissatisfied with a supplier and want to change. This means that in one of every seven cold calls you make, a prospect is probably receptive to what you have to say. Cold calling serves as an excellent supplement to other prospecting efforts if it is carefully planned for maximum effectiveness.

Direct Mail

The success of direct-mail prospecting depends upon the management of mailing lists. Some lists are better than others, and the best investment of your time and budget demands careful planning and analysis. The product or service you sell has a great deal to do with what kind of list you use. The goal is a list of people or businesses that are already at least partially qualified as prospects. Exhibit 7.2 has some suggestions for sources of direct-mail lists.

If you are using a computer to store lists, develop a coding system to show which types of lists produce the highest percentage of responses. Code the names of people who actually respond. Even if you do not sell to them immediately, they have some interest in your product or service and might become active prospects at some later date.

Ron Knox, a 30-year sales pro with Northwestern Mutual Life Insurance Company, wanted a systematic way of contacting existing clients and prospects on a regular basis. Ron sends out a cover letter attached to a newsletter to 400 clients and 100 prospects, four times a year. He has never received less than two reply cards back and often gets eight or more. Ron knows: (1) this database marketing tool provides useful information, a value-added benefit to his clients and prospects; (2) it keeps his name in front of them; and (3) it gives people the opportunity to say they have had a change in their situation and want to review their insurance needs.

Exhibit 7.2

Suggested Sources for Building Direct-Mail Lists

Membership rosters
- Professional societies and trade associations (medical, accountancy, manufacturers, air conditioning, electricians)
- Country clubs
- Civic clubs (Kiwanis, Lions, Civitan, Optimist)
- Religious Groups
- Women's organizations (Altrusa, AAUW, Junior League)
- Special-interest groups (Audubon Society, garden clubs, environmental protection groups)
- Community business groups (Chamber of Commerce, Jaycees, Business and Professional Women)

City directories and telephone books
- White or yellow pages, depending upon need

People you have done business with in the past
- Such as home repair or building, banking, auto service and repair

Power of Observation

No matter what other methods of prospecting you elect to use, your own keen powers of observation provide many of your best prospects. Keep your eyes and ears open because prospects are everywhere. The daily newspaper, for example, is an excellent source of prospects.

Exhibit 7.3 tells of one salesperson's success in using the newspaper for additional prospects and sales. Wedding announcements, business promotions, reports of civic activities, winners of contests, lists of graduates, notices of new business openings, new partnerships or planned mergers — all these and many others focus your attention on people who may be prospects. Clip an item, attach a personal note of congratulation, and mail them to the person or company featured.

THE HANDBOOK FOR RELATIONSHIP SELLING

Joining Civic Groups

Membership in civic groups can give you opportunities to meet people who are prospects for your product or service. Their meetings provide you with regular times to meet more people and to build relationships. Exhibit 7.4 lists some tips for using membership in civic clubs as prospecting opportunities.

In selecting groups to join, consider the kinds of prospects you need to meet. Choose organizations to which decision makers belong. Join a group whose purposes you can wholeheartedly support and one that will stimulate your own thinking and creativity. Look for ways you can assume a place of leadership in the organization, preferably in a position with high visibility so that you become known to most of the members as soon as possible. Perform your leadership role competently so that your name is automatically associated with excellence in the minds of all the members, and give unselfishly of yourself to the group. If you are interested only in what you can get from the group, other members will soon see through your facade of insincerity.

Exhibit 7.4

Tips for Using Membership in Civic Clubs for Prospecting

- Carefully select the groups you join.

- Assume leadership responsibilities to work for positive visibility.

- Set contact goals for each organization meeting.

- Follow up with contacts.

- Maintain an information file on the contacts made in each organization.

- Use "remeet" goals to help you develop closer relationships with people.

- Reach out to new members.

Networking

Networking is the active cooperation between people in businesses to share information about the business climate, specific happenings in the business community, and prospects. Networking incorporates the three C's — connecting, communicating, and cooperating.

In many cities, formal networking groups are organized specifically for the purpose of sharing business information. Alina Novak, founder of New York City's Networks Unlimited, calls such networking the planned acquisition of contacts for mutual support, the exchange of information, and the transaction of business. Members meet weekly and bring their business cards and sales brochures. The members, who were primarily women, are learning to use influence and power to accomplish their career goals. Now the value of such organizations has become obvious to both men and women, and many of the groups contain both men and women from the business world who find value in sharing information and ideas.

One innovative way to gain information is an organization entitled LeTip International, which has over 400 chapters across the U.S. and Canada. Most of the members are salespeople who exchange tips and leads. Each chapter meets precisely for 75 minutes once a week between 7:16 and 8:31 a.m. You must attend 90 percent of the meetings and pass on at least two qualified leads a month — or else be terminated from the club. One particular member made six sales which he credits to receiving information directly from his chapter of LeTip.

Using Directories

Don't overlook directories as a source of prospects. The most accessible directory is the Yellow Pages. We are accustomed to looking there when we want to buy something, but telephone books also tell you where to look when you want to sell.

Directories are gold mines of information if they are used correctly. They cannot replace other means of prospecting, but they are excellent supplements. Some directories are useful in identifying possible prospects; others are helpful in learning more about prospects to determine whether they have the potential to become customers. Many companies have copies of the directories that supply information directly related to their businesses. Other directories are available at public and university libraries. In this age of information technology, many directories are now available on CD-ROMS.

Specific industrial groups publish directories, too. Use them to locate architects, contractors, air conditioning manufacturers, computer software companies, and many others. If the library does not have a directory that fits your needs, ask one of your customers what directory would help you find other customers in that same field.

Company-Initiated Prospecting

The purpose of company-initiated prospecting is to free up time for salespeople to concentrate on the top priority of all sales activity — face-to-face interviews with fully qualified prospects. This is where results are generated. Everything else is merely preparation for the true sales arena.

Make the Most of Telemarketing. Telemarketing is an industry that is experiencing incredible growth. Some firms rely almost completely on a particular chosen form of telemarketing for gaining leads; others use it as a supplement to other prospecting methods. Other companies train their telemarketing specialists to ask additional questions and attempt to set up an appointment for the sales representative. If an appointment is made, you are almost sure to make a presentation. The closing average can be improved, however, if you use some ingenuity to discover additional information about the prospect before the presentation.

Make Use of Current and Past Customers. A study of 183 company executives conducted by the Patrick Marketing Group (PMG) of Calabasas, California, found that 70 percent said expanding relationships with existing customers is the biggest factor challenging the success of their sales forces. These numbers suggest the importance of existing customers as sources of new revenue, says Craig Shields, senior marketing consultant at PMG. Firms realize that it is easier and less expensive to penetrate existing accounts and fully flesh out their potential than to prospect for new clients. It is estimated that it costs 5 to 10 times more to go out and get a new customer than to keep the customer base you currently have. Some companies take the initiative in furnishing salespeople with the names of past customers who, for one reason or another, are no longer active. If they do not, you can certainly ask for this information.

Trade Shows. Trade shows in the United States attract over 100 million visitors each year. And, globally, trade shows are a more significant part of the marketing process than in the United States. Companies use trade shows to demonstrate new and existing products, enhance their corporate image, provide information to those who visit the booth, and also use the opportunity to examine competing products. The decision to exhibit at a trade show is a complex one that must be based on consideration of a number of variables:

- Which trade shows will produce the largest number of prospects and the best qualified prospects?

- Is the goal on-the-spot sales or discovery of leads for future sales?

- What kind of display should be planned?

- How many salespeople will be needed to staff the booth, and which ones are the best choice for this activity?

- How can we ensure high visibility for our exhibit and our name?

- How will we preserve the information gathered?

A company has just 20 seconds to send out a powerful message to get people to visit their booth. For that reason, many companies set up creative and memorable exhibits designed to catch visitors' eyes. Many trade show visitors are using the Internet to plan their attendance. Time constraints have created a new breed of attendees who use the Net to plan their time at exhibitions.

Harnessing the Power of the Web

Salespeople and small companies can set up a home page with a nominal initial expense and use these home pages to advertise their services, offer special deals, tap into lucrative foreign markets or add sales reps halfway around the world. People can market their businesses very inexpensively because of the online relationships they form.

Streamline the Sales Process. Suppose you need distributors to sell your product in Spain and Italy. Just a few years ago you would have had to contact reps who sell there. The process would take months. Now you get on a search engine and type in photography, bronze sculptures, or whatever the product is you sell, and in a few hours have a number of solid leads who you then e-mail. Not only have you located and identified your prospects, you have also contacted them. Contracts can be e-mailed to the ones you select so they can make modifications and fax it back. Consequently, you spend a few days rather than a few months putting the team together.

Make Use of Affiliate Program Marketing. The Internet is also a great prospecting tool, especially as a way to partner with others. Are there Web sites that sell to the same types of customers that also buy what you sell? If so, your products might complement what they're doing in a way that would allow for an affiliate-type of arrangement. An innovative e-marketing tactic to drive traffic to your Web site is to target your marketing at specific groups of prospects that are likely to have an interest in your product. This is done by compensating the referring site for any sales that are made to customers that link from its site to yours. Unlike banner advertising, where you are ostensibly paying for impressions, this approach allows you to only pay for results.

MANAGING PROSPECT INFORMATION

All your good work in prospecting goes down the drain if you do not have a system for managing and using the information you find about prospects. The type of system you use is not the primary consideration; what is important is accuracy, completeness, and ease of use. You can use a file box and individual cards. However, if you use a computer, you can easily achieve the same results with the added advantages of handy printouts and provisions for additional listings of names by any category you desire that can be added to your coding system. Whether you use manual or computer records, the purpose and result are the same.

Initial Recording of Leads

The initial information you need about prospects depends a great deal upon the product or service you sell, but it will, in all likelihood, include these items:

1. Prospect's full name, address, and telephone number (both business and home)

2. Name of company, address, and telephone number; type of business

3. Position in company

4. Family: spouse, names and ages of children

5. Personal information: hobbies, clubs and associations

6. Approximate income (if your product or service is to be sold to the individual rather than to the company)

Classification of Prospects

When you first find the name of an individual or company prospect, assign a classification indicator to the name. One handy classification system uses the letters A, B, and C.

- **Class A prospects** are those about whom you have adequate information to make a good presentation. You know they have the money to buy and the authority to make a decision. Ideally, you also have a referral from someone they respect.

- **Class B prospects** are those about whom you have inadequate information to make the best possible presentation. You may not know enough to be sure they need your product or service. You may not know whether they have the authority to make a decision or whether they can afford to buy. You may not have a referral to help open the door. When one or more of these items is missing, your proper action is research rather than approach.

- **Class C prospects** are people whose names you have found in some way, but about whom you have little or no information other than a name. They are leads, not prospects.

Prospecting activity involves not only finding new leads but also qualifying existing leads by adding information that allows you to move them up to Class A status.

Scheduling Contacts

When you have classified a prospect as Class A, determine when you will initiate contact, either by telephone, personal visit, or direct mail, according to the method of approach you choose. Use a tickler file arrangement of your prospect cards or computer records to see that you take the proper action on the date assigned. The same tickler file will help you schedule later contacts if your first attempt to schedule an interview is not successful. Once a prospect's name enters your file, it stays there permanently until you close a sale or determine that the person is not a prospect for any product or service of your company. If you make a presentation and do not close, choose a time for a new attempt and schedule an appropriate time for contacting the prospect again.

When you discover that a person is not a viable prospect for you and will probably not become one in the foreseeable future, that person can still be an important contact. The impression you have given of your company by your professionalism may cause that person to recommend you to someone who will prove to be an excellent prospect. Passing on the information you have is the basis of networking among salespeople.

Automating Prospect Information

Sales professionals no longer have time to organize prospect information on 3 x 5 blank file cards or in loose-leaf binders. It would be very difficult to go through handwritten or typed notes every time you're on the phone or in a client's office. However, as your client base grows the need to interact with them, and other individuals from the various departments within your own company requires the use of computer technology. This is why the most widely used software programs in selling, outside of word processing, are contact management programs. These powerful programs were developed to help you collect, organize, classify and keep track of prospect information. It's like having a super Rolodex for your desktop or laptop computer.

Applications for database technology are limited only by the creativity of the salesperson. For example, you might begin your day by calling up a list of follow-ups from the corporate database. Check the best way to organize the day based on where you'll be, and what prospects or customers are in that area. Then order form letters to go out to all the customers and prospects you visited the day before and print them on your own letterhead. In addition, you can generate call schedules and short-range forecasts, provide scheduled contact lists in chronological order and account summaries, expedite long-range forecasting and sorting by a variety of criteria (zip code, alphabet, amount of last sale), and prepare graphs showing likely trends in sales for your current customers.

Mastering the basics of prospecting puts you at the top.

Becoming a Master Prospector

- Prospecting is the skill that keeps salespeople in business. Once you have leads, qualify them to determine whether they are true prospects that have a need for your product and are in a position to make a buying decision.

- Make sure they pass the MADDEN test.

- Two of the most effective prospecting methods are referrals and centers of influence. When someone they respect makes the introduction, you have a built-in sales assistant — the influence of the person who provided the lead and the initial contact.

- Group prospecting is securing names of possible prospects at trade shows, through speaking engagements, or in any situation where you have the opportunity to meet a number of people. Cold calling also provides a supplemental source of new prospects.

- Networking is a valuable source of new prospects for salespeople who are willing to share information about their customers or clients. It's all about connecting, communicating and cooperating.

- Efficient management of information means that needed data is always at your fingertips. Utilize filing systems to keep track of prospects as you record initial information, upgrade prospects, and schedule the time you want to contact each one.

Time Saving Tips

Be sure to handle each piece of paper only once.

— Alan Lakein, author of *How to Get Control of Your Time and Your Life*

To keep staff meetings short, I always try to sandwich them between two scheduled appointments.

— Dan McNamee, president, McNamee Consulting Company

I look for the kind of guy who says, "Forget that, it'll take ten years. Here's what we gotta do now."

— Lee Iacocca, from *Iacocca: An Autobiography*

Put a dollar value on what you have to do; if it doesn't add up in dollars and cents, don't do it.

— Edward J. Feeney, consultant, Edward J. Feeney Associates

Simplify expense reports by keeping an envelope in your pocket. Write the date, city, and names of customers to be visited on the flap; note expenditures on the envelope; then put each day's receipts inside.

— Merrill Douglas, chairman, Time Management Center, Inc.

Yesterday is a canceled check: forget it. Tomorrow is a promissory note: don't count on it. Today is ready cash: use it!

— Edwin C. Bliss from *Doing It Now*

Chapter 8

Preapproach and Telephone Techniques

FOCAL POINTS

- **Importance of the preapproach**
- **Objectives of the preapproach**
- **Prepare for an effective preapproach**
- **The preapproach as an extension of prospecting**
- **Effective methods for making telephone calls**
- **The six-step telephone track**

THE IMPORTANCE OF PREAPPROACH PLANNING

The path to success in selling is often described by this formula: Seeing enough of the right people at the right time. That sounds logical enough! The most exacting part of the formula however, is the "right people." How can you be sure that you are investing your time in calling on qualified prospects? The answer lies in your diligence in collecting information about the leads you record in your prospecting system.

When someone gives you a referral, ask questions to learn what you need to know about that prospect. Do some research about the prospect's business or industry and about the company itself. Discover some personal information that will help you know what kind of personality to expect. The various activities that provide this necessary personal and business information are called presale planning or the preapproach. The preapproach is the planning and preparation done prior to actual contact with the prospect.

In gathering such information, you are learning who to call on, why, when, and where. What seems to be insignificant might be the key to the exact approach that spells the difference between success and failure. Leave nothing to chance. For example, details such as the correct pronunciation of the prospect's name can be secured in advance. Roger Capps, an industrial salesperson, thought he was well prepared to call on an important new prospect, only to find himself sent on his way after less than a minute. The prospect, Mr. Hajovsky, had no time for Capps, who made the fatal error of mispronouncing Hajovsky's name. Capps could have avoided the lost sales opportunity by taking a few seconds to ask the receptionist for the correct pronunciation.

EXTENT OF THE PREAPPROACH

The sales cycle is a continuous process with no clear break between one phase and the next. In practice, you cannot separate the prospecting, preapproach, approach, and need discovery elements into different segments. They seem to blend together and become one. They are discussed separately for convenience, but the exact point where one phase ends and the next begins is never clear. Figure 8.1 illustrates the absence of clear dividing lines between these steps in the relationship selling process.

Figure 8.1

Four Phases of the Sales Process Work Together Turning a Lead into a Qualified Prospect

Lead

Prospecting   Preapproach   Approach   Need Discovery

Qualified Prospect

THE HANDBOOK FOR RELATIONSHIP SELLING

The numerous types of selling vary so widely that few broad generalizations can be made about the amount of preapproach information that should be gathered. Depending on the type of selling job you will be doing and the product or services being sold, the preapproach differs considerably. Qualifying prospects at times can only be accomplished during the approach and need discovery process by asking questions and through observing, listening, and interpreting verbal and nonverbal signals.

PREPARATION AND PREAPPROACH

The type and quality of information uncovered during the preapproach is vital. Just as students dislike doing homework after school, many adults have a similar aversion to the preliminaries to the "real work" they prefer to do. However, this step is a must. Successful sales professionals rarely make even a cold call without some sort of preparation. When they are ready for a formal sales call, professional salespeople have studied and analyzed the prospect's personality, company, operations, needs, and financial position before ever entering the office. One of the most thorough ways to prepare is to develop a checklist of questions to answer before you make the sales call. Exhibit 8.1 presents a checklist designed to help gather the essential sales information you need.

Exhibit 8.1

Checklist of Sales Essentials for Collecting Preapproach Information

- What business is the company in? What are its products and markets? Who are its primary customers?

- How big is the company? Where does it rank within the industry? Can this company give us enough business to make this call worthwhile?

- Who is the actual decision maker in buying the product or service I sell?

- Who else influences the buying decision?

- How often does this company buy my type of product or service?

- How well is the company satisfied with its present supplier?

- What plans does the company have that could affect its future need for my product?

- What are the background and personal interests of each person concerned in the buying decision?

- Is the company's staff technically well informed? Can we help them develop greater expertise?

- Do we (or can we) use their products or services in our company?

- Do any of our top executives know any of their executives personally?

For Dean Cormier, sales manager for Catapult Systems, thoroughness is what it is all about. Before giving a sales presentation, Cormier gathers information about the company, researches the industry, interviews potential clients, and finds out exactly how his product can benefit a specific company. Cormier says, "when I give a presentation to a dot-com company, I know exactly how a dot-com company works; when I give a presentation to an oil company, I know exactly how an oil company works." Maren Rupel, a human resources executive at Chevron, cited Cormier's in-depth knowledge and confidence in his product and its capabilities for their business needs as the key in her company's decision to buy from him.

Prepare for the Presentation

Do your research to find out about the prospect and develop a purpose for the call, linked to a potential client benefit. Set a goal for each contact with a prospect, know what you want to accomplish, and how you plan to do it. There is much more to preparation than simply gathering and reviewing information. Rehearsal eliminates the stammering, nervous speech habits, and repetition that sometimes result from lack of preparation. Allow time in your daily schedule to prepare the sales approach and presentation you will use in each call. Decide how you can make the best possible use of sales literature and other tools provided by your company in this specific call. Plan how to incorporate visual aids into your approach and presentation for maximum effectiveness.

Videotaping your presentation allows you to see how you really look. "That's the best way to coach people," says Ken Taylor president of Decker Communication Inc. Videotaping also allows you to hear your use of non-words — such as "um," "uh," and "you know." Here are some rehearsal tips:

- Practice your presentation with specific customers in mind.

- Videotape presentations to show sales reps their strengths and weaknesses.

- Make large, exaggerated motions until you feel comfortable making more natural-looking gestures.

Visualize Successful Selling

Salespeople can learn a great deal from the training habits of world-class athletes. Many track stars use visualization techniques to help them focus on a specific event. An integral part of their training consists of what is called "mental toughening sessions." They run the race over and over in their minds. Edwin Moses, over a 10-year period, won 122 consecutive races in the 400-meter hurdles. His power of visualization became so acute that when he mentally visualized hitting a hurdle, he actually felt the pain in his leg.

You can practice this same type of mental exercise. You can positively affirm the feeling you want to create and visualize the outcomes you want to obtain. Think about what you will say and anticipate the prospect's responses. Create a mental hologram and live it over and over in your mind. Practice out loud; your mind believes the sound of your own voice. *Remember that your mind cannot separate a real experience from an imagined one.*

SOURCES OF PREAPPROACH INFORMATION

When you know what information you need, you can identify a number of valuable sources for obtaining it. The information you gather will help you get in to make a presentation as well as guide you in preparing a strategy for the interview itself. For example, you can ask colleagues on your company's sales team for information they have on particular prospects. Current customers are also excellent sources of information, and they may be happy to share what they know with you. There is nothing wrong with calling personally on prospects without an appointment. At the very least, this cold call gives you the opportunity to observe their facilities and you learn something that validates them as, at least, partially "qualified" prospects. You simply cannot predict the most beneficial sources of information. Keep your eyes and ears open!

Imitation is the Sincerest Form of Flattery

Kelly Immoor, national sales manager for Bedford Communications Inc. in New York, says, "If you want to stand out, then blend in." Before sending anything to potential clients she researches their product lines, Web sites and media advertising. Companies place "about us" links on their products and Web sites for a reason. With this unlimited company information available she puts together communication pieces that match the particular style of the company being targeted. She finds their slogan, the motto the company lives by, and uses the phrase as a headline in the proposal. Immoor further tailors her proposals by including such subtle features as the prospects' colors and images. Based on the company's mission statement and goals, she specifies how her product will help them reach their objectives.

Here's a useful tip — read magazines and newsletters that are related to your customer's industry. You read publications that are pertinent in your field, so obviously your clients also read publications relevant to their fields. This is a great way to uncover ideas to serve their needs better. However, just researching and reading are not enough. You must know what to look for.

Here are six items to consider that may give you valuable information;

- **Mergers**. Will new alliances give you better opportunities to see companies that have denied you access in the past?
- **Personnel Changes**. Watch for new appointments by your customers, prospects, and competitors.
- **Changing Product Lines**. Firms that drop or add products may be suggesting a new emphasis that gives you a reason to call.
- **Advertising Plans**. Have your competitors or customers changed advertising agencies? Are they creating a new approach or pushing certain products?
- **TV and Magazine Ads**. Television commercials and print ads are a source of invaluable clues. Look at the features being stressed and the image being portrayed.
- **Sales Training**. The news media highlight new sales training endeavors. Is your customer or prospect developing a sales training program you can make use of?

Excellence in selling requires an awareness that the hardest work takes place during the preapproach, but all that hard work adds up to a closed sale. You must be prepared to answer the questions that are in the minds of prospects when you first contact them. Exhibit 8.2 lists ten questions that buyers have, although they don't often volunteer to ask you these questions.

Building Your Self-Confidence

One of the real benefits of pre-approach planning is to build personal self-confidence. Knowing that you are prepared gives you an added measure of self-confidence that is transmitted to the prospect. The opposite of self-confidence is fear, and fear comes primarily from the unknown.

Exhibit 8.2

Ten Buyer Questions

1. What are you selling?
2. Why do I need it?
3. Who is your company?
4. How much will it cost?
5. Who else is using it and are they satisfied?
6. What kind of a person are you?
7. Is your price truly competitive?
8. How does your solution compare to other alternatives?
9. Why do I need it now?
10. What is your record for support and service?

A definite plan for each prospect means you are more likely to be accepted. A purchasing agent for a large, multinational food processing plant who sees many salespeople described his reactions like this:

> *I turn away salesman after salesman because they come in like lost sheep. . . . They hope that somehow they'll stumble into an order. I get the impression that they figure I'll do the selling for them. I haven't got time for people like that.*

In your career, you will make calls on professional buyers whose job is to make sound purchasing decisions for their companies. These professionals expect to interact with another professional, not an unprepared amateur. By giving off an air of self-confidence and getting down to business immediately without wasting the prospect's time with unnecessary questions, you increase the likelihood of a successful close.

SETTING UP THE SALES INTERVIEW

Timing

With a little research, you can determine the best time to call a prospect you have not previously met. For example, Powell Kenney, vice-president of Clampitt Paper Company in Fort Worth, sees salespeople only between 5:30 and 8:30 a.m. each weekday morning. He does not want his regular work routine disrupted by listening to sales presentations.

Ordinarily, sales calls can be scheduled for almost any time during the business day. Like Mr. Kenney, however, most prospects have a time when they are more receptive to your presentation. Some like to see salespeople the first thing in the morning. Others prefer to handle routine matters first. Fortunately, prospects have different preferences to the extent that salespeople can fill the workday with appointments.

If every buyer insisted on appointments before 8:30 a.m., salespeople would be in serious trouble. If a particular prospect does not seem to have a preference for a time of day to see salespeople, try to discover when most salespeople call on this prospect. If most call in the morning, schedule your call for late in the afternoon. Many executives work past 5:00 p.m. and will see you. In fact, they may well appreciate your work ethic.

Gaining Entry

Before an actual face-to-face meeting can be arranged, you must choose a way to contact the prospect and set up the interview. Appointments can be set up in three basic ways. You may send a letter requesting an appointment, make a cold call or telephone the prospect and schedule a specific time and date for the interview. Writing a letter for an appointment may produce no answer or may require several contacts to set a mutually convenient time. Cold calls have a low probability of finding the prospect available for an interview.

Today, more and more business is being conducted by telephone. Just a few minutes are required to make an appointment. Good telephone techniques and habits are important to anyone in professional selling.

Using the telephone successfully requires the same basic selling skills as a face-to-face call, plus some additional skills to meet the special challenges of telephone use. Finding a prospect in a bad mood or under a time constraint, the surprise element of a call, and the lack of visual contact are some of the elements that may prevent you from feeling as comfortable with the telephone as you do in a personal contact.

Busy executives have receptionists or administrative assistants who screen their incoming calls and mail. These so-called gatekeepers also do an excellent job of protecting and conserving the time of their superiors by determining who gets in and when. It is important to build a relationship with these gatekeepers, because statistics show that approximately 60 to 80 percent of them have "significant influence" over the purchase of certain products and services. It is a mistake to view them as barriers to overcome, and the best way to get to the main buyer is to sell yourself at the door. Exhibit 8.3 outlines eight ways to build rapport with gatekeepers.

TELEPHONE TECHNIQUES

Because of the ever-increasing cost of a sales visit to a prospect, the telephone call for many companies is replacing the unsolicited or cold call approach in making the initial contact with a prospect. The proper use of the telephone helps you qualify prospects, budget time, and save money. In addition, good telephone techniques enhance your image and preconditions the prospect to receive you favorably. Phoning for an appointment implies that you are courteous and considerate of the prospect's time. The phone call helps to create a selling situation because, just by agreeing to see you, the prospect tacitly indicates interest in your product or service.

Exhibit 8.3

Building Rapport With Gatekeepers

Adjust Your Attitude

Be friendly, but not fake. Gatekeepers appreciate respect, and they can recognize insincerity.

Honesty is the Best Policy

Don't lie just to increase your chances of seeing the decision maker. Gatekeepers will discover your fib, and once this happens the possible sale has ended before it has begun.

Get Personal Information

Find out the names of gatekeepers, their interests and family names without being too nosy. They appreciate being remembered by name.

Sell to the Gatekeeper

Gatekeepers have influence over buying decisions. So if you show them how their company can benefit by using your product or service, the chances of you making the final sale increase.

Question Gatekeepers

Ask them what the needs and goals of their company are, and they just might be willing to tell you.

Be Thoughtful

Remember to thank gatekeepers for their help, but also remember special occasions such as birthdays and holidays. Don't go overboard, and don't use these gifts as payoffs. Gatekeepers are intelligent and know what's going on.

Keep a Sense of Humor

This keeps things light, and maybe this will encourage the gatekeeper to accept you in a favorable way.

Be Patient

It may take longer than you expect to get through the door, but if you keep your patience and persistence, a positive outcome is the result.

Getting the Appointment — A Mini Sale

You must regard the use of the telephone to set up appointments as a true sales activity and not just a necessary evil. You must also remember what you are selling. The mini sale is selling the prospect on the idea of giving you an appointment; your purpose is not to sell your product or service on the telephone.

You can make a large number of inquiries in a fraction of the time it takes to make personal visits. You will likely find that personal visits made with a telephone appointment not only reduce waiting time, but prospects will likely be more receptive because those who are not really interested do not schedule appointments.

Making First Impressions

Do you come across as being sincere, honest, confident, knowledgeable and likable? The quality of your voice, the hesitation in your voice, the volume, the strength of your speaking style all convey an image to another person. If you sound weak and tentative or use words like well, sort-of, kind-of, maybe, perhaps, that says to the prospect, "I'm not one bit sure that this is going to a good investment of time for you." Lots of people also include phrases like, "Well, to be honest with you," which says to the prospect that you aren't always honest.

Remember you're projecting your personality over the phone. How you say something can be as important as what you say. Try to put a smile in your voice. The most successful salespeople project positive voice qualities such as sincerity, courtesy, and confidence. A survey conducted for Jacobi Voice Development revealed the type of voice characteristics prospects find the most annoying. Table 8.1 illustrates the most negative or annoying qualities.

Table 8.1

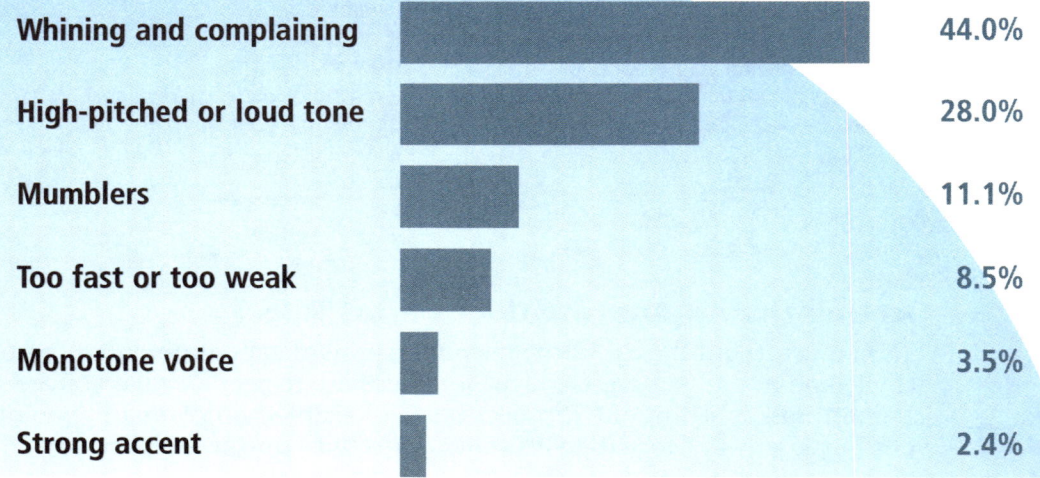

Most Annoying Voice Characteristics

Whining and complaining	44.0%
High-pitched or loud tone	28.0%
Mumblers	11.1%
Too fast or too weak	8.5%
Monotone voice	3.5%
Strong accent	2.4%

Organizing the Call

Inadequate preparation reduces the effectiveness of your delivery. Ask yourself these four questions to help you stay on track:

1. **Why am I calling?** Do you want to make an appointment, check on a customer's need to reorder, or follow up an inquiry?
2. **What is my proposal?** Your plan should have two parts: (1) what do you want from the person you call, and (2) what commitment you will make. Jot down some notes. Be specific!
3. **What would make this person want to grant my request?** Before calling, determine why the person you are calling will do what you request.
4. **How does my telephone script sound?** Identify those key words or phrases in your telephone sales call that you can emphasize to make your message more convincing.

Before you ever pick up the telephone, go through a mental checklist to ensure that you are fully prepared. Exhibit 8.4 presents ten strategic checkpoints to consider when you are preparing to use the telephone to set up appointments.

Exhibit 8.4

Key Points to Consider When Preparing to Use the Telephone

1. Arrange a definite time each day to telephone. Determine a specific number of calls to make during that time period.

2. Arrange for privacy to avoid interruptions. Make as many calls as you can in the allotted time. Your attitude is critical; without a positive attitude, using the telephone is mentally exhausting.

3. Develop a well-written, structured script. Know exactly what to say before you call. However, never make your call sound like a canned spiel.

4. Verify that you are actually talking to the person you intended to call. Be sure you have the correct pronunciation of the name. Use the name several times during the call.

5. Tell the prospect just enough to get the appointment. You know a lot more than you need to tell at this time.

6. Show excitement and enthusiasm in your voice. Give your voice the emotional feel of shaking hands over the telephone. Put a smile in your voice. Place a mirror by the phone and watch your expression.

7. Never argue; be sure to ask for the appointment. Always offer a choice of times so prospects can choose a time that is convenient.

8. Sell your own name. Ask the prospect to write it down to be sure you are remembered when you arrive for the appointment.

9. Be courteous. Say thank you and begin sentences with phrases like, "May I ask . . ." and "If I may . . ."

10. Watch your language. Choose words carefully for impact. Repetition of nonfunctional expressions like, "I see," "uh huh," "you know," and "fantastic" are irritating and unprofessional.

Figure 8.2

The Six-Step Telephone Track

Introduce yourself
and your company

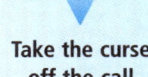

Take the curse
off the call

State the purpose
of the call

Make an interest-capturing
statement

Request an
appointment

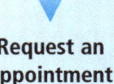

Overcome
resistance

THE SIX-STEP TELEPHONE TRACK

The key to using the telephone effectively is to engineer conversations that sound like talk. They have to be two-sided, but cleverly get people to sell themselves on seeing you. When you try to set an appointment by phone, you don't have the advantage of being able to show your prospect what a great product you offer. Instead, you need a careful strategy that allows the prospect to take an interest in what you're saying and agree to meet with you face-to-face. Use the six-step outline in Figure 8.2 to plan your appointment-setting calls so that the next time you talk to prospects, you're sitting face to face with them.

Step 1: Introduce Yourself and Your Company

Most sales relationships depend heavily on initial impressions. When you call on the telephone, the prospect will make a judgment about you before your first twelve words are said. How you introduce yourself, therefore, and what you say immediately thereafter are vitally important. A weak or tentative opening puts you at a severe disadvantage throughout the rest of the call. Your opening words should tell who you are, indicate the company you represent, and confirm that you are speaking to the correct person:

Good morning . . . I am Larry Henley, sales representative for Express Media. Am I speaking to Mrs. Teresa Ridings? . . . Good. Mrs. Ridings, . . .

Be sure the person you reach on the phone is someone who can make or influence a buying decision. Smile as you speak so that you transmit the impression of a warm, friendly personality. Watch the rate at which you speak. Prospects instinctively pay more attention to someone who speaks at a moderate rate. A too rapid rate of speech seems nervous or sounds as though you are reading a canned pitch. If you are too slow, you come across as lazy or unconcerned, or the prospect feels that talking to you will be a long, time-consuming process.

Step II: Take the Curse Off the Call

The telephone call is an interruption of your prospect's work. To sell people on the idea of granting you an appointment, you must detach their attention from what they were doing or thinking when the phone rang and attract it to what you propose. It helps if you think and talk about your call as a service you are offering rather than as an interruption for which you must apologize. You can take the curse off the call with a statement and a question to soften the impact of the interruption. For example,

> 1. *It will take just about a minute to explain why I'm calling. Is it convenient for you to talk now?*

> 2. *Mrs. Ridings, do you have a minute to speak with me now, or did I catch you at a bad time? . . . (If the prospect indicates the time is inconvenient) . . . When would be a better time?*

A prospect who is totally preoccupied with other matters may refuse to speak with you. In this case, calling back at a time the prospect suggests is better. When you do call back at the suggested time, the odds will be greatly improved that your message will receive a favorable hearing.

Step III: State the Purpose of the Call

Follow Step II (assuming the prospect does have time to speak) with a brief, hard-hitting, lead-in statement about why you are calling — just enough to capture the prospect's attention but short of describing the benefit(s) you will present in Step IV. Use these ideas to spark your creative thinking about possible lead-in statements you can use:

- Refer to a direct-mail piece you have already sent to the prospect.

- Mention the person who referred you to this prospect.

- Say that your company has designed a program or service to benefit clients like the prospect.

A letter, product literature, newsletter, or any other direct mail piece sent to a select sampling of prospects gives you the opportunity to call and inquire if they received it. This tactic gives you a purpose for calling and provides an acceptable type of lead-in statement. Here is a sample:

> *Mrs. Ridings, thank you for taking a minute of your valuable time to speak with me. My purpose in calling is to find out if you received the newsletter I sent you last week describing a specialized investment service that my company has recently developed for professionals like you.*

Whatever the answer, you can use this beginning to move on to the next step.

Perhaps the best reason you can give for calling is that you have been referred by a third party the prospect respects. The value of using a third party as an introduction is the immediate endorsement it provides. The prospect automatically assumes that you are reputable and reliable and that you deserve a hearing.

In the majority of instances, a referral alone is enough to get the prospect to hear you out during this first telephone call. Then you must generate enough interest to motivate the prospect to agree to give you an appointment. Here is an example of how to use a referral as a purpose for calling:

> *Mrs. Ridings, I recently performed a service for the DM Bass Company that was extremely well received by their employees. Martha Bass was so pleased with the service and the results that she asked me to get in touch with you and see whether it might also be helpful to you.*

After you have established a legitimate purpose for the call, you are ready to move to the next step.

Step IV: Make an Interest-Capturing Statement

Once you have the prospect's attention, your task is to convert attention into interest so that you can expect a favorable hearing. Interest is established primarily by promising a benefit or offering a service. Use product benefits, company services, or financial rewards to answer the prospect's unspoken question: "What's in it for me?"

Offer the prospect a benefit from listening to you, offer a service, or offer to do something for — not to — the prospect. Be sure to say how long the actual personal visit will take, and assure the prospect that everything you have to say can be covered in that length of time unless the prospect wants to explore certain areas in greater detail. Here are two examples:

1. *Mrs. Ridings, we have designed a service for companies similar to yours that could increase the effectiveness of your business from 10 to 25 percent with a decrease in the cost of operation. It will take about 20 minutes for me to show you how.*

2. *The benchmarking results from our design department show that many managers have been pleased with the quality and reliability of our new design simulator. Our clients report saving tens of thousands of dollars. In fact one client, Shelby Engineering, saved more than $50,000.*

Rather than making a statement, you may ask a question to capture the prospect's interest:

My company has an idea that could give complete protection to your entire plant and decrease your present costs. You are interested in cutting costs, aren't you?

Most business people want to see their operations run more efficiently and would answer this question in the affirmative. You could then suggest that you have a specific plan and request a personal visit to discuss it with the prospect.

Step V: Request an Appointment

Remember that your goal at this point is to secure an appointment with the prospect so that you can make a complete presentation. Avoid giving interview information over the phone; the more information you give, the more problems the prospect may see. The prospect can easily say, "I'm not interested" into a telephone. Then you have nowhere to go. The conclusion could be much different when you give an excellent presentation in person. Next time, try the "KISS" approach to setting the appointment: Keep It Simple, Salesperson! The telephone itself encourages brevity, so just ask for the appointment confidently and directly.

1. *I'm sure you agree that we should get together to discuss how we can accomplish this for you. Would this Thursday at nine be good for you? . . . or perhaps Friday morning would be better?*

2. *The best time for me would be tomorrow afternoon at 2:00 or Thursday morning at 11:00. Which would be more convenient for you, Mrs. Ridings?*

Notice that in each example the prospect was given a choice of times rather than asked, "When would it be convenient to see you?" which makes saying no too easy. You simply want to create enough initial interest to set up an appointment. Resist every temptation to get into specifics on the telephone. You are *selling an appointment*, not the product or service.

After you have set up the appointment, be sure to say "thank you" and then allow the prospect to end the call. It is important for you to *hang up last*, because the prospect may think of something at the end and should hear your voice instead of a click.

Step VI: Overcome Resistance

Using the telephone to set up appointments gives rise to two types of objections: An objection to receiving a telephone call and an objection to granting an interview. A prospect who was engaged in an activity of interest or importance may feel irritated by an interruption and prefer to resume that activity. This prospect's goal is to get you off the phone by refusing to become interested in what you have to say.

Prospects who do not want to grant an interview often fear that they cannot successfully defend their own ideas or decisions when faced by an experienced salesperson. They are afraid that they will buy. This type of objection can be overcome in three steps:

1. Agree sympathetically with objections to build the prospect's ego.
2. Switch from the prospect's objection to your idea or purpose for the interview.
3. Ask for the appointment.

Design the telephone approach in the six-step format presented above and then practice it until it feels comfortable and natural. *Internalize it rather than just memorize it.* When you combine the six-step telephone approach with confidence and friendliness, you are likely to find yourself dealing with more responsive and receptive prospects.

Sample Telephone Script

The following is an example of a telephone script written by Ben Phillips, an agent with Northwestern Mutual Life Insurance Company. Ben's example is a referred-lead telephone script. This is just one of five scripts he has developed depending upon the type of prospect he is calling. You can see how closely he follows the six-step telephone track.

Step 1: **Introduce Yourself**
   Agent: Good morning, I am Ben Phillips with Northwestern Mutual Life Insurance. Am I speaking with Mr. Jones? Good!

Step 2: **Get Approval to Continue**
   Agent: Mr. Jones, it will only take a minute to explain to you why I am calling you today. Is it convenient for you to talk now? Thank you!

Step 3: **State Your Purpose for Calling**
   Agent: Mr. Jones, as I mentioned I am with Northwestern Mutual Life. Our mutual friend Mrs. Smith is a customer of mine, and she felt that some of the ideas that I shared with her might also be of interest to you. Mrs. Smith has been pleased with the service that I provide and thought that it might be good to check with you to see if you too might benefit from my services.

Step 4: **Capture Interest**
   Agent: Mr. Jones, I would like the opportunity to share with you how Northwestern Mutual is helping people just like you explore their family's financial security. It will take me about twenty minutes to show you the kind of work I do, and if you feel like some of the ideas I share with you would improve your situation I would consider it a privilege to help you in that way.

Step 5: **Request Appointment**
   Agent: Mr. Jones, I am sure that you are interested in providing financial security for you and your family aren't you? Then I think we should get together for a few minutes and explore how our services may help you accomplish that.

Step 6: **Overcome Resistance**
   Prospect: I already have insurance!

   Agent: Great! Because our system takes into account your existing insurance. So we can take a look at your entire situation.

   Prospect: I have enough insurance!

   Agent: I am glad you mentioned that. Many people feel the same way, but a current review is nearly always beneficial. That way you will know that your program is staying current.

Preapproach planning means the difference between success and failure.

Preapproach and Telephone Techniques

- Planning and preparation are essential to securing an appointment for a personal sales interview.

- Your preapproach planning may utilize cold calls designed to meet the prospect and request an appointment, a letter to introduce yourself and your company, or a telephone call to request an appointment.

- The attempt to set up a sales interview is a mini sale in which the product is a live sales interview, and the purpose of the phone call is to sell the prospect on the idea of granting that interview.

- Save the detailed description of your product and its benefits for the actual face-to-face meeting. Keep the telephone discussion focused solely on getting the appointment.

- It is vital that you hang up last. The prospect may be thinking of something and should hear your voice instead of a click.

- The six-step telephone track for making appointments includes:
  - Step 1: Introduce yourself and your company
  - Step 2: Take the curse off the call
  - Step 3: State the purpose of the call
  - Step 4: Make an interest-capturing statement
  - Step 5: Request an appointment
  - Step 6: Overcome resistance

Part IV

The Face-to-Face Relationship Model of Selling

EXCELLENCE

Excellence is never an accident. It is achieved only as a result of an unrelenting and vigorous insistence on the highest standards of performance. It requires an unswerving dedication to continuous quality improvement.

Excellence is contagious. It infects and affects everyone in an organization. It establishes the criteria for planning. It provides zest and vitality to the organization. Once achieved, excellence has a way of penetrating every phase of the life of an organization.

Excellence demands commitment. It requires a tenacious dedication from the leadership of the organization. Once it is accepted and expected, it must be nourished and continually reviewed and renewed. It is a never-ending process of learning and growing. It requires a spirit of motivation and boundless energy.

Excellence inspires. It potentializes every phase of the organization's life. It unleashes an impact that influences every program, every activity, and every individual. To instill it is difficult; to sustain it, even more so. It demands adaptability, imagination and vigor. But most of all, it requires from the leadership a constant state of self-discovery and discipline.

Excellence is a company's lifeline. It is the most compelling answer to apathy and inertia. It energizes a stimulating and pulsating force. Once it becomes the expected standard, it develops a fiercely driving and motivating philosophy of operation.

Excellence is a state of mind. Once put in action, it is a road map to success. Success is getting what you want. Happiness is liking what you get. Successful people form the habit of doing what unsuccessful people don't like to do.

Excellence in life is important . . . because it is everything. The quality of a person's life is in direct proportion to their commitment to excellence regardless of their chosen field of endeavor.

Chapter 9

Approaching the Prospect

FOCAL POINTS

- **The purpose of the approach**
- **The importance of first impressions**
- **Surface language**
- **Elements of the greeting**
- **Ways to get attention and capture interest**
- **Types of approaches and when to use them**

PURPOSE OF THE APPROACH

Your prospecting and preapproach efforts have uncovered potential clients, and you have successfully arranged a personal meeting with a prospect. What happens during the opening of the face-to-face encounter profoundly affects the success of the whole presentation and your ability to close the sale. The approach is important because it determines the character of your future relationship with a prospect, including how receptive the prospect will be to your presentation and whether the close will be difficult or easy.

Although the overall success of the interview depends on more than the approach, an effective approach creates a favorable buyer-seller environment. The approach is often overlooked or taken for granted. Although the approach is usually considered in the context of the first call on a prospect, every meeting with a new prospect or an established customer begins with an approach.

You never get a second chance
to make a good . . .

FOLLOW the river and you will find the sea. Determination is the key.

INDIVIDUALS cannot consistently perform in a manner which is inconsistent with the way they see themselves.

REMEMBER . . . If you fail to plan, you plan to fail.

SOME people dream of worthy accomplishments, while others stay awake and do them.

THE single most important ingredient in the formula for success is knowing how to deal with people.

IF you don't take care of the customer . . . somebody else will.

MANAGE your time and your choices — and you'll manage your life.

PREPARE yourself for leadership. Be a living example of the excellence you expect from others.

RUNNING a business is no trouble at all as long as it's not yours.

EVERYTHING you say and do is a reflection of the inner you.

SINGIN' in the rain of life is better than letting it dampen your spirits.

SELF-ESTEEM, commitment and action determine your outcome.

IF we could kick the person responsible for most of our problems, we wouldn't be able to sit for a week.

ONE way to avoid criticism is to do nothing and be a nobody. The world will then not bother you.

NO one is useless in this world who lightens the burden of another.

Choose a job you love and you will never have to work a day in your life.

Salespeople tend to use the same approach over and over, but prospects and situations are not the same; instead, salespeople ought to make a practice of using various types of approaches that fit the needs of a specific situation, whether calling on new prospects or on old customers. An effective approach achieves four key objectives:

1. To make a favorable or **positive impression** on the prospect

2. To gain the prospect's **undivided attention**

3. To develop **positive interest** in your proposition

4. To lead **smoothly** into the need-discovery phase of the interview

FIRST IMPRESSIONS

In his book *Contact: The First Four Minutes*, Leonard Zunin says that the first four minutes of initial contact with a prospect are crucial. He suggests that four minutes is the average time the prospect takes to decide whether to buy from you. Impress the prospect with a show of good manners, clear enunciation, good grooming, and appropriate dress; when you look and act like a professional, the prospect, consciously or subconsciously, begins to trust you. People make quick decisions based on feelings, emotions, or hunches. The more positive their feelings, the more they hear and accept what you say. The opening moments of the approach must be designed to create an atmosphere of trust. The first twelve words you speak tell volumes about you.

Although some buyers base purchasing decisions on first impressions, others do not. Doug Bartulis, a sales representative with Applied Data Systems Inc., based in New Haven, Connecticut, has several clients who admit that they did not like him at first. Remember, too, that you are not forced to like all prospects personally; you can sell to them in spite of a lack of personal attraction. A relationship salesperson must be able to work effectively with a prospect even in the presence of a personality clash. Look further than your first impression of a prospect before making an unalterable judgment.

> Successful salespeople have a knack for making people feel important. It does not matter how knowledgeable they are about their product lines or how many closing techniques they have memorized, unless they earn their prospect's trust and confidence, they are not going to make the sale — *period*.

Every personal characteristic is watched and evaluated; your approach must be impeccable. Exhibit 9.1 presents some guidelines for making the first impression favorable. After all, *you never get a second chance to make a good first impression.*

Exhibit 9.1

There's No Second Chance to Make a Good First Impression

When meeting a prospect for the first time, pay attention to:

Visual factors

- Correct any detail that could become a visible distraction: a tattered briefcase, a messy car, or inappropriate grooming.
- Nonverbal communication is powerful. Pay attention to what the prospect sees in your body language as well as in what you wear.
- Don't wear jewelry such as lapel pins, tie pins, or rings that advertise your membership in a specific organization that may not be recognized or admired by some people.

Organization and Professional habits

- Be prompt, even early. Set your watch five minutes ahead if necessary.
- Present a clear agenda. State the purpose of your call right away. Make it clear that you are not there to waste the prospect's time.
- Be prepared with as much information as possible about the prospect (individual and company).

Building rapport

- Be sure to pronounce the prospect's name correctly. A person's name is a personal identifier; mispronouncing it takes away some of the owner's status.
- If you pay the prospect a compliment, make it specific and of personal interest.
- Recall the importance of proxemics. Respect the prospect's personal space.
- Look for common ground like mutual friends, membership in the same religious or civic group, or similar hobbies.

Your Actions

- Shake hands, maintain eye contact, and greet the prospect warmly, but never say, "How are you?"
- Refrain from personal habits like smoking or chewing gum or careless language that might be offensive to some people.

Your Attitude

- Be enthusiastic. Enthusiasm is infectious if it is sincere.

Although first impressions may be dependable signposts, first impressions do have some weaknesses:

- They are likely to be based on feelings and emotions.

- All behavior traits do not show up simultaneously, and an initial short interview may not provide enough time for all traits (either favorable or unfavorable) to surface.

- The prospect may deliberately control behavior and allow you to see only certain chosen personality traits.

- Some event immediately preceding the interview may strongly influence the prospect's current behavior.

Be willing to wait before you conclude that you and a prospect have a personality conflict that cannot be overcome. Your job is to establish rapport, build confidence, and make the prospect feel comfortable. Do everything in your power to satisfy the needs of your prospects, and refuse to allow first impressions to prevent a mutually beneficial sales experience.

SURFACE LANGUAGE

Surface language — including grooming, clothing, accessories, posture, and all other aspects of appearance — vitally affects first impressions, even though surface language factors actually provide limited or shallow insight into the true person. Salespeople must be sure the statements they make with their surface language are favorable because the impressions formed during the first few minutes of an initial encounter between two people could be lasting. Successful salespeople increase the odds in their favor by taking advantage of the power of first impressions. Visual impressions almost always come first. Fortunately, you can do a lot to shape the visual impact you make when a prospect first sees you.

Projecting an Image

"As an effective salesperson you want your clothes to command respect, inspire credibility and create trust — you must come across as the authority on the product that is offered," points out Sherry Maysonave, head of Empowerment Enterprises in Austin, Texas. Your clothes speak volumes about you, your company, your work, and how you relate to customers.

When you know that you are dressed appropriately, you feel good about yourself. When you are confident and at ease, you emanate an air of competence that the prospect unconsciously accepts and interprets as credibility. Total appearance is important because the prospect's initial attention is focused on you and not on your proposition. If you want to be successful, you must look successful. A salesperson who wears an obviously cheap suit, for example, creates a negative impression and sets up this line of thinking in the mind of the prospect:

- *This salesperson is dressed cheaply. He must not be making much money.*

- *Because he's not making much money, he must be having difficulty selling his product.*

- *If the product is not selling, something must be wrong with it.*

- *I don't want an inferior product.*

Dress Conservatively. Your objective is to focus the prospect's attention on the benefits of buying your product or service. Anything that detracts from that focus works against you. Conservative dress gives the prospect the impression that talking with you is safe and that you are familiar and dependable. Although "conservative" varies from one region to another and from one industry to another, that variation is not extremely wide. Dressing conservatively suggests stability and dependability; following extreme fads of color, cut, and pattern may suggest just the opposite.

Casual corporate dressing has become a trend, and it appears to be a growing one. This new style is not intended to convey a lack of professionalism, just a more comfortable, perhaps less boring way of projecting one's best. "Professional" is the key word to remember when dressing business casual. But be aware that you do not dress too casually. Rather, make sure your clothes reflect your position and the message you wish to convey to your clients.

Dress Appropriately. You should plan to dress as well as your prospect. People feel comfortable dealing with those who seem to fit into their own lifestyle. Joe Girard, who according to the *Guinness Book of World Records* is the world's greatest salesman, says, "I believe a salesman should look as much as possible like the people to whom he sells. . . . I never wear clothes that will antagonize my customers and make them feel uneasy." Customers buy the salesperson long before they buy the product. If your clothes are too formal or carry too much of an aura of power, you cause the prospect to feel overpowered; the result may be rebellion against what is perceived as your snobbish attitude. If you dress too casually or carelessly, prospects may unconsciously feel that you do not consider them or their business important. Exhibit 9.2 indicates what the clothes you wear say about your image.

Exhibit 9.2

Dressed to Sell

What do your clothes say about you? That you're sophisticated? Disorganized? Powerful? Your professional image should work for you, not against you. How you look goes a long way toward establishing your identity. Your clothes say much about your character and credibility.

Consider these style tips

- Clothes should be professional and understated. Flashy clothes detract from your image and take attention away from the work at hand.
- Absolutely nothing you wear should be wrinkled, frayed or sloppy.
- The most powerful color is blue. This is why police uniforms are blue.

- Keep your shoes shined (men often judge others by the condition of their shoes).
- Make sure your socks match your suit and shoes.
- Keep accessories simple: ties, watches, and jewelry. Clients should be looking at you, not your accessories.
- Dress in line with your superiors, but never more casually than subordinates.
- Dress appropriately for your business. Bankers always look like bankers.
- Be prepared for unexpected meetings. Have a spare sports jacket/blazer cleaned, pressed, and ready in your office.

THE PROPER GREETING

Choice of Greeting

In order to increase the odds of making a good impression, use the business etiquette *Rule of Twelve*. The first twelve words you speak should include a form of thanks: "Good morning, Mrs. Eubank. Thank you for agreeing to see me," or "Good afternoon, Brian. It's a pleasure to meet you." Casual questions like "How are you?" or "How ya' doing?" have lost all semblance of meaning. How does the prospect respond? "Great" or "Just fine, thank you," but what if the prospect is not feeling great and what if business is not going great? If a prospect covers up real feelings with a conventional answer, a vague feeling of uneasiness results from the untruth. If the prospect responds to your question with a long list of ills or problems, no response you make can turn attention naturally toward your sales presentation. How might you answer the simple question "How are you?"

You may want to try the response used by Pat Shemek. When prospects or clients ask Shemek "How are you doing," his response has become a real attention-getter. Pat replies, "Super duper" — an answer certainly different from the typical response, but it seems to give him an edge over competitive salespeople. The clients have come to expect this response. They look forward to it. Shemek's attitude seems to be — fake it until you make it! If this sounds too impractical for your style, come up with your own unique response delivered with a smile on your face and enthusiasm in your voice. Your customers will appreciate your positive attitude.

The Handshake

Your voice inflection and how you shake hands are as important as what you say. These three elements of the greeting taken together tell a prospect your mood. The handshake, particularly, is a revealing form of nonverbal communication. Exhibit 9.3 presents helpful guidelines for an effective handshake.

Exhibit 9.3

Guidelines for an Effective Handshake

- Maintain eye contact for the duration of the handshake.

- You may wait for the prospect to initiate the handshake (to avoid offending those people who "do not like to be touched").

- If your palm tends to be moist from nervousness, carry a special handkerchief with powder and pat your hand several times just before entering the prospect's office. Be careful not to leave a residue of powder on your hand that might be transferred to the prospect's hand or to your clothes.

- Apply firm, consistent pressure on the hand. Avoid the limp-wristed, wet-fish or bone-crusher handshakes.

- The hands should meet equidistant between you and the prospect in a vertical position. If you turn your wrist so your hand is over the prospect's, this nonverbal gesture implies the intention to be dominant. If you turn your wrist so that your hand is on the bottom, you are signaling a submissive nature.

Small Talk or Get Down to Business

In the initial face-to-face meeting, both parties may experience what might be called *relationship tension.* Prospects fear being sold something they do not want, and salespeople face the fear of being rejected. The opening few minutes of conversation are designed to find a comfort level for both parties so that rapport can be established. The purpose of small talk at the opening of the interview is to gain an advantageous, positive beginning that breaks the ice and eases the tension. Small talk may be a discussion of topics entirely unrelated to what you are selling. Al Angell, a very successful sales professional in Dallas, says this warm-up period usually takes him five minutes or more. Al calls this time "chit-chat with a purpose." He asks four basic questions that he feels are nonthreatening, easy to answer, and objective:

1. **Are you a native of this area?**
2. **Were you educated there?** (Based on answer to Question 1.)
3. **Are you a family person?**
4. **How did you happen to get into this business?**

This type of socializing at the beginning of the interview eases tension and may give you some insight into your prospect's behavioral style. It warms up a cold environment and has the side benefit of providing additional information about the prospect. If the prospect seems withdrawn or even hostile, this warm-up conversation helps you determine whether that is the prospect's real personality or whether you have arrived on an especially bad day.

People love to tell you what they do in their spare time, talk about their accomplishments, or tell you about their families. This non-selling conversation is important. An ideal topic for initial chit-chat is one that relaxes the prospect, is of interest, and relates — if possible — to your objective so that you can move easily into the attention getter and then into need discovery.

> **PEOPLE HAVE NO CONFIDENCE**
> in salespeople whose only
> interest is self-interest, who
> seek to use their clients instead
> of being of use to their clients.

Use of the Prospect's Name

People do not like to have their names forgotten, misspelled, or mispronounced. Typically, when we are introduced to someone, we hear our own name, then we might hear the other person's name. In *How to Win Friends and Influence People*, Dale Carnegie says, "A person's name is to them [sic] the sweetest and most important sound in any language." If we forget a name or mispronounce it, we send out this message: "I care more about me and my name than I do about you and your name." Imagine how a prospect feels when you say, "So you see, Mr. . . . ah . . . uh . . . excuse me (shuffle for prospect card or appointment calendar) uh . . . Mr. Danner, I mean, Tanner." The prospect probably stiffens, the environment turns a bit frosty, and you may well walk out without an order. Now recall how pleased you were when someone remembered your name after just a casual meeting several weeks previously. You would stand in line to do business with such a person.

Improving your memory for names is not as difficult as it may seem. Several books are available to help you devise a method to correct a careless memory for names. Table 9.1 gives some suggestions for remembering names.

Table 9.1

How to Remember Your Customers' Names

Five steps to remembering names:

Pay attention
Ask to have the name repeated (even spelled). It will impress the person.

Concentrate
Look for characteristics that distinguish this person from others.

Associate
Relate a characteristic with some gimmick to help you recall the name.

Observe
Study people regularly to strengthen your ability to see characteristics and practice your imagination.

Repeat it
Use the prospect's name several times during the interview.

THE HANDBOOK FOR RELATIONSHIP SELLING

You should remember not only the names of prospects and clients but also the names of their secretaries, assistants, and associates. These people also have feelings and can be instrumental in helping you secure an order. Executives depend on their personnel to help evaluate you after you leave.

Suit the Approach to the Person

Most people today have more work than they can hope to complete during regular working hours. Individual consumers, purchasing agents, engineers — anyone a sales representative might contact — feel time pressure and quite naturally regard you as an intruder. Prospects may react with resentment toward anyone who appears intent upon "stealing" precious time to engage in "small talk." How much or how little time you give to small talk or chit-chat depends on the behavioral style of the prospect, the circumstances of the moment, and the nature of your visit. If you sense that the prospect wants to get on with the interview, then move on.

Gain Attention and Capture their Interest

As the cartoon states, first you have got to get their attention! Develop a carefully constructed, attention-getting statement that focuses the prospect's attention solely on you and your proposition. Remember that prospects are thinking, "What does this person want with me? Why should I allow my work to be interrupted?" Unless prospects want to listen, they won't. Give them a reason. Just as the newspaper uses a headline to make you take notice, you must also develop an attention-getting opening statement that breaks through their preoccupation and focuses attention on the selling situation.

"First you've got to get their attention!"

The two basic methods of getting attention are: 1) through an appeal to the senses and 2) through the introduction of a benefit.

Appeal to the Senses. An appeal to the senses gets the prospect involved in the presentation. Use a little dramatization. Show something the prospect can see; hand the prospect something to hold.

Introduction of a Benefit. Introduce a benefit by a statement that relates to the prospect's need for your product or service. Highlight the value of the product or service. The prospect always wants to know, "What's in it for me?" Phillip Proctor, vice president of sales and marketing for Associated Printing in Ft. Lauderdale, certainly knows how to get a prospect's attention. He routinely uses a corny but effective prop: a simple bag of bread with a note that reads, "Our clients say we're the greatest thing since . . . sliced bread."

TYPES OF APPROACHES

Because every prospect and every selling situation is different, you ought to have several approach methods available and use the one that best fits the particular circumstance. Learn the principles of each of the different types of approaches so that you can use whichever one is appropriate for a particular situation. How many approach techniques are enough? You cannot have too many. The personality style of prospects, the mood they're in as you greet them, and your own feelings and mood that particular day suggest the need to have an opening for every occasion and every situation. You may have to deviate 180 degrees from the opening and presentation you had planned.

Self-Introduction Approach

This approach is commonly used but is probably the weakest approach to use alone. A smile, a firm handshake, and a relaxed but professional manner should accompany the introduction. Address the prospect by name, pronouncing it correctly, state your name and company, and present your business card. Although the business card is optional, it is a useful reminder of your name, and the prospect is not embarrassed by finding it necessary to ask you to repeat your name. Here is an example of a typical self-introduction:

> *Good morning, Mrs. Fritts. I am Heath Smith, representing the Xerox Corporation.*

To increase the effectiveness of the self-introduction approach, follow it immediately with one of the other approaches. The consumer-benefit approach, for instance, is generally a good fit.

Consumer-Benefit Approach

Give the prospect a reason for listening and suggest a risk for failure to listen. The benefit statement should be unique and appeal to the prospect's dominant buying motive. It should be sincere and must never sound like a gimmick. Something new and different about your product or service that paves the way for the rest of the interview is a good choice.

> *Good morning, Mr. Carter. I am Kevin Davis with McLee and Associates. I stopped by to see if I might take fifteen minutes to introduce you to a concept that will, first of all, keep your name in front of your customers for . . . maybe a year; second, it will allow you to provide each and every one of your customers with a value of up to $85 just as a way of expressing your appreciation that they are doing business with you; and third — and probably the best part of all — is that it should end up costing you not one cent.*
>
> *Do you have fifteen minutes?*

This example combines both the self-introduction and the consumer-benefit approaches. Because most business people want to offer value to their customers, presenting this benefit statement may cause the prospect to seek more information about the concept. Such a statement often sparks questions from the prospect that lead directly into the presentation.

Curiosity Approach

The curiosity approach works best when you know something about the prospect. Used sensibly, this approach is an effective opener. Suppose you are selling a telecommuting software package so a sales force can get up to date information on their laptops when they are out in the field selling. You might say something like this:

> *Mr. Wanke, have you ever been in a meeting when a written report analyzing a new competitive product is brought to your attention for the first time, and you want to share parts of it with your salespeople immediately? Do you know how much time you are losing by having to edit the report manually?*

People with certain behavioral styles, particularly analyticals and drivers, may find this approach offensive, especially if it sounds gimmicky.

Question Approach

The question approach quickly establishes two-way communication. It enables you to investigate the prospect's needs and apply the benefits of your product or service to those expressed needs. This type of approach suggests your interest in the prospect's problems and draws attention to the need to identify problems.

You may frame a leading question designed to obtain mental commitment from the prospect and at the same time show a major benefit. Here are two examples of how this might be done:

1. *Mr. Fisher, you do want to have distinctive-looking, quality-driven reports and the most up-to-date pricing information to share with your customers, don't you?*

2. *Do you feel you could get more accomplished in meetings if you had complete and current information at your fingertips? Wouldn't you also like the capability to easily edit that information, thus enabling you to provide your customers the best support possible?*

Qualifying Question Approach

A variation of the question approach seeks a commitment from the prospect. This qualifying question approach asks the prospect to consider buying the product; it can help determine whether you have a prospect who is cold, lukewarm, or red hot toward your opportunity.

Here are two illustrations of how this technique could be used:

1. *Mr. Armstrong, if I can satisfactorily demonstrate to you that the long-distance service provided by LDS will save you at least $1,000 within the next three months, would you be willing to do business with us?*

2. *Mrs. Woods, I am looking for individuals who have the discretionary funds to invest in an opportunity that will produce a return on their investment of at least 25 percent. If I can show you the evidence to support this claim, would you be willing to invest $125,000?*

If the prospect says yes, you have a sale, provided you can back up your statement with valid proof.

Compliment Approach

Opening with a compliment is like walking on eggshells, but this opening is highly effective if used properly. Follow the same guidelines you would use in any situation: Offer compliments with empathy, warmth, and sincerity. The purpose is to signal your sincere interest in the prospect. Sources for information upon which the compliment is based vary. Information from a person who provided a referral or from an item you saw in a newspaper or trade journal about the prospect can tell you about significant accomplishments that you genuinely admire. You can also see hints in the company offices as you come in or in the prospect's private office that suggest items that can be the basis for compliments.

Camco Inc., with international headquarters in Houston, sells gas-lift equipment, well-completion systems, safety systems, and wireline tools and units to the oil industry. At a time when the oil industry is experiencing a recession, a Camco salesperson would be out of line to compliment a prospect on the company's "obvious prosperity." Instead, a compliment should center on some other commendable factor:

> *I have been impressed with your continuous emphasis on safety on your offshore drilling rigs. I noticed the recent announcement that your company ranked first in safety ratings last year. You must be proud of that achievement.*

This type of compliment not only builds rapport but also directs the prospect's train of thought toward safety and the related products that Camco has to sell. Whenever a compliment is used as an opening, it must be *specific*, of *genuine interest* to the prospect, and *sincere*.

Referral Approach

The referral approach is especially useful because it helps you establish leverage by borrowing the influence of someone the prospect trusts and respects. If you use a referral card signed by the person who provided the prospect's name, you can give it to the prospect to introduce yourself and your company. This approach enhances your credibility and increases the likelihood that the prospect will give you full attention. Here are two good examples:

> 1. *Miss Reid, your neighbor Ray Thornton has recently completed one of our courses in personal leadership. He told me that you are also interested in growing as a person and in becoming a better leader, and suggested that you would like to hear about what our company has to offer. (Give the referral card to the prospect.)*

2. *Mr. Carpenter, I am Don Edwards with MC Designs. Melanie Jacobs, for whom we just completed a large order, suggested that I contact you. She thought you would like to have an opportunity to consider whether our T-shirt products and prices also could be of benefit to you.*

Product Approach

This approach consists of actually handing the product, or some physical representation of it, to a prospect to produce a positive reaction. The product approach provides a visible image of the product or service. This approach should focus on the uniqueness of the product and, as far as possible, allow the product to tell its own story.

Bringing the product to the prospect stirs interest, permits a demonstration, makes a multiple sense appeal, and usually creates in the prospect a feeling of commitment to listen and to participate actively in the presentation. For example, a PDA or handheld computer sales representative might say,

> *"Mrs. Wampler, chances are, your busy field reps rarely have time to sit down. So why give them a computer that needs a lap? Our new light-weight, pen-based computer helps them work better anywhere. Here, catch."*

Sometimes you cannot bring the actual product with you because of size or other constraints, but you can use other devices to simulate the actual product. A piece of literature, a sample of the output of the machine, a small working model, a picture — any visual tool that the prospect can hold and look at helps to focus and hold attention.

If you are selling a service, such as a time-management program, hand the prospect a letter from a satisfied client that identifies specific benefits of the program. Statistical data that shows the return on investment earned by satisfied clients can accomplish the same purpose.

To summarize, whatever approach device you decide to use, it should be directly related to your plan for beginning the need discovery phase of the presentation. The exchange of conversation in the approach phase allows you to move smoothly into the questions you plan to ask to discover the needs of the prospect. Because the actual presentation of benefits cannot begin until the prospect agrees to having a need for what you have to offer, whatever you can do to make need discovery seem a natural process will be helpful.

Approaching the Prospect

- What you do and say in the initial moments of the face-to-face interview has a profound effect on the success of the close. Plan those initial moments carefully. The first 12-15 words out of your mouth are crucial.

- Be aware of the power of first impressions. You never get a second chance to make a good first impression.

- Proper dress and grooming give the prospect the feeling that you are competent. Appropriate choices in dress and grooming let the prospect focus on your sales message instead of on your physical appearance.

- The greeting is important to create a favorable first impression. Use the prospect's name often and begin with some "chit-chat with a purpose" to feel out the mood and behavioral style of the prospect.

- Have a firm handshake, maintain eye contact and make use of voice properties that reflect confidence.

- Confirm or modify your impressions of the prospect's behavioral style and adapt your plans for the presentation accordingly.

- A number of different types of approaches are available: (1) the self-introduction, (2) consumer-benefit, (3) curiosity, (4) question, (5) qualifying question (6) compliment, (7) referral, and (8) product. A good approach forms a natural transition into the need-discovery phase of the selling process.

Relationships are like a two-way street, but you have to meet each other halfway.

Chapter 10

Identifying Needs by Questioning and Listening

- **The purpose of asking questions**
- **Questioning tactics appropriate for the sales situation**
- **Specific questioning techniques**
- **SPIN® Selling and its application**
- **Functions served by various types of questioning methods**
- **The importance of listening**
- **Improving listening skills**

THE PURPOSE OF ASKING QUESTIONS

Telling isn't selling; asking is! For many years, salespeople were told that selling is talking. The message seemed to be to tell the prospect everything you know in hopes that something you say will touch the right spot and the prospect will buy. The result of this kind of thinking was a salesperson who kept the prospect pinned down with constant chatter that resembled oral machine-gun fire.

The problem created by that theory of selling lies in its assumption that every prospect uses the product or service for identical purposes and in the same manner. But in actuality, each prospect has unique needs. Of the many benefits you have to offer, only a few will be the key motivators for a particular prospect. The challenge is to determine their buying criteria before beginning your presentation and then use only the specific benefits that address their particular situation.

Salespeople are diagnosticians. If you went to your family doctor complaining of severe back pain, and the doctor — without asking any questions — wrote a prescription for a medicine to be taken three times a day for the next month, would you take it? Of course not! You would not believe the doctor could make an accurate diagnosis and prescribe the appropriate medicine without making a thorough examination and asking a number of probing questions about the problem. You would expect the doctor to understand your problem—not the problem of back pain in general — before prescribing for you. Your prospect has the right to expect the same professional attention.

Need Discovery and the Sales Cycle

The evolution of relationship selling has reached the point where the need discovery step in the sales cycle is more important than making the presentation, handling objections, or closing. Figure 10.1 shows the relationship between need discovery and the other basic steps in the face-to-face sales process. At this point of need discovery—not in the close—the sale is most often lost. The dotted line around need discovery in Figure 10.1 is a reminder that this step is often skipped or given inadequate attention by the traditional salesperson. In reality, more time should be spent in the approach and in discovering needs than in any other steps of the process.

Figure 10.1

Relationship Between Need Discovery and Other Steps in the Sales Process

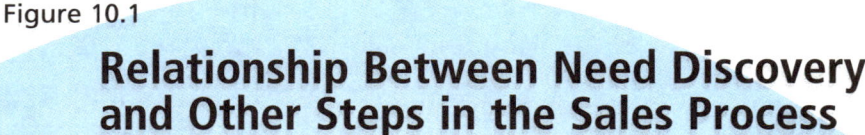

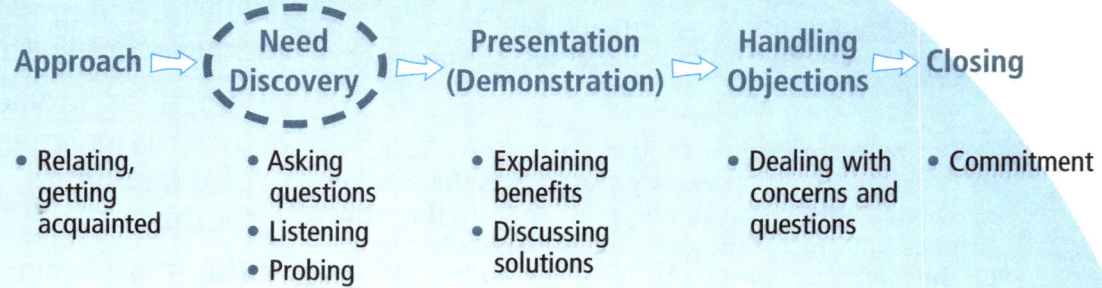

Need discovery is the foundation upon which a successful sale is built. Telling prospects what they need is a mistake. Asking questions that allow prospects to discover their own needs and share them with you sets you up as a sounding board for the solutions they "discover" while considering your proposal. Prospects are more receptive when they feel that the solution is their own idea.

THE HANDBOOK FOR RELATIONSHIP SELLING

Specific Planning of Questions

You must retain control of the questioning phase of the interview so that you obtain the required information and do not detour into irrelevant areas. The old standbys — *who, what, when, where, why, and how* — are a vital part of the sales interview. Decide in advance what you need to know, and then plan what types of questions will elicit that information in the quickest and most efficient manner consistent with the prospect's social style and situation.

Because the sale is made in the mind of the buyer and not in the mind of the salesperson, using the questioning process to gain agreement on key issues is paramount. Then you must assist the prospect in prioritizing those issues and agree that those are the problems or concerns that must be addressed before they make a decision to buy. Research shows that prospects are more likely to buy if you establish points of agreement early in the interview. To accomplish this. . . .

- **Plan** your questions in sequence to gain information in a logical order.

- **Predict** beforehand all the possible answers to each question so that you are never left wondering what to do next.

- **Prepare** a smooth transition from every possible answer into the next question.

Some salespeople hesitate to ask questions because they are afraid the prospect will refuse to answer. However, prospects that refuse to cooperate during the need discovery phase are unlikely to cooperate at the end of the sale either. Communication is a two-way street that demands participation by both you and the prospect. If you are to involve prospects in the sales process, you must be prepared to ask the questions that maximize participation. The right questions never materialize out of thin air. Your questions should attempt to achieve four objectives:

- To discover the prospect's "hot button" or dominant buying motive.

- To establish the purchase criteria or specifications.

- To agree on a time frame for completion of negotiations.

- To gain prospect agreement on the problem(s) before making the presentation.

STRATEGIC RECOMMENDATIONS

As you select specific questioning methods, keep these tactics in mind:

Avoid Technical Language That Might Confuse the Prospect. An account executive selling ad space to a small business owner should avoid terms such as *kerning, bodoni extra bold, mistral fonts,* or *bleed page* unless certain that the prospect is technically sophisticated and would expect to use such terms. In the same way, using company stock numbers, codes, or abbreviations may confuse the client. Your goal is to promote understanding and not to demonstrate your own personal erudition.

Transition from the Approach. Chapter nine presented four specific objectives of the approach: To make a favorable first impression, to gain attention, to create interest, and to serve as a logical transition into need discovery. This transition into need discovery requires that you tell the prospect exactly what you intend to accomplish during the interview session. You are to provide a clear agenda for the sales interview. Always let the prospect know what you want to accomplish. You can set up the desired atmosphere by requesting permission to ask questions. Here are two practical permissive questions:

1. *I believe I can offer you a service that will be of considerable value to you, but in order for me to be sure, and to know a little more about your particular situation, would it be OK if I ask you a few questions?*

2. *The only way for us to know how my company can best serve your needs is for you to give me permission to ask a few personal questions. Will that be all right with you? Oh, and may I make some notes while we talk?*

Phrase Each Question So That It Has One Clear Purpose. An ambiguous question or one with multiple meanings creates misunderstanding between you and the prospect. Proceed logically, one topic at a time. Murphy's law operates here: Anything that can be misunderstood will be misunderstood. A corollary to this principle is equally important: Phrase each question to produce the maximum amount of information so that the number of questions needed to elicit the required information is as small as possible. Exhibit 10.1 gives a good example of how not to do it.

THE SPIN TECHNIQUE

Neil Rackham is president and founder of Huthwaite Inc. and the author of the book *Spin Selling*. His corporation's 12-year, $1 million research into effective sales performance resulted in the unique sales strategy, the SPIN® method — Situation, Problem, Implication and Need-payoff questions. Successful salespeople don't ask random questions. This model represents how relationship salespeople probe. These are guidelines, not a rigid formula. There is a distinct pattern in the successful call. The answers you get will be used during the presentation to help underscore how the benefits you give support, reinforce, and solve the answers to the questions you have asked during need discovery. Its questioning sequence taps directly into the psychology behind the buying process. The questions provide a road map for you, guiding the sales call through the steps of need development until explicit needs have been agreed upon. You want to allow customers to discover for themselves the problems they have. People don't like to think, and certainly don't want to admit, their problems are that obvious.

Exhibit 10.1

Focusing the Questioning Process

A real estate agent wants to find out how many children the prospect has, their ages and gender. Poor planning produces a scenario like this:

Agent: Do you have any children?

Prospect: Yes.

Agent: How many?

Prospect: Three.

Agent: How old are they?

Prospect: 11, 9, and 7.

Agent: Are they all boys or all girls?

Prospect: Two boys and one girl.

Agent: What age is the girl?

Prospect: She's the 7 year-old.

At this rate, the agent will be asking questions all day. Why not simplify the process with one straightforward question:

Agent: What are the ages and genders of your children?

SPIN® Selling in Action

Let's take a specific example of a company and demonstrate the SPIN® method just as they might use it. A business with overdue accounts receivables has three options: It can hire a conventional percentage-based agency, a flat-fee agency, or do the collecting internally. Transworld Systems Inc. (TSI) is one of the largest collection agencies in the country. TSI works with over 40,000 clients helping them to recover their slow-paying and delinquent accounts without having to pay up to 50 percent of the collection as charged by a conventional agency. Many clients with a wide range of account balances have found the TSI system to be the only economical method of obtaining professional third-party collection results. TSI pays the money they collect directly to the client, the client maintains control of their accounts, and they do not have to pay a percentage. TSI has a low flat fee that enables clients to assign their accounts in the early stages of delinquency, thus providing the best opportunity for successful recovery. Here is the SPIN® technique in action:

Situation Questions: These questions are designed to find out about the customer's situation. These are data-gathering questions. They ask about the prospect's general state of affairs or circumstances as it relates to the services TSI has to offer. They help the TSI sales rep get to know the prospects and obtain initial information about their background and situation. You are looking for a general understanding of the prospect's needs. The following questions have an important fact-finding role, are non-threatening, and help to build an atmosphere of trust and cooperation:

- *Do you make the purchasing decision?*
- *How many active accounts do you bill each month?*
- *Do you do all the collection of overdue accounts internally?*
- *About what percentage of your customers do not pay their bills on time?*
- *Do you have out-of-state accounts?*
- *Is the billing and follow-up done in this office?*
- *Do you currently use a collection agency?*

Problem Questions: Once the TSI sales reps feel comfortable about the buyer's situation, they move on to a second type of questioning technique. These questions explore needs, any difficulties they may be having, and dissatisfactions in areas where TSI's service could be the solution. The goal in this step is to have the prospect say, "I really do have a problem with the collection of my accounts receivables."

TSI wants to determine explicit needs or uncover the prospect's "hot button." Remember: *The sale is made in the mind of the buyer, not in the mind of the TSI salesperson.* Customers don't want to be told they have a problem; allow them to discover it for themselves. Whatever they say is true; when you say it, they doubt it!

You're searching for areas where the services TSI offers can solve their specific problem. If you can uncover problems your service can solve, then you're providing the buyer with something useful. Ask these kinds of problem questions:

- *Do you know how much it costs to do your collecting internally?*

- *Do you ever get mail back? Wrong address? No longer at the address?*

- *When do you consider an account to be a concern or problem?*

- *Do you ever get checks back NSF or ACCOUNT CLOSED?*

- *Do you have a service to help recover these checks? If yes, is it a guaranteed service?*

Implication Questions: Implication questions build up the magnitude of the problem so that it's seen as serious in the mind of the prospect, and then the sales rep uses need-payoff questions to build up the value of the solution. Implication questions are the language of decision-makers, and if you can talk their language, you'll influence them. In larger sales you need to ask this third type of question. The phrasing of implication questions is critical because you want the prospect to discuss the problem and how it might be improved.

Attach a bottom-line figure to the implication questions. The TSI sales rep wants the prospect to agree that the implications of the problem are causing such things as loss of revenue; ill-will with some of its customer base; prohibitive cost of time and money in trying to do the collection themselves; percentage-based collection agencies are too expensive. The prospects must see that the problem is serious enough that it outweighs the cost of the solution, namely, using the services of TSI. The TSI sales rep might ask these questions:

- *Would it help if the money was paid directly to you? Last year we collected over $500 million for our clients and the money was paid directly to them.*

- *Do you know most collection agencies deposit the money they collect into their own bank account and hold it up to 60 days?*

- *Would it be important to you to recover a larger share of delinquent accounts and bad checks faster than a conventional collection agency and put the money directly into your hands and let it work for you?*

- *Is it safe to say that you would like to collect delinquent accounts quickly, without disturbing ongoing relationships with those customers?*

Need-Payoff Questions: How would that help? What benefits do you see? Why is it important to solve this problem? Is it useful to solve this problem? These questions get the customer to tell you the benefits that your solution offers. These types of questions actually get prospects to name benefits and tell you why they should buy. These questions help you build up the value of your proposed solution in the customer's mind. You want to focus the customer's attention on the solution rather than on the problem. This creates a positive problem-solving atmosphere.

In the words of an 8 year-old named Quincy, "Implication questions are always sad; while need-payoff questions are always happy." That's because implication questions are problem-centered, while the following need-payoff questions are solution-centered:

- *Would it be useful to speed up the rate of collection, and at the same time be guaranteed that you will recover at least twice as much as you pay for our service?*

- *If you could create the perfect agency, what would you want them to do for you?*

- *If I can show you how TSI has been able to help others in your industry, and we can determine what kind of results you might expect, can we get started today? Let's take a look at your aging report.*

- *We automatically send out a report detailing the status of each account assigned for collection. Does this sound like something that would interest you?*

- *Do you want the account handled diplomatically or intensively? We have another division that handles the hard-core collection problems. Would you like to have that option?*

- *Would you like us to send a "thank you" card to the debtor after the account has been paid?*

COMMON QUESTIONING TECHNIQUES

General Types of Questions

The major types of questioning techniques are summarized in Exhibit 10.2. Questions are generally classified by the type of answers required and by the purpose they are intended to serve. Begin the questioning process with closed-end questions or fact-finding questions that are easy to answer and therefore not threatening to the prospect. If the first few questions are reasonable, the prospect begins to gain confidence and feel comfortable with the questioning process. The next questions then, although progressively more challenging, seem easier to handle.

Exhibit 10.2

Types of Questions and Probing Techniques

General types of questions

Closed-end questions

Provide a series of responses from which the prospect selects one, are easy to answer, used to get feedback, and can be used to get prospect commitment.

Open-end questions

Identify a topic but do not provide structured alternatives for responses, usually begin with "how" or "what", cannot be answered "yes" or "no", and are designed to stimulate the prospect's thinking.

Classification of questioning techniques

Amplification questions

Ask prospect to expand on an answer. Do not direct thoughts but encourage prospect to continue talking. (Nonverbal gestures, silence, and continuation questions)

Getting agreement on the problem

Make a formal statement of the problem, get prospect to agree, and attempt to get commitment.

Internal summary questions

Assimilate information presented, put it in perspective, and ask if the interpretation is correct; may repeat all of prospect's last response in the form of a question. (Reflective or internal summary question)

Closed-End Questions: These questions are direct, fact-finding questions designed to reveal background information about the prospect's business and/or family. They ask an either-or question or request a choice from a series of suggested responses. Closed-end questions are usually answered with a very brief response, often a single word. They often ask for a yes or no response or a choice between two alternatives. They are directive questions for which you want specific answers:

- *How many employees do you have working the day shift?*
- *What interconnect companies are you familiar with?*
- *Is a rear-window defogger important to you?*
- *Does your company pay the full cost of employee health insurance, or do the employees pay part of the cost?*

You may also phrase closed-end questions to get feedback or to gain commitment.

- *Would you like delivery Friday, or is Monday of next week all right?*

- *Who will be involved in deciding whether to purchase from a competitor or from us?*

- *Do you know what your customers do with your product after buying it?*

- *Do you prefer to pay cash, or would you like to arrange a monthly payment plan?*

Use closed-end questions as a substitute for telling the prospect something. A question can sometimes make a point in a more telling manner than a statement because the prospect must think to answer it, and thinking makes a stronger impression than hearing. Consider these two ways to impart the same message:

1. *Our procedure will completely eliminate waste in your welding operations.*

2. *How much cost savings would you have if you used a procedure that completely eliminates waste from your welding operations?*

The first method tells the prospect something. You hope the prospect is impressed, but that may not happen. Unless the prospect reacts strongly enough to the statement to break in with a comment, any skepticism is buried until some later point, where it emerges as a vague objection or stall like, "Well, we're not thinking of making any changes just now." The question method, however, gains attention because the prospect has to think about an answer. Disbelief surfaces immediately where it can be dealt with instead of being postponed until later when you are trying to close. Exhibit 10.3 lists the various purposes served by asking closed-end questions.

Exhibit 10.3

Purposes of Closed-End Questions

- Uncover specific facts.

- Reduce prospect tension because they are easy to answer.

- Check understanding and receive feedback.

- Maintain control by directing the flow of conversation.

- Reinforce prospect commitment to a specific position.

Open-End Questions. These broadly phrased questions allow prospects plenty of room to answer as they wish. They call for explanations. Open-end questions encourage prospects to explain their needs by explaining their preferences, expectations, or judgments. Open-end questions tend to be general rather than specific. Use them when you want the prospect to talk freely. You can encourage the prospect to verbalize feelings by asking questions that begin with "What do you think?" or "How do you feel?" Talking out loud often helps people clarify and organize their thoughts. Real feelings are often not in the conscious awareness until they are verbalized.

Open-end questions help you and the prospect sort out ideas and begin to make decisions. Here are some examples of questions that give prospects the freedom and responsibility to express their own thoughts and use their own information in the decision-making process:

- *What options would you want on your new Mercedes?*
- *How do you think I might be able to help you?*
- *In a perfect world, what would you like to see us deliver?*
- *What are five unique characteristics of your business?*

- *What benefits would you expect from our ten-week, self-paced time-management program?*

Open-end questions reveal attitudes that you must be aware of if the sale is to be closed. You cannot easily ask a prospect, "Are you motivated by pride?" but you can ask open-end questions designed to detect this emotion, and you then have the answer to the direct question you cannot ask. Exhibit 10.4 lists the properties of open-end questions.

Exhibit 10.4

The Properties of Open-End Questions

- Allow the prospect to move in any direction.

- Cannot be answered with "yes" or "no".

- Ordinarily begin with "how" or "what".

- Designed to stimulate the prospect's thinking and increase dialogue.

- Help determine dominant buying motives (rational or emotional).

- Uncover the social or behavioral style of the prospect.

CLASSIFICATION OF QUESTIONING TECHNIQUES

The questions you ask can be classified by the purpose they are intended to perform. Three basic classes of questions can be used: Amplification, internal summary or reflective, and questions to gain agreement on the problem. Either open-end or closed-end questions may be asked for any of these purposes, depending upon the situation. If one type of question does not provide all the information needed, another type can be used to get a more specific response or to elicit a better sense of the prospect's point of view.

Be careful how you phrase the questions you ask. Place responsibility for not understanding on yourself rather than on the prospect. "Do you understand what I said?" or "Did you get that?" or "Are you with me?" seems to imply that the prospect may not be too bright. You must take responsibility for any possible misunderstanding by asking, "Have I explained this clearly enough? Is there some part I need to clarify or go over again?"

Amplification Questions

Ask probing questions and listen to your customer. These questioning techniques encourage prospects to continue to provide enlightening information and encourage them to explain the meaning of a statement made. Amplification questions help both salespeople and prospects. At times prospects may not make themselves clear; they may wander off the subject or may stop talking before you can fully understand their position. In a subtle manner, these techniques ask the prospect to expand on or clarify the meaning of a statement and help identify the frame of reference used.

Nonverbal Gestures. *Visual cues* such as nodding the head or leaning forward show that you are listening, believe the prospect is on the right track, and understand what the prospect is saying. You may also *inject appropriate words* or phrases to encourage the prospect to continue: "You don't say?" "Is that right?" "That's interesting!" You may imply a question by the nonverbal choice of silence accompanied by a slightly raised eyebrow or furrowed brow.

Silence. *Silence* is a powerful sales tool. When prospects avoid telling you the whole truth, the knowledge that they are being less than honest makes them uncomfortable. Your silence convinces them to go ahead and tell you the whole story. Silence allows you to slow down and relax the pace of asking questions. Some prospects want to think and contemplate longer than others before responding to your questions. Give people time to reply at their own pace. Silence also gives you valuable time to formulate your own next question or comment.

Continuation Questions. *Continuation* questions encourage prospects to keep on talking by making a positive request for more information. Such questions do not push for a particular response or for agreement; they just encourage more communication from the prospect. Here are three examples:

- *What additional thoughts do you have on that topic?*

- *That's just the kind of information we must have to help pinpoint your needs. Please go on.*

- *Could you tell me in a bit more detail why you feel that way?*

Exhibit 10.5 lists the advantages of amplification questions.

Exhibit 10.5

Advantages of Using Amplification Questions

- **Encourages the prospect to continue to provide revealing information.**
- **Allows you to rephrase what the prospect appears to have intended.**
- **Invites the prospect to expand or clarify any point of disagreement.**
- **Narrows down generalizations and clears ambiguities.**

Internal Summary Questions

Probes designed to get prospects to think, see, and consider your interpretation of the situation may be called internal summary or reflective questions. Summarize what you understood the prospect to mean. You want to assimilate the information provided, place it in the perspective that suits your purpose, and ask if the interpretation is correct. You achieve this by repeating all or part of the prospect's last response in the form of a question or by rephrasing the entire idea expressed by the prospect, feeding it back in a slightly different form, and asking for confirmation.

These types of questions are useful throughout the interview. Successful salespeople know about summarizing the key benefits just before asking for the order: "Now, as I see it, we've agreed that a complete line, with these particular items featured, will move for you with the proper promotion. Am I right about that?" Such summary techniques are especially useful during the close.

The summary question may be used to underscore points on which you already agree. An occasional summary of the points to which the prospect has already agreed will fix them firmly in the mind of the prospect and demonstrate just how wide an area of agreement there is between the two of you.

Getting Agreement on the Problem

In *Open the Mind, Close the Sale*, John Wilson says that the salesperson's failure to confirm the problem is one of the biggest mistakes in selling. The whole purpose of asking questions is to determine whether the prospect has a problem or need that you are capable of solving. State the problem in your own words and get the prospect to agree, "Yes, that's it." Never begin the actual presentation phase of the sales interview until the problem has been clearly established in the minds of both you and the prospect. Begin the formal statement of the problem by using such phrases as these:

- *Let me attempt to summarize what we have been saying.*

- *As I understand it, here is (are) the problem(s) we must solve.*

- *Based on your answers to my questions, I see the problem as . . .*

After you pinpoint the problem, you must seek confirmation. Get the prospect to agree by following your summary of the problem with questions like these:

- *If I show you some comparisons demonstrating that my company can save you money without sacrificing quality, would you commit to our program?*
- *Is that a fair statement of the way things stand?*
- *If I can satisfactorily demonstrate a solution to these concerns of yours, would it be enough to earn your business?*

If the prospect agrees with the problem statement, you are ready to present the specific benefits of your product or service that can solve the problem. Even if the prospect disagrees with your summary of the problem, you have both learned by sharing information.

LISTENING

About 80 percent of waking hours is spent communicating, about half of that listening. Effective listening is not just hearing what the prospect is saying. Faulty listening results in misunderstanding and lost opportunities. Research indicates that 60 percent of misunderstandings in business are due to poor listening. Fortunately, improved listening skills can be learned.

To succeed in professional selling, you must be able to offer a product or service that satisfies the buyer's needs. Presenting features and benefits is not always enough. How they are presented may be as important as what is presented. Listening is the key to finding ways to present benefits that enhance the possibility of a close.

Effective listening helps sales professionals catch verbal and nonverbal signals indicating a prospect who is interested in buying their product or service. "Unfortunately, good listening skills usually require a change in our behavior," says Barry Elms, CEO of Strategic Negotiations International. Psychologists claim that listening uses only about 25 percent of our brain. The other 75 percent either thinks about what to say next or stops listening if the conversation is boring or of no interest.

Improving Listening Skills

To improve your listening skills, practice these five mental activities as you listen:

1. Avoid Prejudgment. Not only should you allow the speaker to complete a message before you comment or respond, but you should also wait until you have heard the entire message before judging it. Making value judgments colors your thinking and creates *emotional blind* spots that block your ability to make a buying recommendation. Jumping to conclusions is a common fault of poor listeners. As the cartoon indicates, assuming you know what is coming next can seriously damage your understanding of the actual meaning intended.

YOU KNOW THAT DELUXE COMBINE YOU SOLD ME LAST WEEK? WELL, FOR YOUR INFORMATION MR. GILL, THAT *©!!% COMBINE IS . . .

HIS WIFE MAKES HIM CALL FROM THE BARN WHEN HE WANTS TO TALK "MACHO."

HE SAID HE'D RUSH RIGHT OVER AND HUNG UP. I JUST WANTED TO SAY IT'S THE BEST *©!!% COMBINE I'VE EVER COME ACROSS.

I'LL BET IF YOU CALLED FROM THE HOUSE THIS WOULDN'T HAVE HAPPENED.

2. Be Patient. Listen more and give "verbal nods" of encouragement. This allows speakers plenty of time to answer questions and encourages them to express their ideas. Speak at the same speed as the other person: Matching speed is a rapport builder. In addition, find the person's *mental rate of speed* and then adjust or modify your thinking to that rate. Even though the speaker is saying something exciting, wait until the message is complete and you are sure that you understand it all before you contribute your own thoughts.

3. Take Notes. Remembering everything a person says is difficult. Use the pencil-and-paper approach to selling. Divide your notepad into two columns. On one side note what the prospect says. Then in the other column sketch out your proposal to meet those expressions of needs, requirements, or desires. The mere physical action of writing down a few key words reinforces your memory and understanding. You can go back to the prospect's own words to help you show your product's applicability to the problem.

4. Reinforce. Anchor — in your mind and in the prospect's — the points made by the prospect. Use your own reinforcing responses to achieve this purpose. If the prospect says the mileage per gallon a car gets is important, respond, "Yes, that is very important." Later, tell what mileage the prospect could get with your car. If the prospect says, "Our secretaries spend too much time making copies," respond, "That has to be a problem." Then later emphasize how your copier cuts secretaries' time by copying on both sides of the paper in one operation and by running more copies per minute.

5. Capitalize on Speed of Thought. We can process about 600 words a minute, but even a fast talker gets out only 100 to 150 words in that time. Thus you can think about four times as fast as the average prospect talks. All that spare time is valuable. The poor listener uses it to fidget impatiently, to think about what happened earlier in the day or what will happen later, or to plan what to say as soon as the prospect takes a breath. Successful salespeople have a plan to follow for using this time profitably:

- **Anticipate where the prospect is going.** If you guess right, your thinking is reinforced. If you are wrong, compare your thoughts with the prospect's; look for the point the prospect is making.

- **Mentally summarize the message.** Pinpoint problems, misconceptions, attitudes, objections, or misunderstandings. What you learn can be an excellent guide to the items that should be stressed in the presentation and at the close.

- **Formulate a response,** but not before you hear everything the prospect wants to say. Listen, understand, and then turn the prospect's words to your advantage.

- **Listen between the lines.** Nonverbal messages are as important as verbal ones. Watch facial expressions, body movement, and position; listen to the tone of voice and volume changes.

Salespeople are first diagnosticians.

THE HANDBOOK FOR RELATIONSHIP SELLING

Identifying Needs by Questioning and Listening

- Asking questions is the primary tool for identifying problems. Need discovery lays the groundwork for the presentation and close. When you ask the right questions, prospects clarify problems in their own minds as well as in yours.

- No standard set of questions is universally applicable. The product or service, your preapproach information, and the prospect's behavioral style help determine the questions you ask.

- Questions may be either closed-end or open-end. A closed-end question asks for a yes-no response or a choice between alternatives. Open-end questions ask for opinions, explanations, or judgments.

- Ask questions according to their structure, Amplification, internal summary, and questions designed to gain agreement.

- Listening is one of the most neglected skills in any type of training program. Taking notes focuses your attention on what the prospect is saying and avoids prejudgment of ideas. Reinforce what you hear by comparing the prospect's ideas with your own.

- People can think at a rate much faster than they talk. Use this spare thinking time to anticipate where the prospect is going, mentally summarize what you hear, form a response, and refine the message as your listening continues.

CHECKLIST OF SUCCESS FUNDAMENTALS

	YES	NO
Goals		
Increase size of existing accounts	_____	_____
Contacts and networking daily	_____	_____
New appointments daily	_____	_____
New prospects daily	_____	_____
Closing Interviews		
Three today	_____	_____
Three yesterday	_____	_____
A minimum of 12 last week	_____	_____
Prospecting		
New qualified prospects each day	_____	_____
Five referrals on every sale	_____	_____
Adequate information on those referrals	_____	_____
Three methods of prospecting	_____	_____
Appointment Getting		
Call from same place and at same time everyday	_____	_____
Prepare names and numbers to call before phone time	_____	_____
Make at least 3 new appointments a day	_____	_____
Use the Six-Step Telephone Track	_____	_____
Presentation:		
Complete the sales presentation in 30 minutes	_____	_____
Close a minimum of four times	_____	_____
Use an organizer or visual aid presentation	_____	_____
Attitude Adjustment		
Use a personal goals program to help achieve success	_____	_____
Work on two of the Wheels of Life this week	_____	_____
Personal Organization and Self-Management		
Use a daily and weekly plan sheet	_____	_____
Use a monthly goal calendar	_____	_____
Know how much an hour of your time is worth	_____	_____
Schedule appointments geographically	_____	_____

THE HANDBOOK FOR RELATIONSHIP SELLING

Chapter 11

Making the Presentation

- **Make an engaging presentation**
- **Develop units of conviction**
- **Effective tactics for making a sales presentation**
- **Different methods for getting the prospect involved**
- **The significance of a demonstration in the presentation**
- **Different types of sales aids available**
- **Using technology to make winning presentations**

DEVELOPING A PERSUASIVE PRESENTATION

Some experts are predicting that salespeople are soon to be corporate relics on the road to extinction. Not true! Relationship salespeople will prosper in the future if they understand this: There are big differences between data and information. In the past, traditional sales reps simply presented data. How "data dense" are most sales presentations?

Here are some interesting and surprising facts about most sales presentations:

- The typical salesperson presents six to eight features or benefits during the sales presentation. Twenty-four hours later the average prospect remembers only one benefit.

- In 39 percent of those cases they remember the one benefit incorrectly.

- In 49 percent of the cases they remember something that wasn't mentioned at all.

Prospects demand a product that does what they want it to do, explained in a language they understand. The future of professional, relationship selling is going to be based on real-time value and how well sales professionals become trusted advisors in guiding clients to a solution to their problems. Salespeople must become better knowledge managers and not just people who are trying to close a deal.

Strive for Passion, not Perfection. More often than not, customers buy because of the rapport building established over time. "Selling is all about relationship building. There are hundreds of competitors chomping at the bit," says Diane DiResta. It all comes down to the way you present yourself and your product or service, and the value you create for the customer. Sales presentations must be listener-centered. People want to have their problems solved. People-reading skills help salespeople adapt to their prospect's social styles.

Mark McCormack in his book *What They Don't Teach You at the Harvard Business School* said there are three fundamental selling truths: (1) If you don't know your product, people will resent your efforts to sell it. (2) If you don't believe in your product, no amount of personality or technique will cover that fact. (3) If you can't sell your product with enthusiasm, the absence of it will be infectious.

Nobody buys from a dispassionate seller. If you don't believe in the product, no one else will. The more options a sales rep creates for the prospect, the greater the chance for a sale. Don't worry about making the perfect presentation. It probably will not happen! Besides, the prospects are looking to you for knowledge of what you're selling and how it can help them solve a problem or become more successful. You must truly believe in what you're selling and show some passion when doing it — that is far more important than perfection.

Calling on Regular Customers. If you are calling on the same person or dealer on a regular basis, you may tend to give the same old presentation over and over or even skip the presentation entirely and merely ask, "What do you need today?" If you are unwilling to put some real work into your selling and are content just to "take orders" all your life, your best opportunity to become rich is to win the lottery! Vary your presentation. Provide new ideas to help your customer make money, save time, or increase efficiency. Plan to use ideas like these:

- Give the customer a new advertising or merchandising idea.
- Help the customer develop an overall marketing plan for improving the business.

- Tell some new product fact that the customer needs to know.
- Share a piece of industry or trade news of personal interest to the customer.

Begin with Planning

Does everything begin with planning? Yes, everything important begins with planning. Exhibit 11.1 is one man's account of the results he suffered from his failure to plan his immediate future. Random, haphazard action never leads to success in any worthwhile endeavor, and in this respect, selling is no different from any other undertaking. How well you plan what takes place during the sales interview plays a major role in the success you achieve when closing time arrives.

Exhibit 11.1

Failing to Plan My Immediate Future

I am writing in response to your request for additional information. In block #3 of the accident form I listed "not planning my immediate future" as the cause of my accident. I trust the following details will be sufficient.

I am a bricklayer. On the date of the accident I was working alone on the roof of a new six-story building. At the end of the day, I discovered about 500 pounds of bricks left over. Rather than carry them down by hand, I decided to lower them in a barrel by using a pulley that was fortunately attached to the building at the sixth floor..

Securing the rope at ground level, I went to the roof, swung the barrel out, and loaded the bricks. Then I went back to the ground and untied the rope, holding it tightly to ensure a slow descent of the 500 pounds of bricks. Block #11 of the accident report shows that I weigh 135 pounds. Due to my surprise of being jerked off the ground so suddenly, I forgot to let go of the rope. Needless to say, I proceeded at a rapid rate up the side of the building. In the vicinity of the third floor, I met the barrel coming down. This explains the fractured skull and broken collarbone.

Slowed only slightly, I continued my rapid ascent, not stopping until the fingers of my right hand were two knuckles deep into the pulley. Fortunately, I had regained my presence of mind enough to hold tightly to the rope in spite of my pain.

At approximately the same time, however, the barrel of bricks hit the ground and the bottom fell out of the barrel. Devoid of the weight of the bricks, the barrel now weighed approximately 50 pounds. I refer you again to block #11. As you can imagine, I began a rather rapid descent down the side of the building.

In the vicinity of the third floor I met the barrel coming up. This accounts for the two fractured ankles and the lacerations of my legs and lower body. The encounter with the barrel slowed my descent enough to lessen my injuries when I fell onto the pile of bricks. Fortunately only three vertebrae were cracked.

I am sorry to report, however, that as I lay there on the bricks, in pain, unable to stand and watching the empty barrel six stories above me, I again lost my presence of mind and let go of the rope. Now the empty barrel weighed more than the rope, so it came back down on me and broke both of my legs.

I hope these details explain sufficiently that my accident was caused by failure to plan my immediate future.

Call Objective

The most successful salespeople have specific objectives for each sales interview. In many instances, the call objective is to present your product or service and secure an order. In others, your objective is to discover the prospect's needs so that you may prepare a proposal for later consideration or to persuade the prospect to set up a presentation to a group of people who are jointly charged with the responsibility for a buying decision. In these latter instances, you will probably plan several interviews that, taken together, contain all the elements that may be considered parts of "the presentation." The difference is that you accomplish the various steps in successive interviews rather than in a single meeting with the prospect.

Whether you intend to complete the presentation and the close in a single call or in a series of calls depends upon the type of product or service you sell and the size of the expected order. The single-call close is appropriate for selling items that can be ordered upon the decision of one person; if a buying center is involved, multiple calls are usually necessary.

John Zavitz is a business development manager for a major telecommunications company. John's role is to seek out new prospects and handle a small group of customers. He usually works on a four-interview system. The sale may be closed on any one of the calls, but often it requires many more than four calls. Here is his system:

1. **Initial call.** Develop rapport and establish a need. Judge how far to go by how quickly a relationship is established. Take notes all along to help build a trust level.

2. **Survey call.** Interview all key decision makers to get information. The decision is ultimately based on three factors: cost, quality, and service. Discover which one is most important to this client.

3. **Proposal call.** Present a buying recommendation. Recognize the fact that this is a joint or buying center decision, and give each person what that individual needs to reach a decision. Use trial closes.

4. **Closing call.** Get verbal and/or written commitment.

5. **Continue meeting** with executives, managers, and department heads until a solution is reached. Consider each meeting as a minicontract negotiation.

THE HANDBOOK FOR RELATIONSHIP SELLING

Sales Call Planning Sheet

Many companies, especially those whose product or service entails extensive research into customer needs, require salespeople to prepare a presentation plan in written form. The plan reveals the need for any additional information, makes it possible to check needs and goals against suggested solutions, and makes sure you have a clear picture of the entire situation before arriving for the personal interview. Exhibit 11.2 is an example of a sales call planning sheet that may be used for this purpose.

Exhibit 11.2

Sales Call Planner

1. Company Name _____

2. Type of Company _____

3. Address _____

4. Individual(s) to contact

   _____ (position) _____

   _____ (position) _____

5. Background and profile of buyers_____

   _____

6. Major competitors to be aware of

   _____ (sales rep)_____

   _____ (sales rep)_____

7. Objective for this particular call _____

8. Best time to see buyer _____

9. Expressed needs or problems _____

10. Strategies and tactics useful for this situation

    a. Best approach to use _____

    b. Specific fact-finding questions _____

    c. Features and benefits to stress _____

    d. Anticipated objections _____

       (techniques to answer them) _____

    e. Closing techniques to be used _____

    _____

11. Sales tools to take (audiovisual, flip-chart presentation, etc.) _____

    _____

12. Results of this sales call _____

    _____

PRESENTATION STYLES

As long as people have been attempting to analyze the selling process, a running controversy has raged over the use of "canned" presentations. Opponents point to presentations that are obviously memorized, and delivered in a hypnotic manner likely to produce a mesmerized listener in the shortest possible time. Supporters of memorized presentations point to the many advantages of knowing exactly what to say and when.

The question is not likely to be settled once and for all because the difference lies more with the salesperson than with the method of delivery itself. In deciding how you will deliver the message you want the prospect to receive, consider the advantages and disadvantages of three basic choices: the memorized presentation, the outline presentation, and the extemporaneous presentation.

Memorized Presentation

Some companies supply their salespeople with a printed presentation and require them to memorize it. A few words of caution are in order when considering the use of a memorized presentation. Even though it is memorized, the presentation should never sound memorized.

A memorized presentation should be practiced and its delivery polished until it becomes natural. It should be internalized to the point that it is a normal, personal message. The memorized presentation must be used as a framework or guide to lead you and your prospect through the sales process.

A well-prepared, memorized presentation offers a number of important advantages, especially to new salespeople.

Quick Productivity. If you are new to the company or to the selling profession, you can memorize a good presentation in much less time than one can be developed. Using a standardized presentation gets you into production quickly. Enough sales can be made during the initial learning period to supply basic income needs while you gain knowledge and experience.

Reliable and Proven Effectiveness. The memorized presentation makes sure you give the right information to the prospect. Nothing vital is omitted, and nothing erroneous is inserted. The presentation a company supplies to salespeople has usually been tested and refined over a period of years in actual selling situations.

Confidence Building. When you know the presentation has worked for others with no more experience than you have, you feel capable of using it successfully. When you succeed in closing a sale with the presentation, you gain even more confidence. Each success builds on the previous one, and you are earning and learning at the same time.

Outline Presentation

The outline presentation takes a great deal of thought and preparation. With this presentation technique, exact words are not planned in full detail. You know what content will be presented at each stage of the presentation but are confident enough of both knowledge and skill to believe that the right words will be available as needed. This is the same process that most experienced public speakers use.

Using an outline presentation successfully depends upon the development of numerous *units of conviction* that are thoroughly internalized. The outline is built by considering all the information available about the prospect. Most salespeople who use an outline method follow the same general outline for most presentations. They may, however, have several approaches or openings from which to choose, numerous features and benefits to present, and all sorts of evidence to present—all of which can be combined and recombined to meet the needs of the specific situation. Ideally, you make the choice in advance and know which pieces of material will be used. The use of the outline presentation generally calls for more judgment about people and broader product knowledge than the memorized presentation.

Extemporaneous Presentation

Some highly successful salespeople, particularly those who have many years of experience, may be heard to say that they "don't prepare" for a sales presentation. Actually, their preparation time is distributed in a different way than that of the less experienced salesperson, but they do prepare.

The extemporaneous presentation follows the same principles that any other presentation would incorporate, but experienced salespeople who use the extemporaneous approach are master people watchers. They understand people; they ask questions and listen. They are experts in discovering problems and identifying dominant buying motives. They know their product so thoroughly that they can seize almost magically upon the one feature or benefit that will best appeal to the prospect. They possess such charisma that the air of trust and credibility they create makes objections nonexistent and painlessly places the client's name on the order form. People love to buy from them.

As a result, these master salespeople spend most of their "preparation time" in gathering additional information about the prospect rather than spending time in *consciously* matching features and benefits to prospect qualification information. This step is almost automatic and subconscious as a result of their long experience.

PRODUCT-ANALYSIS WORKSHEET

Prospects have neither the product knowledge you have nor an understanding of the type of service you are prepared to render. You must not only know all the facts about your product but also be able to relate your knowledge directly to the specific needs of the prospect. If you can quote prices, catalog numbers, shipping dates, delivery schedules, and credit terms but have no solid, convincing evidence of the product's value to offer upon which the prospect can base a buying decision, you are afflicted with what has been called the *salesman's curse*: "You know your product better than you know how your client's business can use it."

Before you can expect a signed order form, you must figure out how to improve your customer's business and then find a way to persuade the prospect that the solution you offer is the best possible. You can do this by preparing *units of conviction.*

Units of Conviction

Units of conviction are concise, carefully prepared "mini-presentations" used as building blocks to construct the information you present. When the individual units of conviction are combined, they form what is referred to as a *product-analysis worksheet.*

Preparing a written product-analysis worksheet helps you evaluate the various characteristics of your product so that you are better able to present it to your prospects. When you prepare units of conviction and add them to your store of available options, they become a permanent part of your selling arsenal. A single unit of conviction consists of five elements:

1. A feature of your product or service
2. A transitional phrase
3. The benefits the feature provides
4. Evidence to support your claims
5. A tie-down question to gain the prospect's agreement

Features and Benefits. *Features* are the tangible and intangible qualities of the product or service you sell. Features are facts that are the same no matter who uses the product or service. The tangible features of a product include observable factors such as color, size, capacity, speed of performance, material from which it is made — anything that can be detected through one of the five senses. Intangible features are also important: the service given by the company, price, delivery, availability of service, and even the service and support that you promise.

Benefits, however, are the value or worth that the user derives from the product or service. Of the numerous benefits a product or service has to offer, only four or five will be key motivators to a prospect, and these will be different for each prospect. Your task is to find out which ones are the key motivators.

Every feature of your product has numerous benefits. Remember, *one feature does not equal one benefit.* Examine the insert that follows and challenge your mind to perform some mental gymnastics to prove this point.

Features and Benefits

Every feature of your product has numerous benefits. Here's an exercise to give your mind a healthy benefit workout: What are the benefits of a 270-horsepower engine in a luxury car? They could include a smoother ride, power to spare when passing a slower car, quick acceleration away from a hazard, the feeling of being in charge, less wear and tear, higher resale value, etc.

The point is, one feature does not equal one benefit. List your product's top ten features, then come up with at least five different benefits for each feature. Remember, features only justify the price; benefits justify the purchase. This gives you 50 new ways to close more sales.

Transitional Phrase. The ability to translate features into benefits is one of the strengths of a relationship salesperson. Even if you know which feature can fulfill the buying motive, you cannot expect the prospect to make the connection automatically. You must make the verbal transition. The prospect does not know your product as well as you know it and has to have features and benefits connected by transitional phrases. Some salespeople call these bridges. While the actual words may vary, they are all designed to accomplish the same purpose: to connect, in the prospect's thinking, features and benefits. These phrases all serve the purpose of answering the prospect's question, "What's in it for me?" Some common transitional phrases are:

"This is beneficial to you because . . ."

"This lets you . . ."

"This heads off all the problems of . . ."

"What this means to you . . ."

Evidence to Support Claims. Just as you present benefits to head off the prospect's question "So what?" about the features of your product or service, you must present evidence to support the claims you make to head off the questions "Can you prove it?" and "Who says so?" Even if you have been unusually successful in establishing a high degree of credibility and trust with the prospect, you are unlikely to be looked upon as an all-knowing sage with all the answers whose statements are to be accepted without question. You must be prepared to back up what you say with: (1) demonstrations, (2) testimonials, (3) facts and statistics, (4) samples, and (5) examples or case histories.

1. **Demonstrations**. Show the product being used. The demonstration is especially effective for some types of prospects if they have hands-on use in the demonstration. Audio and stereo salespeople encourage prospects to listen to their speakers to hear the high definition sound. Furniture salespeople suggest that prospects sit on the furniture and experience its comfort. Some office machines are left with the prospect for several days' trial.

2. **Testimonials**. The best possible testimonial is for one of your satisfied customers to call the prospect ahead of time and suggest that you be given an appointment. At this time, your customer expresses satisfaction with the product or service; this predisposes the prospect to accept what you say.

Other types of testimonials are also effective with the right type of prospect. Use customers' letters expressing their pleasure with your product and the service you have provided. Such letters are easy to get. Just ask for them! You may even write the testimonial yourself and ask the prospect to read and sign it to save the client's time and make sure the letter is worded to fit your needs. When a client thanks you for some help, just say you would appreciate a letter saying the same thing.

This kind of testimonial is especially helpful when it comes from a person who has influence in the community or with the particular prospect or when it is written on the letterhead of a respected company. You may have pictures of your clients using your product, with their signatures on the back. All of these are excellent testimonials.

3. **Facts and Statistics**. Call attention to manufacturer's ratings, such as the energy ratings of air-conditioning and heating units and the estimated mpg ratings of

automobiles. Show earnings of stocks or other investment vehicles over the past five years. The U.S. Census Bureau projects that the 65-and-older group will grow 75 percent by the year 2050. Hispanics over 65 will increase by 150 percent, faster than any other ethnic group in that age bracket. This type of niche marketing information is useful to a wide variety of companies in various industries.

4. **Samples**. A sample of the product itself or of the material from which it is made gives the prospect something concrete to use as the basis of decision-making. Supermarkets offer customers a taste of a featured food: cheese, sausage, pizza — anything that can be served from a small table, cooked in an electric frying pan, or stuck on the end of a toothpick. The demonstrator then indicates the display of the food item and asks the customer to try it. A salesperson for operating room scrubs for hospitals might give the purchasing agent a swatch of the material from which they are made to feel as the quality is described. Samples are intended to provide an appeal to one or more of the five senses.

5. **Examples or Case Histories**. The use of examples or case histories is another way to present the satisfaction of other clients and customers. You may tell the prospect about other people whose circumstances are similar and how you were able to solve their problems or how they are enjoying some benefit from using the product. Use these guidelines when planning this type of evidence:

- The case history must be *authentic*. It should be about someone the prospect knows or can contact for verification.

- Use *many details* to let the prospect know you are intimately familiar with the situation.

- *Back up* the example with pictures, personal letters, newspaper articles, and other evidence.

- *Relate it directly* to the prospect's circumstances.

The Tie-Down. The "tie-down" is an essential step in building units of conviction, although it usually consists of no more than a single question that asks for the prospect's agreement. Your goal is to translate features into benefits for the prospect, to provide the necessary evidence to prove your points, and to gain a commitment to act. Here are some examples of tie-down questions:

- *Considering these facts, you agree with me that this is a safe tire, don't you, Ms. Craft?*

- *I believe you will agree with me, Mr. Sanders, that this is a better way for handling this process than your present method, won't you?*

- *I think you can get an idea of the enormous advantage you will have with one-tenth of a minute billing, can't you, Ms. Grimmett?*

The tie-down is important throughout the presentation to check on understanding and agreement and to make sure the prospect is ready to proceed to the next point. One of the functions of the tie-down is to ask a series of questions, all of which the prospect can be expected to answer yes. Then when you attempt a close, the prospect more easily says yes again. Suppose, however, that you ask, "You agree with me about this, don't you?" and the prospect says, "No, I don't." Where are you now?

You are in a better position than you were before you asked the question because you now know you have a problem. Had you not asked this question and found out about the lack of agreement, you would have pushed on to the close and to failure. Now you are warned about the existence of a problem and can go back to find its source and correct it, ask another tie-down question, and move forward again when agreement is reached.

EFFECTIVE PRESENTATION TACTICS

You have the option of approaching the task of telling your story to the prospect using a variety of sales tactics. Which tactics you choose depend upon what you have learned about the prospect during preapproach qualification, what you observe in the opening minutes of the interview, what you personally want to do, and what kind of environment you find in the interview location. The only limit to the number of different presentation tactics is your own creative imagination.

The most common tactics are presented here; you will use all of them at one point or another as they fit into your sales activity. You will probably find yourself developing your own personal mixture of tactics — a blend that fits your personality, your product, and the needs of your prospects.

Participation

Every presentation — no matter how it is organized or what other method is used — must get the prospect involved in the selling process. When prospects are shut out of the presentation process or choose to remain aloof, say nothing, and contribute nothing, they also buy nothing. The prime tactic for gaining the participation of the prospect is asking questions and then listening to the answers.

Plan the questions to be asked during the presentation to gain maximum participation by the prospect.

Beyond asking questions yourself, you should encourage prospects to ask questions about any benefit of the product you present or any factor involved in its application or use. Their questions prevent misunderstanding and give you the opportunity to direct your presentation to the problem or need that is most important to them.

Demonstration

Showmanship sells if it is more than mere carnival hoopla. There is a big difference between showmanship and *show-off-manship*. A well-timed dramatic touch seizes and holds the prospect's attention. A demonstration is an effective method of adding showmanship to the presentation while achieving the purpose of the presentation. A good demonstration provides you with these benefits:

1. Catches the buyer's interest

2. Strengthens your selling points

3. Helps the prospect understand the proposition

4. Stimulates your own interest

5. Cuts down on the number of objections

6. Helps you close the sale

The value of a demonstration is that it involves more than one of the physical senses in the selling process. Remember these three points when determining how you will deliver your message to the prospect:

1. If you rely solely on "telling" the prospect about your product, only the auditory sense is involved. If you add a demonstration, you include the visual sense.

2. If you involve the prospect in the demonstration, you add the sense of touch. The more of the senses you can involve, the more quickly the prospect absorbs the information that leads to a sale.

3. People remember 20 percent of what they hear and 20 percent of what they see. But they remember *50 percent* of what they see and hear. By mapping your information out visually, you unquestionably increase how much your clients retain.

Here are three principles to follow in using a demonstration as a part of your sales presentation:

1. **Concentrate the Prospect's Attention on You**. The CEO of a large corporation once called a meeting of his associates in his office. When they came in, he was juggling several tennis balls. Finally, he tossed aside all but one and said, "We all have many things on our minds — like these tennis balls. But we must put them aside and concentrate on one problem at a time or we'll waste time trying to juggle them all." This demonstration illustrates the situation when you go to call on a prospect. You must focus the prospect's attention on one thing — what you are saying. A planned demonstration is an excellent tool for accomplishing this purpose.

2. **Get Your Prospect Into the Act**. Invite the prospect to operate your device, taste your food, smell the fragrance, feel the depth of the tread on the tires, or listen to the quiet sound of your machine in operation. If you are selling an intangible, hand the prospect photos, charts, or a prospectus. Get as many senses as possible involved.

The Gulf Coast Regional Blood Center in Houston asks a prospect to put a thirty-letter word puzzle together. The sales representative hands the prospect a small box full of letters that, when properly arranged, spell: **WILL YOU HAVE BLOOD WHEN YOU NEED IT?** This demonstration dramatically illustrates how crucial a company-sponsored blood drive is to the community and to individuals.

3. **Paint a Mind Picture Using Metaphors**. Metaphors imply comparisons between otherwise dissimilar things without using the words "like" or "as", often creating a dramatic visual image. Remember, "facts tell, stories sell." Painting a mind picture is a hook that grabs prospects and reels them in.

Steve Becker, west regional manager for Amersham Life Science, has used this creative metaphor with prospects: *Picture yourself in a desert without a canteen. In the distance you see a water well. There's a bucket with a rope nearby. Now, would you jump into the well headfirst or would you use the bucket and rope? What my firm can do for you is supply you with the bucket and rope — the tools you need to succeed.*

Metaphors, analogies and similes can bring special life to sales presentations. These are effective ways to reinforce concepts, while building rapport and winning people over to your way of thinking.

PRESENTATION SALES TOOLS

Sales aids fall mainly into the categories of audio, visual, or audiovisual. Many people are visually oriented. That's why exciting, illustrative slides, overheads, and computer-driven programs are effective presentation tools. Sales aids are used primarily to help the prospect visualize or otherwise experience the benefits of the product or service or to help you organize the presentation so that your prospect receives an ordered, logical message that is easily remembered.

The Organizer or Flip Chart

Companies may provide their salespeople with standard visual sales kits in the form of a small flip chart suitable for standing on a desk or in the form of a ring binder. When such an organizer is provided, a planned sales presentation usually accompanies the visual and is coordinated with it. The presentation and visual, used together, help you cover features and benefits and overcome objections. The organizer not only provides additional input for the prospect but also prompts your memory about what to cover next and keeps the interview on track.

A well-designed organizer has these characteristics:

1. It is built around user benefits.

2. It fosters two-way communication because you can concentrate on listening attentively to the prospect rather than worry about what to say next.

3. It increases the closing rate by leading naturally to that point.

4. It helps you tell the complete story in less time.

5. It helps the interview get back on track after an interruption by reminding both you and prospect what was being discussed.

Although the company-prepared organizer is a good beginning tool, most successful salespeople develop additional visuals that are useful for their personal style and type of selling. Here are some of the visuals you can prepare for yourself:

1. Letters from existing customers expressing satisfaction with the product, the company's responsiveness, and your personal service.

2. Business cards of existing clients, preferably with a note thanking you for service.

3. Pictures of clients actually using the product.

4. Pictures of product installations in customers' plants or offices.

Exhibit 11.3 gives guidelines for preparing visuals.

Exhibit 11.3

Guidelines for Preparing Visuals

- Visuals should be kept simple.

- Don't use complete sentences. Text should be in phrases.

- Leave plenty of white space and place text in similar location on each slide or overhead.

- Use colors that are functional, not decorative. Colors should be easy on the eyes; hence, use red sparingly.

- Never put the whole presentation on a visual and then read it to the prospect.

- Tables, charts, or graphs with complex data must only be used for groups that intend to study the information closely.

- Each chart or graph should present only one idea to ensure clear understanding.

- Line charts are used to show how several variables change over time.

- Bar charts show relationships between two or more variables.

- Pie charts are used to show relationships among parts of a whole at a given point in time.

Touch, Turn, and Talk. These are the most basic presentation actions. The touch, turn, and talk method of presention is commonly used and highly effective in keeping your clients engaged in what you are saying rather than getting distracted by your visual aids. When you are speaking to prospects, follow this easy three-step formula:

1. **Touch.** Point and look at your visual presentation to draw their attention to your illustration or exhibit.

2. **Turn.** While still pointing at the visual, turn to your clients to reestablish eye contact.

3. **Talk.** Once you have their attention, stop pointing so they will focus on you, then talk about the visual.

Liven Up Your PowerPoint Presentation. Salespeople should try to put some sparkle in their presentations, but avoid turning them into a three-ring circus. Use some bells and whistles without going overboard. A little color and some type-font changes can spruce up a presentation. There are a lot of electronic devices and special effects available today to create what is anything but a boring slide show. For example, liven up your PowerPoint presentations with tools to grab your client's attention such as spinning titles, TV-style transitions, and animated photographs. Try to make the presentation interactive, fun, and as concise as possible without eliminating main points. Exhibit 11.4 discusses another new and innovative idea for your presentations.

Exhibit 11.4

Voice on the Internet

A new technology called Brainshark uses the power of voice mail with the convenience of a PowerPoint presentation. It works this way: You upload your PowerPoint slides onto the Web site. Then you call a special telephone number and record your message to be delivered in synch with each slide. You use your telephone keypad as the record, play, rewind, and erase buttons. Once the slides are narrated, you can forward the presentation to a prospect or targeted audience. Tony Swierkot, marketing manager for Ricoh Company Ltd. in Canada, used it to send a presentation to Ricoh's sales force. The sales reps were delighted because the technology allowed them to actually hear the presentation from one of their own sales managers.

ADJUST THE PRESENTATION TO UNIQUE CIRCUMSTANCES

Situational Selling

Master salespeople have a specific plan for every sales interview, but they never feel slavishly bound by that plan. Relationship selling requires flexibility. No matter how much you learn about a prospect before you appear for the interview, you can never be absolutely sure what kind of situation to expect when you arrive. Instead of finding a calm, receptive prospect ready to listen and evaluate your product, you may find one who is angry, resentful, or emotional. If planning has been adequate, you can shift gears and make a different kind of presentation, switch to another purpose for the interview, or even delay the presentation until a better time.

Bill Hamilton finds his handheld computer ideal when making sales calls. This way he doesn't walk into a buyer's office "lugging equipment" during the initial call. Instead, he can reach into his pocket and be prepared to take an order, calculate it, offer "what ifs," and make any changes right on the spot. The ability to exercise this type of flexibility is called situational selling — fitting yourself to the situation and making each contact with the prospect beneficial to your ultimate purpose of closing a sale.

The Setting. Where the sales interview takes place is often a vital factor in determining its success. The prospect's own office is usually the best place if interruptions can be controlled. If the prospect has a private office, the door can be closed and calls can be held. The prospect feels at ease and in control in familiar surroundings and is not required to put forth effort or travel time to accommodate you. You are a guest and automatically a person to be treated politely and with respect.

If your information tells you that this prospect customarily tries to control every interview and every person, however, you might decide that meeting at a place where you are the host or even on neutral turf would give you more potency. Some salespeople make effective use of what is called a *power lunch*. Inviting the prospect to lunch at a carefully selected restaurant gives you an opportunity to present your product or service with several distinct advantages:

- You are away from an office where interruptions may occur.
- You are the host, and the prospect, as your guest, feels obligated to listen politely.
- The atmosphere is nonthreatening.
- Relaxing over the meal relieves some of the stress of making a decision.

Making the Presentation

- You can memorize a presentation or use an outline that allows you to present each of your selling points in an orderly and systematic way.

- Personalize each presentation to the needs of the prospect. One of the most important tactics available is prospect participation.

- One way to choose what you will present is to develop units of conviction. Each unit of conviction includes:
   A feature of your product or service
   A transitional phrase
   The benefits the feature provides
   Evidence to support your claims
   A tie-down to gain agreement

- Sales aids include all sorts of visuals and audiovisuals. Many people are visually oriented, which is why exciting, illustrative slides, overheads, and graphics are effective presentation tools.

- Interruptions represent anything that distracts the prospect's attention from your message. The setting of the sales interview requires that you be prepared to take advantage of any situation. You must learn to control these distractions and transform them into buying opportunities.

The key to maintaining a positive sales environment is to disagree without being disagreeable.

Chapter 12

Handling Objections

- **The truth about objections**
- **Types of objections**
- **A six-step plan for identifying objections**
- **When to answer objections**
- **Five specific techniques for overcoming objections**
- **Specific tactics for handling price concerns**

THE TRUTH ABOUT OBJECTIONS

Objections Are Buying Signals

The problem with the word objection is that it conjures up an adversarial relationship between the salesperson and the prospect — someone must win and someone must lose. In reality, the relationship sales cycle is a mutually beneficial process that produces a jointly satisfying long-term connection.

The most successful salespeople look positively at the objections prospects offer. Objections move prospects nearer to the close and reveal what they are concerned about. An objection often reveals the key to closing the sale.

An objection is anything the prospect says or does that presents an obstacle to the smooth completion of the sale. Objections are a normal and natural part of almost every conversation — not just in sale situations, but whenever people discuss any current topic. A purchasing decision usually involves some risk. To ease the fear of risk, people object, raise concerns, or ask questions in hopes of getting answers that will convince them that the buying decision is in their best interest.

If the prospect has been properly qualified, objections are really buying signals. Offering an objection is another way for the prospect to say, "Here are my conditions for buying," or "I want to buy as soon as you answer a few more questions or reassure me that buying is the smart thing to do." Welcome all objections! They are the verbal and nonverbal signs of sales resistance that give you the chance to discover what the prospect is thinking. These objections become *leverage* for closing the sale.

Objections actually indicate that the prospect is interested in what you are saying. Successful sales presentations, those that end in a sale, have twice as many objections as those presentations that are unsuccessful. Qualified prospects will not raise objections to a proposal in which they have no interest. They simply wait and say no!

Why Prospects Have Sales Resistance

Sales resistance contains elements of both logic and emotion. When people really want something, logic goes out the window and emotion takes control. The heart tends to rule the head. The first task in answering an objection is to calm the prospect's emotions by proving that you are open to reason. Pause before responding; then acknowledge that you respect the prospect's opinion and find the views expressed worthy of consideration. Show a measure of empathy. People are open to changing their opinions and attitudes when they are convinced that others value their opinions, understand how they can feel that way, and grant them the right to those opinions. Thus, *the key to maintaining a positive sales environment is to disagree without being disagreeable.*

Arguing with a prospect, particularly in response to objections, is one of the easiest and most disastrous mistakes you can make. Your purpose is to remove the objection without being objectionable. Remember that relationship selling is a win–win proposition. The negotiation process is not a battle that you win and the prospect loses; rather, it is a situation of mutual cooperation and mutual benefit. You may well win the argument and prove that you are right, but lose the sale in the process. *People who are forced to agree seldom actually change their minds.* Never force a prospect into making a decision. Prospects are more likely to stay sold and come back to you for repeat business if the decision to buy was their idea.

TYPES OF OBJECTIONS

The difficulty with objections is that they all sound like obstacles that will stop the sale. When the prospect objects, you must understand what type of sales resistance is being offered before you can handle it effectively. Sales resistance may be separated into four general types: the *stopper*, the *searcher*, the *stall* or *put-off*, and the *hidden objection*.

The Stopper

Prospects often have legitimate reasons why they feel unable to buy. One type of valid objection is called a *stopper*. Even Harry Houdini could not solve this one. The stopper is an objection to which no satisfactory solution can be found. For instance, if you can promise delivery no sooner than six months from now and the prospect absolutely must have the product in three months, you cannot — or at least, you should not — make that sale.

The Searcher

A second type of objection is called a *searcher*, a request for additional information. Some prospects object simply to get more information, even though they have already mentally decided that they want to buy. The customer just wants to be convinced that buying your product or service is the right thing to do.

Handle Valid Searcher Concerns with Finesse

How Negotiators Might Respond to Four Common Searcher Objections

I'm not interested.

- There is no reason why you should be interested until I show you how my service can help you make money and solve your problems. May I show you how the product can do that for you?

- Do you mean you are not interested at this time, or at all? I'll call back in four weeks; hopefully, things will be less hectic for you.

I don't have any money for this.

- I can certainly respect that. If I could show you two ways the product will pay for itself, would you be interested?

- If you did have the money, would you want it? Good! Allow me to present some facts and statistics illustrating just how affordable our product really is.

We are satisfied with what we have now.

- What do you like most about the product you are using now? [Then demonstrate how your product is better.]

- You don't like to change without a good reason, right? I certainly can understand that. Here are five reasons why more and more managers are switching to our online sales training material.

I really like the competitor's product.

- I am not surprised to hear you say that. Their product does have some interesting features. I know some of my happiest customers are people who used to own that other company's product.

The Stall or Put-Off

When the prospect offers a *stall* or *put-off* objection, look for the true meaning. Frequently, the prospect is simply avoiding a decision. You should never experience a stall if you have properly qualified a prospect at the beginning. The stall could mean that you have not presented a compelling enough reason to buy. A stall is a classic sales killer unless you can create a sense of urgency to buy **NOW**. The stall is actually the prospect's way of saying, "I really don't want to think about your proposition right now because I would then be forced to make a decision." Here are some examples of how stalls are phrased:

1. "I have to leave in 15 minutes; I have an important meeting."

2. "Just leave your literature with my secretary. I will look it over in the next day or so and then call you."

3. "I must talk this over with my partner."

Handling a stall is a test of your *attitude*. If you believe you have a qualified prospect whose needs will be satisfied by your product, then you will not allow a *"put-off"* to put you off. Here are some suggestions for responding to stalls:

1. "We are both busy people. Can I have five minutes to show you something that would save you hundreds, perhaps thousands, of dollars?"

2. "Mr. Ray, I thought that I had adequately covered the points summarized in the literature. Obviously, I have not made myself clear at some point. Would you tell me what I have not explained to your satisfaction?"

3. "I certainly understand wanting to involve your partner in a decision of this magnitude. Can we ask him to join us now, or may I drop by his office this afternoon?"

The Hidden Objection

A fourth type of sales resistance is the *hidden objection*. This kind of resistance is more difficult to overcome. John Utter, regional sales manager for Motion Technology, defines *hidden problems* as "unspoken hesitations which, if not addressed, can delay or prevent a sale." The prospect refuses to let you know the real concern. Many times the reason is quite personal, and the prospect prefers not to reveal it or has a vague feeling that cannot be easily articulated. You know the prospect has a hidden objection when the answers fail to make sense. The

THE HANDBOOK FOR RELATIONSHIP SELLING

reasons for not buying are not logical based on the interview up to that point. For example, a prospect may dislike revealing these six concerns:

1. "Circumstances have changed since you first qualified me. Recent family problems have caused severe financial hardships, and I do not have the ability to pay for your product."

2. "I find this whole situation distasteful, and I don't want to deal with you. I don't like you, but social convention prevents my being blunt enough to tell you so."

3. "I really don't know what my objection is. It just doesn't feel right. Quite frankly, the product looks like a cheap imitation to me."

4. "I really wasn't in the market for your product. I just wanted to hear what you had to say for future reference."

5. "It sounds good on paper, but how do I know the system will really work for my company?"

6. "I've been burned in the past by lack of technical support with similar products. How do I know your company won't do the same?"

GETTING TO THE HEART OF SALES RESISTANCE

The relationship salesperson must get to the heart of the prospect's objection before it can be negotiated successfully. Before you can marshal the appropriate facts, logic, and evidence to resolve a vaguely stated objection, you must know the basis for the prospect's point of view. To make intelligent responses to customer resistance, you must know the underlying circumstances.

Most objections that an experienced salesperson hears are not original. If you have been selling for any length of time, your chance of encountering an objection you have not heard before is remote. Eighty percent of buyers will give you the same five or six objections. You should therefore be ready to handle each one in advance, and have practiced them in a training course or sales meeting first.

Adopt the attitude described by Ann Barber, a top sales representative for Sportswear International in San Jose, California. When Ann hears an objection, she says to herself, "Hot dog, another sale!" Ann knows she has the knowledge and experience to answer every legitimate objection. Prior preparation and a servant's heart allow relationship-oriented sales pros like Ann Barber to adapt such positive attitudes toward objections.

To deal effectively with the objections you hear, develop a worksheet to categorize them and the responses you use to answer them effectively. Write out your responses word for word, commit them to memory, and practice delivering each one so that it becomes a reflex action. Polish and refine your responses; keep a record of how they are received. You will soon be able to choose the best possible response from your prepared list for each situation you encounter. Exhibit 12.1 lists six basic categories of buyer resistance with examples of what the prospect might say or, in the case of hidden objections, might think.

Exhibit 12.1

The Basic Categories of Buyer Objections or Sales Resistance

Product Objection
- The materials are not up to industry standards.
- The product is poor quality.
- The product won't hold up over time.

Objection to Salesperson (Hidden)
- You are poorly prepared.
- I don't like you.
- You have tried to dominate me from the moment you arrived.

Company Objections
- Your company is not very well known; I prefer to deal with a large, established company.
- Wasn't your company charged with some unethical sales practices?

Don't Want to Make a Decision
- See me on your next trip.
- I want to think it over.
- We don't have room for your line.

Service Objection
- I can't live with your delivery schedule.
- We need same-day response on all service calls.
- Your maintenance contract doesn't meet our needs.

Price Objection (Possibly Hiding Real Objection)
- I can't afford it.
- Your pricing structure is out of line.
- I'm going to wait until prices come back down.

A SIX-STEP PLAN FOR IDENTIFYING OBJECTIONS

Professional salespeople handle prospects' objections successfully by first identifying them, and then placing them in the proper perspective. They realize that well-handled objections become powerful aids. To handle them skillfully, you need a definite negotiation strategy so that you react naturally to buyers' concerns. Knowing that you have a strategy gives you confidence. Then you can welcome objections instead of shuddering at the very thought that the prospect may not go along with your proposition. The six-step plan presented in Exhibit 12.2 should be internalized so that you use it instinctively and automatically.

Exhibit 12.2

A Strategic Negotiating Plan for Overcoming Buyers' Concerns

1. Listen carefully and hear the prospect out.

Learning to listen is not difficult, just unusual. We were born with two ears and one tongue. Listen twice as much as you talk. The buyer will tell you what you need to know. Just listen!

2. Confirm your understanding of the objection.

The key is to clarify and classify the objection. What type of objection is it and into what category does it fall?

3. Acknowledge the prospect's point of view.

Prepare the prospect for your answer. Don't just tear into your answer. After all, the buyer has a reason for stating the objection. Show concern for his or her feelings. Practice empathy.

4. Select a specific technique.

No one technique works best for all prospects. It must fit your behavioral style as well as that of the prospect.

5. Answer the objection.

The answer must satisfy the buyer if a sale is to result, and it must be complete and prompt. Get a commitment from the prospect.

6. Attempt to close; if the close is not completed, continue the presentation.

After answering a major objection, ask for the order. The worst that can happen is that the buyer will say no. If that happens, continue with the presentation.

Listen Carefully and Hear the Prospect Out

The relationship salesperson is happy when the prospect raises an objection, because it provides the information needed to complete the negotiation. Never interrupt a prospect who is expressing an opinion. Listen carefully to what the prospect says. Observe the prospect's verbal and nonverbal behavior, and listen to what is not being said. Recognize the prospect's right to express opinions and concerns. The prospect is telling you what to do: "Give me more information," "Go over that service agreement again; it wasn't clear," or simply "Reassure me one more time that this is a good decision."

Confirm Your Understanding of the Objection

Restate the prospect's objection to make sure you understand just what it is. This is a critical negotiation tactic. Use your own words and repeat what the prospect was saying to clarify and classify the real objection, and to indicate to the prospect that you understood what was said. In addition, you give yourself time to formulate an answer. Restating the objection in a sympathetic manner dissolves the prospect's defensiveness and helps you avoid the temptation to argue. Say, "Now as I understand it, your position is . . . ," and then explain the prospect's position in your own words. When you prove you understand, the prospect will be ready to listen to you.

Your purpose here is to evaluate and isolate the stated concern. Determine whether the reason given for not buying is the real reason, simply an excuse, or a statement hiding the actual objection. You may decide to answer immediately, not answer, or seek more information. If you need more information before you can answer, ask questions until you have the information you need. There are a number of questions you might ask the prospect that can help you isolate the real issue and confirm your understanding:

1. Other than that, is there any other reason that would prevent you from purchasing?

2. I am glad you brought that out into the open. Is this your only concern?

3. If we can work together to find a solution to this important concern, would that help you make a purchase decision?

It may help to ask the prospect to explain the objection. At times, the prospect may not know fully what they are objecting to, and explaining it will help clarify the issue for both you and the prospect. This keeps you from having to search for an objection before it can be dealt with.

Acknowledge the Prospect's Point of View

All successful negotiators find points of agreement with the prospect before beginning to answer an objection. Agree as far as possible before answering, and take responsibility for any misunderstanding. If the prospect indicates a bad experience with your company or your predecessor, believe it. Find a way to cushion your response so that it has a chance of convincing the prospect. After all, prospects believe they have good reasons for not buying, and they give you those reasons. Instead of arguing directly, soften your answer and say something like this:

1. *I can certainly understand how you feel, Mr. Maloney. Others have had much the same feeling when I first presented the concept to them. (Then provide a plausible explanation.)*

2. *I appreciate your concern, Ms. Torres, and you do have a relevant point. Thank you for bringing it to my attention. (And you really should appreciate it.)*

Select a Specific Technique

The last two sections of this chapter detail eight specific techniques for use in formulating answers to the types of sales resistance you may encounter. Not all of them work all the time. In deciding which of the techniques to use, take these factors into consideration:

- The prospect's behavioral style.

- The stage of the negotiation process in which the objection is raised.

- The mood (argumentative or receptive) of the prospect.

- How many times the objection has come up.

- The type of objection (searcher, excuse, stall, product or service).

You must decide quickly on the technique you will use and avoid showing that an objection has upset you. Keep in mind that far too many variables operate in a given selling situation to guarantee that every objection can be answered satisfactorily.

Answer the Objection

Negotiation is persuasion, not manipulation. Avoid explanations that merely cloud the issue and cause prospects to feel that you are trying to pressure them. The answer, however, must be conclusive; don't close off your answer with the question still up in the air. Present only as much information as required to gain the prospect's cooperation and commitment. Minimize the objection by not dwelling on it. Say just enough to dispose of it to the prospect's satisfaction. Be honest and factual, and do not promise anything that you, your company, or your product or service cannot deliver.

Prospects have their own needs, viewpoints, and ways of looking at things. Be sure to consider the prospect's ego and help the prospect to win. Your answer should include a benefit and should be shaped to fit the behavioral style of that prospect. Finally, confirm that your answer satisfied the prospect. Gain agreement by suggesting, "Am I correct in assuming that I have completely satisfied you regarding . . . ?"

Attempt to Close

Closing opportunities exist at various times throughout the entire negotiation process. Recognizing those times and capitalizing on them is up to you. When you have successfully answered a major objection, you have created an opportunity to close, especially if you are near the end of the presentation. Attempt a trial close before continuing with the presentation. The trial close gets a prospect's reaction without exerting any pressure to make a definite decision. It may be used at any point in the sales presentation to test the water, to see whether you have presented enough information for the prospect to make a decision. Typical trial closes start with "If you were to buy . . ." "In your opinion . . ." or "How do you feel about . . .".

If you receive positive buying signals from the prospect at this point, you can attempt to close. If the close proves unsuccessful, get back on track and continue the presentation until another opportunity presents itself.

WHEN TO ANSWER OBJECTIONS

A lot more has been said about how to overcome objections than about when to answer them, but choosing the proper time to answer an objection is just as crucial as the answer itself. In determining when to answer, you must consider the type of objection, why it was raised, in what phase of the interview it was raised, and the prospect's mood. Timing is important in any negotiation. Prospects introduce an objection at a time that favors their position. Why shouldn't you choose to handle it when the timing favors your position? Normally, there are four logical times for responding to the buyer's concerns:

1.   Answer them before they arise.
2.   Postpone the answer until later in the presentation.
3.   Answer them immediately when they are raised.
4.   Do not answer an excuse.

Anticipate and Forestall Objections

Every product or service has both strengths and weaknesses. Because no product is perfect, a prospect may well identify a negative feature or shortcoming in what you sell. Hoping that the prospect will fail to notice a negative feature is futile. Instead of waiting for the prospect to raise a specific objection, anticipate the objection and forestall or answer it in the presentation before the prospect can ask. You are thus able to make a more orderly presentation of benefits and maintain better control of the entire interview.

Weave into your presentation factual answers to anticipated objections, so they are answered before the prospect verbalizes them. Anticipating objections requires a well-thought-out, planned presentation delivered from the prospect's point of view and focusing on value. As an example of how you might forestall objections that come up over and over again, consider the two objections Fred Bass, a venture capitalist in Phoenix, was constantly hearing from prospects: "I don't have the money" and "I have to talk this over with my (partner, wife, agent, etc.)." After the opening, get-acquainted chit-chat, Fred gets down to business by saying:

> *Mr. Goode, I am working with professional athletes who have enough discretionary income that they can invest at least $75,000 in a business venture they are convinced is sound and who can also make their own investment decisions without consulting someone else first. Do you fit into these conditions?*

This opener is admittedly forceful, but Fred prefers not to spend 45 minutes presenting his proposition and then hear one of these familiar objections. Of course, dealing with an objection early in the presentation does not guarantee that it will not be raised again. However, you are at an advantage in such a situation for two reasons:

- The objection has much less impact the second time.
- You may recall the original answer, expand upon it, and then move on into a close or back into the presentation if necessary.

Postpone the Answer

Answers to some objections are better postponed. This tactic is logical when you are planning to cover that very point further along and the prospect has simply jumped ahead. To answer early might disrupt the flow of the presentation and make the answer less effective. For example, the prospect may ask about price — "How much is this going to cost me?" — before you have established the value of your product. If you answer immediately, the price may seem too high because the prospect has not yet learned enough about the product to make a value judgment. The price may depend on options selected; in that case, you cannot quote an accurate price. You may need to build a better foundation before risking a confrontation with the prospect. You can postpone answering an objection by saying something like this:

> *That's an excellent question, and I can certainly understand why you want to ask it. Let me write it down so I won't forget to answer it. And if you don't mind, let's postpone the answer until later. I have some information we need to consider first. Is that all right?*

Salespeople often get price questions early in the interview. Here are two ways to postpone the premature price question:

1. *I can appreciate that you would be interested in the price, and I assure you we will discuss it completely, but before we even consider the price, I want to be sure that my service can satisfy your needs. Will that be all right?*

2. *Ms. Osmond, your concern for price is quite understandable. The actual amount paid for the product, however, will depend on the options you ultimately select. Let's consider the price for the system after we establish the specific features you will require. Is that fair enough?*

The price question should be answered near the end of the presentation, after need, value, and benefits have been discussed. Should the prospects absolutely insist that you answer immediately, then by all means do so. You do not want to risk having the outstanding question keep them from hearing everything else that follows.

Answer Immediately

Most valid objections should be answered when they are raised, unless you have a logical reason to postpone answering. If you feel the objection is valid and postponing an answer could cause problems, by all means handle it immediately. Answering an objection right away prevents it from festering in your prospect's mind and blocking out the more important information you are presenting. The rule of thumb is: Never answer until you are sure of the real concern, and once it is discovered, answer in 30 seconds or less. A sincere and immediate response conveys professionalism and respect for the prospect's point of view.

Do Not Answer an Excuse

A final alternative is simply not to answer an objection that is really an excuse. Some issues don't have a worthwhile answer. On some sales calls, prospects raise concerns that have nothing to do with your discussion. They say things that have no relevance to the point you are trying to make. In reality, they are offering excuses for not buying rather than valid resistance. Never try to answer an excuse. By acknowledging excuses, you may actually turn them into real objections in the prospect's mind. If you must reply to excuses, suggest to the prospect that you will answer them at the end of the presentation. If the question is a serious objection, the prospect will repeat it later. Exhibit 12.3 summarizes the factors to consider in choosing the best time to deal with objections.

Exhibit 12.3

Timing Answers to Objections: Points to Consider

Anticipate the Objection and Answer It Before It Arises

This option should be considered only when you are fairly certain that the prospect will bring up the objection.

Anticipating the objection prevents a future confrontation and shows your objectivity.

Postpone an Answer Until Later

Postponing an answer allows you to present many more benefits that have the effect of reducing the significance of the objection.

Postponing an answer allows you to maintain control of the interview by keeping to your agenda rather than to that of the prospect.

Postponing an answer gives you time to think about how you will answer the question. Better a good answer later than a poor one now.

Answer the Objection Immediately

Answer immediately so the prospect can concentrate on the rest of the sales story.

Answering immediately shows the prospect your sincerity.

An immediate answer prevents prospects from inferring that you are unable to answer.

Do Not Answer an Excuse

Not acknowledging an objection is one way to separate it from an excuse. The serious prospect will repeat the objection.

By not answering, you suggest that the excuse is not relevant and imply that bringing it up again is not necessary.

FIVE SPECIFIC TECHNIQUES FOR OVERCOMING OBJECTIONS

Keep in mind that with any technique, you must produce evidence to prove the validity of what you say. Techniques do not establish belief and credibility; that is your job. Techniques are merely vehicles for organizing your answer and your support for it.

After an objection has been clarified and classified, you are in an excellent position to respond by using one or more of the following techniques.

1. Feel, Felt, Found

This practical technique overcomes a stall or a very personal concern. It can counter prospect hostility, pacify an unhappy customer, or inform someone who does not yet clearly understand the value of the product or service. Answer the prospect with this language:

> I can understand how you *feel*. . . . I have had other customers who *felt* the same way until they *found* out. . . .

This approach serves several purposes. It shows prospects that you understand their concerns, and it reassures the prospect that having this kind of objection is normal. Now the stage is set to introduce information that can change the prospect's way of thinking. This technique says that other people who are now customers had similar misgivings but changed their minds after they found out some new information. These new facts allow the prospect to reevaluate your proposition.

2. Compensation or Counterbalance Method

At times, a prospect may buy in spite of certain valid objections. The prospect may be partly right or may have misunderstood a portion of what you said. Accept and admit any truth in the objection. Admit that your product does have the disadvantage that the prospect has noticed and then immediately point out how the objection is overshadowed by other specific benefits of the product. Your job is to convince the prospect that the compensating benefits provide enough value that the disadvantage should not prevent the prospect from buying. By admitting the objection, you impress the prospect with your sincerity and sense of fair dealing. Then you can select the real strengths of your offering to offset the prospect's negative feelings. A good way to deal with this situation is to provide documentation such as *statistical evidence*, a *third-party endorsement*, or the *case history* of someone who faced a similar situation. This method works because the prospect is approached positively with an acknowledgment of expressed

THE HANDBOOK FOR RELATIONSHIP SELLING

concerns, and then given a series of logical, compensating benefits to counterbalance the stated objection.

3. Ask "Why?" or Ask a Specific Question

This method is helpful not only for separating excuses from real objections but also for overcoming objections. You can use questions to narrow a major, generalized objection to specific points that are easier to handle. If the prospect says, "I don't like to do business with your company," ask, "What is it that you don't like about our firm?" The answer may show a past misunderstanding that can be cleared up. If the prospect complains, "I don't like the looks of your product," ask, "Why do you object to its appearance?" The objection may be based on a relatively minor aspect that can be changed or is not true of all models.

Another value of this method is that some objections sound flimsy once they are put into words. The prospect may conclude that the objection is of little consequence and write it off without your needing to do anything.

4. Deny the Objection

One way to answer buyer resistance is simply to assert that the prospect is wrong. This technique must be used with caution or it will antagonize prospects. You can sometimes tell prospects they are wrong, but you have to be careful how you do it. *You could win the argument but lose the sale.*

The denial technique is useful when the prospect clearly has the wrong information. Either a portion of the presentation was misunderstood or someone else has supplied incorrect information. Point out that the prospect's information is wrong, but not by means of a direct, frontal assault. Present the denial sympathetically, thoughtfully, and with dignity.

> *After listening attentively to the buyer's concern, begin by saying, "I don't believe I quite understand what you are saying." (This response allows the buyer time to cool down emotionally and perhaps to soften the statement. It also gives you the opportunity to regain your composure).*

After the prospect repeats the incorrect information, respond in this manner: "I don't know how you could have gotten that impression. I really must have stated my position poorly; please let me correct it for you." A bit more forceful statement would be, "Fortunately for me, that is not the real situation. I have some other information that does not support what you just told me."

Your attitude is critical. Your goal is to earn the prospect's respect and avoid an angry reaction. However, you do want the prospect to know that you will not be intimidated. Sometimes a direct denial is your only recourse. There are times when you must fight fire with fire. A direct denial is a high-risk method of dealing with any objection, but it is necessary at times, even if you lose the sale.

5. Boomerang Method

The boomerang method allows you to agree with prospects yet show them that their objections need not prevent a purchase. This method is often used in a situation when the point to which the prospect is objecting is actually a sales point in favor of buying the particular product or service. The boomerang method involves agreeing with the objection and then making another statement that *translates the objection into a reason for buying*. For example:

A sales representative for Blue Bell Inc., Brenham, Texas, might hear this type of objection: "Blue Bell ice cream is too new to this area. My customers will not buy something they have never heard of before." Turn the objection into a sales point: "There is no question that our ice cream is new to your area; that's why we are eager to build consumer awareness for the product. We intend to spend over $100,000 to tell your potential customers about our ice cream. Blue Bell uses its advertising messages to presell the product for you. If you agree to carry the product, we will generate a great deal of customer demand (and increase store traffic) for you."

The boomerang method works well when the prospect lacks complete information or perceives a drawback that may not actually exist. Be careful of the image you project when using this technique. If prospects feel that you are directly challenging them or perhaps patronizing them, you could be in for a real battle. In that case, you might as well pull out your boxing gloves, because you will have more use for them than you will for your order book.

SPECIFIC TACTICS FOR HANDLING PRICE CONCERNS

A Mindset for Negotiating Price Resistance

One type of objection surfaces so frequently that it requires additional examination. Your prospects and customers want as much for their money as they can get. While that's not unexpected, you can't provide value-added service at reasonable prices if you give up too much at the negotiating table. How many times each week do you suppose a salesperson hears, "I just think your price is too high." To succeed in selling, you must see this type of sales resistance for what it is and overcome it.

The price objection is more difficult to pin down because it can mean so many different things. The final price paid for a product or service depends on the discounts available, advertising and promotional allowances paid by the seller, service after the sale, free trial periods, warranties or money-back guarantees, sales support service and training, delivery charges, and a myriad of other price-related variables. Then, too, the prospect may not really be objecting to the price, but may just be hiding the real reason for not buying. When prospects says, "I can't afford it" or "Your prices are just too high," they may really mean, "You have not convinced me that the value I will receive is worth the price I have to pay to get it." Often the buyer's concerns or questions about price signal an incomplete sales job!

Your company priced the product or service so it would sell. Never be afraid to ask the full value for your offering, but be prepared with solid evidence to support the price you are asking. Do not be defensive or apologetic. You must believe that the price you are quoting is actually much less than the value your product will give the prospect. If your product has exclusive features that are not readily apparent, convert them to benefits and sell those benefits, as the classic example in Exhibit 12.4 illustrates.

Exhibit 12.4

Sell Benefits to Overcome the Question of Price

Two farm wagons stood in a public market. Both were loaded with potatoes in bags. A customer stopped before the first wagon.

"How much are potatoes today?" she asked the farmer's wife, who was selling them.

"A dollar and a quarter a bag," replied the farmer's wife.

"Oh, my," protested the woman, "that is pretty high, isn't it? I gave one dollar for the last bag I bought."

"Taters has gone up," was the only information the farmer's wife gave. The housewife went to the next wagon and asked the same question. But Ma McGuire "knew her potatoes," as the saying goes. Instead of treating her customer with indifference, she replied:

"These are specially fine white potatoes, madam. They are the best potatoes grown. In the first place, you see, we only raise the kind with small eyes so that there will be no waste in peeling. Then we sort them to grade out culls so you get only full-sized, good potatoes. Then we wash all our potatoes clean before sacking them, as you see. You can put one of these bags in your parlor without soiling your carpet — you don't pay for a lot of dirt. I'm getting $1.50 a bag for them — shall I have them put in your car or will you take them now?"

Ma McGuire sold two bags, at a higher price than her competitor asked, in spite of the fact that the customer had refused to buy because she thought the price was too high!

THREE SPECIFIC METHODS FOR OVERCOMING THE QUESTION OF PRICE

A product often has hidden qualities. The prospect cannot see these qualities and does not fully appreciate them until they are pointed out. You usually get what you pay for. A low price is probably low for a good reason. Competitors can undersell you only temporarily because they have the same basic labor, they are cutting costs somewhere with lower standards of product quality, service, or delivery. A bargain price can turn out to be quite expensive.

Face the fact that you will not always have the lowest-priced product or service to sell. Be prepared to justify your asking price and show that it is fair. Understand and be able to apply the differential competitive advantages you have in product, source, people, or service superiority. There are a number of negotiation tactics that can help you overcome the price obstacle. You may respond to the question of price by using one or a combination of the following methods.

1. Break the Price Down

The price that sounds huge in its entirety often sounds much smaller when you break it down into weekly or monthly payments and compare it to how the customer normally spends extra money. If the prospect is really objecting to the absolute magnitude of the price, then a logical response is to break the total cost down over a period of time. Here is an example of how you might use this technique:

> I am glad you mentioned price, and I can certainly appreciate your concern. The $3,000 does seem like an awful lot of money for an Acme car stereo system. But just imagine, for the price of a daily cup of coffee and a newspaper, you will enjoy your terrific new sound system during that hour-long commute you said you make to and from work every day. What a small price to pay for the increased enjoyment and relaxation that comes from owning such a magnificent system.

Compare the one-time price of your product to the amount of money the prospect will save after years of using it. The clearer you make the distinction between what your prospects pay and what they get, the easier it is for them to recognize your product's great value. Talk about the initial and ultimate costs. Look at the *price-cost-value* comparison from two perspectives: *price* represents the initial amount paid for the product; *cost* is the amount the buyer pays as the product is used over time.

2. Use the Presumption of Exclusivity

What can you do when the price for your company's product is higher than that being asked by a competitor? Stress those features that are exclusively yours. What does your product have that the competition cannot offer? No two products are exactly alike. You will find strengths and weaknesses in any offering. Analyze your competitor's offering to see why the same product has a lower price. If your analysis indicates that you are offering more, then your task is to drive home those exclusive features. You may have to show more interest in the prospect than the competitor that concentrates only on price. Go out of your way to isolate other needs of the prospect with which you can provide assistance.

If your company has a higher price, it must be because you offer more to your customers. Identify your superiority and advantages and convince the prospect that the extras can be obtained only from you. In other words, justify the price with facts. Determine what the prospect wants more than anything else from your product and then identify the features that satisfy those wants. This is what Mack Hannan calls the "presumption of exclusivity." Concentrate on those features until the prospect feels that only with you (your product and/or your company) can his or her needs be completely satisfied.

If a prospect gives you a hard time about price, stop selling price. Show what the money buys. Make the price seem unimportant in comparison to the value received. You might proceed something like this:

> *Ms. Harvey, allow me to share some information with you. The lower price of our competitor may not be the best buy for you. Let's look at the quality of our product and why we are more expensive. We pay our employees a fair wage, purchase superior-grade raw materials, and have a multimillion-dollar advertising program that has made our product nationally known. Our price includes training for your people; our staff is skilled at maintaining and upgrading the product over time. You will have easy availability of parts and a one hundred percent guarantee. We stand behind our product. We don't fight your complaints; we settle them promptly and equitably. The price paid for a solution to your problem should be based on what gives you the best solution. Don't you agree?*

Draw the picture clearly and convincingly. Sell quality and exclusivity when the prospect argues price. If you sell the exclusive features properly, the prospect is not even thinking about price by the end of the presentation. Most buyers are fair-minded if you show why your company must get the price it does.

3. Use Comparison

Be prepared to present logical reasons for the price you are asking. One way you can do this is to compare the quality of your product to that of the prospect's company. For example, you could stress that both are selling superior products:

> *Mr. Becker, your own company makes a high-grade product that commands an exceptionally high price, and deservedly so. Your tool-and-die products warrant their outstanding reputation because of the top-quality materials used to make them. Our high-viscosity, high-grade motor oil is naturally suited for your machines. Oh, you can buy less expensive brands than ours, but you would not be satisfied with their performance.*

Acknowledging the superior nature of your prospect's product and suggesting that the prospect's company and your company are two of a kind makes considerable sense. This approach elevates your product to the same level of pride the prospect's company has in its products.

If you choose to make comparisons, be sure you have facts to substantiate your claims. Case histories and testimonials are useful for this purpose. For example, Dick Randolph sells x-ray equipment to hospitals and clinics by focusing on company performance and referrals to build trust. "My customers are more concerned about what happens after they sign a purchase order than the actual price," says Randolph, account manager at NXC Imaging. He provides prospects with current customers' names and a referral list encouraging prospects to contact any or all of them. Randolph uses his company's reputation to build trust and justify the higher price. A demonstration could also work effectively to show a comparison. Let the prospect see personally how your product compares to other alternatives. Visual evidence and verifiable case histories produce powerful comparisons, regardless of what you are selling.

Always remember, when dealing with price objections, that your prospects know it is unwise to pay too much, but it is actually worse to pay too little. Your customer may pay too much and lose a little money, but when they pay too little, they could lose everything, because the item purchased was incapable of doing what it was bought to do.

The common law of business balance prohibits paying a little and getting a lot — it can't be done. So be patient with your prospects and focus on the benefits if they still seem fixated on price.

Handling Objections

- Success in handling objections depends on your attitude. If you assume that the sale is over when you hear an objection, it will be. If you regard an objection as an invitation to continue negotiating, you are likely to enjoy a successful close.

- Buyers offer objections for a number of reasons, most of which are psychological. Objecting to something enables them to avoid the risk of making a decision that has potentially unpleasant consequences.

- Some objections are valid and indicate either a logical reason for not buying or a need for you to present additional information before the prospect makes a buying decision.

- Classify and clarify the objections according to their type and apply the appropriate plan to overcome them.

- The six-step strategic negotiating plan for dealing with buyers' concerns gives you the opportunity to handle whatever objection you encounter.

- Experts in overcoming objections record the objections they hear, study them to determine which ones they hear most often, and develop logical answers to use whenever these objections come up.

- You will not always have the lowest-priced product to sell. Apply the competitive advantages you have in product, source, people, or service superiority and respond to the question of price by using price breakdown, the presumption of exclusivity, or comparison.

Success in the End is What Counts —
Not Failure in the Beginning

His failures far exceeded his successes:

- 1832 lost his job
- 1832 defeated in the race for the legislature
- 1833 failed in business
- **1834 elected to legislature**
- 1835 sweetheart died
- 1836 suffered a nervous breakdown
- 1838 defeated for speaker in the legislature
- 1843 defeated for nomination for Congress
- **1846 elected to Congress**
- 1848 lost renomination
- 1849 rejected for job as land officer
- 1854 defeated for Senate
- 1856 defeated for nomination for vice-president
- 1858 defeated for Senate
- 1860 **elected sixteenth president of the United States**

Abraham Lincoln

Chapter 13

Closing the Sale

- **The proper attitude toward the close**
- **The function of the close**
- **Reassuring the prospect**
- **The value of persistence**
- **How to deal with rejection**
- **Knowing when to close**
- **Recognizing buying signals**
- **Different types of closes**

A CLOSING FRAME OF MIND

A close can be defined as a question asked or an action taken by a salesperson designed to elicit a favorable buying decision from the prospect. It is always related to the specific objective you identified for the interview.

Closing the sale is not really difficult for the salesperson who is conducting a professional sales interview held under favorable conditions, including the presence of a qualified prospect. Although closing a sale is actually quite natural, far too many salespeople have adopted such a distorted view of the close that they dread trying, even though the close is their only reason for being there. In fact, according to Chris Hegarty, in sixty-three percent of all sales interviews, salespeople fail to ask for the prospect's business. The usual scenario goes like this:

Well, Dr. Bickley, that's about all I have to tell you. Is there anything else you would like to ask me? No? Okay, I guess I'll call you again in a few weeks. Have a good day. I enjoyed talking with you.

When you are standing outside the prospect's office wondering, "What happened? I thought sure I had that order. What did I do wrong?" The usual answer is that you did not do anything wrong. You probably just did not do anything.

The sale has actually been made or lost long before the time arrives to sign the agreement. The final step should be just a formality — a necessary step, but not one that requires making weighty decisions. Unless you complete the selling process by asking for the order, the only title you deserve is *conversationalist.*

When each step in the sales process is handled correctly, the close is the natural conclusion to a successful sales interview.

Closing is not a separate event tacked onto the end of a sales interview. It is something that happens all along during the course of the presentation. Closing would probably be easier to understand if someone had devised a better name for it. Because the word close suggests something that occurs at the end of a process, salespeople seem to feel that it is an isolated segment of the selling process that must be approached in some exact manner to produce success, but the opportunity to close may occur at any time during the sales interview. The wise professional watches for and takes advantage of every closing opportunity. Take the order as soon as you can get it! Closing begins the moment you speak the first word to the prospect and continues throughout the whole process until the order is signed.

Failure at the close is the result of inadequate completion of the prior steps in the sales process: Inadequate prospecting, incomplete qualifying of the prospect, or too little probing to determine the prospect's real needs. As a result, the presentation has focused on the wrong features and benefits, or the wrong evidence has been supplied to support claims for the product. A prospect's failure to buy, then, does not automatically brand you as a poor closer. Studying your entire performance to find the weak link in the chain is necessary. Focusing only on closing as an indicator of sales skill is like expecting to hear Tiger Woods say that putting is all that matters in golf. Of course, that final putt that wins the championship is the most obvious success moment, but secure agreement throughout the sales process and the final step is the easiest one.

FUNCTIONS OF THE CLOSE

The Need for a Close

Even when all the steps leading to the close have gone well, the prospect may still hesitate. Logically, the prospect would gladly sign the agreement when a professional salesperson has a good product or service to offer, has presented meaningful benefits, has a carefully planned strategy for servicing the prospect's account, makes an impressive sales presentation, and successfully answers all of the buyer's concerns. However, the *moment of decision* is difficult for most people. Buyers take many risks: They must live with the purchase and pay for it; they may be forced to justify the buying decision to someone else; they may be responsible for an important impact on the company's productivity or profitability as a result of the purchase. Risks are threatening to most people. Of course, you may also feel some strain at the moment of decision. You may be asking yourself, "Have I told the prospect enough? Did I find the real need? Did I read the verbal and nonverbal clues correctly? Is this the best moment to close? What if the answer is no?"

> **The art of closing sales is not the process of persuading people to make decisions, but the art of making decisions with which people will agree.**

Reassure and Close. Consider how the prospective buyer is probably feeling and thinking. Do you remember the first time you jumped off a diving board? You thought, "the board is too high; I can't swim that far; I'll choke on some water; I think I see sharks." You thought about all the possible bad consequences. Perhaps a friend in the water encouraged you to try. When you finally jumped, you discovered that the water was fine, just as your friend had said. In the sales situation, you are the friend in the water, you know how the prospect feels and you offer the needed reassurance: "Come on in; you'll be glad you took that first dive; I'm here to help if you need me." Your attitude must be that you respect prospects and their decisions, whether or not they decide to jump in. You continue to reassure them until they finally make a decision. The next time you advise them to make a buying decision, they will trust your recommendation more readily.

WIFE asks: Dear, do you have difficulty making decisions?

HUSBAND responds: Well, yes and no.

Once prospects agree that they can benefit from using your product or service, your responsibility is to guide them to a close. You must never be discouraged by no. If you honestly believe that a sale is an exchange of mutual benefits, then a no should set up this train of reasoning: The prospect is asking me to explain once more that this decision will work, so I will continue to reassure and close. Do not be discouraged when the buyer hesitates. People do not like to make decisions; without assistance and reassurance, some simply cannot make decisions at all. *There is no agony like that of indecision.*

A CLOSING CONSCIOUSNESS

A Closing Attitude

The most important factor in successfully closing a sale is not having the lowest price or the best product. *Your attitude* is the crucial factor. You must have an absolute belief in what you are selling, and you must *expect* to be successful. If you assume that you will successfully close the sale, the prospect interprets your confidence as reassurance that the product will provide the needed benefits. Your positive attitude makes the difficult decision, "Yes, I'll buy" much easier. All they have to do is say, "Yes, you're right" when you recommend that they buy. Confidence is contagious; it infects prospects and draws them to your side.

> *Mr. Evert, we have agreed on the capacity of the printer, its speed capabilities, and the cost of supplying paper, and we have clarified your questions regarding the service contract. We could significantly speed up the process if we could settle now on a delivery date. Is Friday okay with you?*

When you maintain a positive mental attitude, a high level of self-confidence, and belief in your product, you create an atmosphere within which you can handle the day-to-day rejections that are inevitable in the world of selling. Steve Simms, noted author and speaker, reveals how to *shake off the shackles of rejection.* When prospects fail to follow your buying advice, you know that the rejection is seldom directed toward you personally but is instead a reflection of their own differing opinion about what will best fill their needs or a result of their personal hesitancy to make a decision that they perceive as a risk. In other words, you have lost nothing except a little of your time, but the prospects who say no have lost the opportunity to benefit from using your product or service and of being your personal customer. The bigger loss is theirs.

Persistence

Diana Smith, a representative for Jim Stephenson and Associates, Inc., says, "You should push, but never be pushy." Smith calls on Houston home builders to convince them to use her company's line of plumbing supplies in their construction projects. She suggests that "making repeat, *meaningful* calls demonstrates to prospects that you are not going to give up. The idea is to be graciously tenacious — without being obnoxious." Focused persistence involves asking whether doing *this* today will get you *that* tomorrow. Successful salespeople like Diana Smith never take no for an answer unless it is in everyone's interest to do so. If the business is worth having, it is worth going after repeatedly — with repeated calls or repeated attempts to close during a single call. The extra effort often makes the difference between success and failure.

How often do you ask a prospect for the business? The answer often given is "one more time." Realistically, you should be prepared to ask *at least* four or five times. A study of several thousand salespeople demonstrates how important persistence really is:

1. Forty-eight percent of those interviewed quit after the first contact with a prospect.

2. Seventy-three percent give up after the second contact.

3. Eighty-five percent quit after the third contact.

4. Ninety percent give up after the fourth contact.

The most dramatic statistic from the study shows that the *ten percent* of salespeople who continue past the fourth contact, end up with *eighty percent* of the business. Exhibit 13.1 describes the kind of persistence needed for success in sales.

Selling should be a side-by-side, step-by-step process, involving both prospect and salesperson, in which you earn the right to close. When you understand the problems faced by prospects, stay with them through the problem-solving process, watch for buying signals, and time the close to fit the prospect's behavioral style,

Exhibit 13.1

Persistence

One of the best examples of persistence is a story you probably loved as a child: *Green Eggs and Ham*. This Dr. Seuss classic describes the attempt of the "salesman," Sam I Am, to induce a wary "prospect" to try a meal of green eggs and ham. When his first straightforward offer is rejected, Sam I Am tries one assumptive close after another: "Do you want them here or there? Would you like them in a box or with a fox? Do you want them in a house or with a mouse?" Finally, the prospect tries green eggs and ham and is surprised to find them quite delicious. His no's seemingly never registered with the persistent Sam I Am. If you have not read *Green Eggs and Ham* lately, visit the children's section of the library and learn the story's important lesson about persistence.

Dr. Seuss, *Green Eggs and Ham* (New York: Random House, 1960)

your chances of a successful close skyrocket. Opportunities to close occur a number of times during the sales process; recognize them, persist, and ask for the order.

Dealing With Rejection

So many salespeople leave the profession because of their inability to cope with the day-to-day sense of rejection they experience. They interpret a prospect's refusal to buy as a message that says, "You are personally worthless." The first thing to remember when facing rejection is that you just can't take it personally. Mary Crowley, founder of Dallas-based Home Interiors, Inc., would often tell her salespeople what Eleanor Roosevelt was quoted as saying: "No one can make you feel inferior without your permission." She feels that this concept is especially important for not only her salespeople, but all sales reps, to internalize.

Sales professionals must learn to deal with rejection by keeping a positive attitude about themselves and how they make their living. True, they feel disappointment if they fail to close, but successful salespeople focus in on the sense of accomplishment they feel when they do close a sale. To keep from being overwhelmed, accept the fact that rejection exists, see it for what it really is, and never make the mistake of allowing it to serve as a measure of your own self-worth.

> "The number of failures salespeople have is not important. What counts is the number of times they succeed, and this is directly related to the number of times they can fail and keep trying."
>
> — Tom Hopkins

What is a good batting average in selling? Professional baseball players who average .300 (three hits for every ten times at bat) or more for a full season are a small minority of players in the major leagues. Imagine failing to get a base hit 70 percent of the time. Consider some of the great names in baseball history:

- Babe Ruth hit 714 career home runs, but struck out 1,330 times.
- Cy Young won 515 games, but lost 313.
- Ty Cobb stole 96 bases one year but was caught stealing 38 times.

Baseball fans ignore the failures and concentrate on the successes of their favorite players. The attitude of all professionals is, "I may have *failed*, but that does not mean *I am a failure*."

A salesperson who never hears a 'no' is no salesperson, only an *order taker*. Rejection is as much a part of sales as getting dressed in the morning, and salespeople who can't or won't deal with it had better find another career. The first thing to remember when handling rejection is that you just can't take it personally. Refuse to permit anyone else to make you feel bad about yourself. Exhibit 13.2 describes seven specific tactics for coping with rejection.

Exhibit 13.2

Seven Tactics for Dealing with Rejection

1. Remind yourself of exceptional salespeople and how many hundreds or thousands of rejections they had to face on their journey to success. You see, you are not alone!

2. Positively anticipate rejection and it will not overwhelm you. Expect it, but don't create it. Think in advance what your response to rejection will be.

3. Give yourself a pep talk. Replace negative thoughts with positive ones such as, "I'm a great salesperson, and after they hear what I have to say, they'll want to buy from me."

4. Remind yourself constantly that persistence is key to success, and that rejection may not be pleasant but you won't let it stop you. Stubbornly refuse to let it get to you!

5. Remind yourself of the difference between self-worth and performance. Never equate your worth as a human being with your success or failure as a salesperson.

6. Engage in positive self-talk. Separate your ego from the sale. The prospect is not attacking you personally. Say to yourself, "This prospect doesn't even know me; the refusal to buy cannot have anything to do with me as a person."

7. When you make mistakes, forgive yourself. Mistakes are great learning experiences, but to benefit from them you have to keep moving forward. Continue to generate, gather and harvest prospects. The more prospects you have, the better you feel.

WHEN TO CLOSE

Most of the sales you make will not close themselves. The closing curve shown in Figure 13.1 illustrates how the closing process works. The will-buy line (WBL) shows that some sales will be closed almost at once, others are easy sales, and that most can be closed with an interest-building presentation. A few can never be closed. The key is recognizing the spots at which a close can be made — when the buyer gives a buying signal. The appearance of a buying signal is the critical moment during the presentation when a successful close is more likely.

When you sense the psychological moment to close do so immediately. A delay of even a few seconds may give prospects a chance to change their mind. If you fail to recognize these critical moments at which the prospect is most nearly ready to make a buying decision and continue to talk past them, the close becomes steadily more difficult. After a critical point is passed, you must buy back the prospect's readiness to decide. In other words, you must once again convince the prospect that buying is the proper decision. Talking too much and overselling is a much greater danger than underselling. Your attempts to close early and often eliminate the possibility of going past the point at which the prospect is ready to buy.

Figure 13.1

The Closing Curve

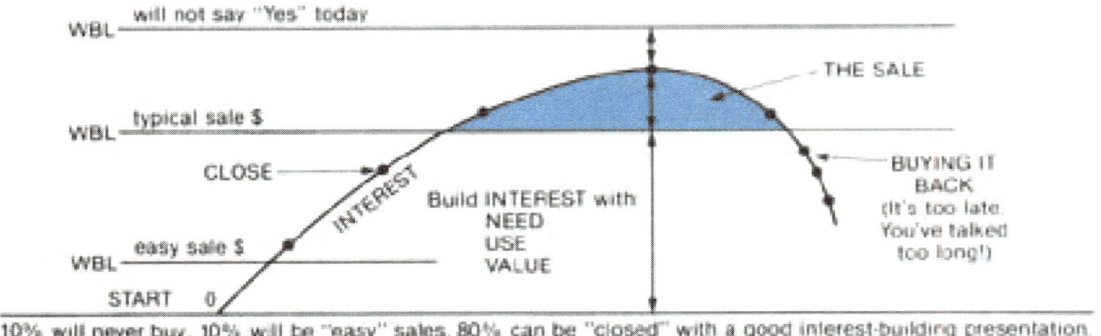

The professional salesperson guides and directs the prospect's behavior. As you reach the point where the final decision is to be made, it's just as important for you to know *when to ask* for the order as it is for you to know *how to ask*. Instead of just watching passively for signs of interest, you must create situations in which interest can be generated and revealed.

The best psychological moment for closing may occur at any time during the presentation. When it does come, prospects *signal* in some way that you have convinced them and they are ready to buy. You never have only one possible moment to close. You may be in the early stages of the presentation, you may have completely exhausted all the selling points you planned to present, or you may be somewhere in between.

RECOGNIZING BUYING SIGNALS

A buying signal is anything the prospect does or says that indicates readiness to buy. Buying signals are all around us if we learn to recognize them. Unfortunately, it's all too easy to become focused on your presentation that you overlook these signals even if they are obvious. Buying signals occur quickly and may be verbal, nonverbal, or both. Genuine buying signals show that the prospect has moved from evaluating your proposal to an appraisal of it. A buying signal may come in the form of a question. A prospect may ask you to repeat some point or benefit previously discussed or stop you right in the middle of the presentation to ask how long delivery will take. However a buying signal comes, take advantage of it and close immediately. Always remember that when the prospect is ready to buy, you will receive a signal.

The CHEF Technique

Just as the experienced chef in a fine restaurant knows precisely the right ingredients to blend to produce exquisite cuisine, similarly professional salespeople can exhibit chef like characteristics as they try to translate the combination of gestures fed to them by their prospects. Use the **CHEF** method to identify prospects' verbal and nonverbal buying signals.

Cheek Or Chin. When prospects touch or stroke their chin or cheek they are signaling satisfaction and gratification. Leaning forward and nodding the head in agreement says, I'm almost persuaded. In this instance, ask if you've answered all their questions, move quickly and ask for their business. Prospects that tighten their jaw muscles or cover their mouths suggest that they are not receptive to what you have to say. This is a critical time to ask questions to open them up.

Hands. Open and relaxed hands, especially with palms facing upward, are a sign that prospects may be ready to buy. Rubbing their palms together signals that they are already assuming ownership. Those individuals who steeple (like a church steeple) their hands together are indicating confidence or superiority. When the prospect's hands are fidgeting or forming a fist, they're more than likely skeptical, or worse yet, irritated. You must stop talking and find out what is wrong!

Eye contact. Maintaining consistent eye contact with you indicates the prospect is probably paying attention to what is being said, and the handling and examination of any visuals shows the intensity of that commitment. This is a good time to request a

buying decision. When the pupils of the prospect's eyes are dilated this signals relaxation, and you are on the right track. However, rolling or squinting of the eyes often means irritation or confusion. In addition, the rate at which a prospect blinks can indicate anger or excitement. A raised eyebrow can mean the prospect doesn't believe what you are saying. Something is wrong and you had better find out what that something is. If you sense this you might say, "You seem a bit uneasy with this. Please tell me what concerns or questions you have."

Friendly prospects. Prospects who are smiling, relaxed, or engaging you in conversation are telling you that you've earned their trust. A prospect indicates readiness to purchase by saying, "It sounds good, but I ought not to buy." Give this prospect another reason to buy. Reassure and ask for a decision. When prospects turn unfriendly, be sensitive and empathetic. After all, the basic reason for becoming experts at relationship selling is to create an atmosphere within which an act of trust can take place! *People like to buy from people who are like them.*

The Trial Close

A *trial close* asks for an *opinion;* a *closing question* asks for a *decision.* A trial close, by asking for an opinion, serves as a thermometer that tells you whether the prospect is warm, hot, or cold to your proposition. It is designed to help you read the prospect's feelings and predict probable reactions. In Chapter 11, the tie-down question was discussed as one element in a *unit of conviction.* The tie-down and the trial close are used for basically the same purpose. When you get the prospects agreeing with you throughout the presentation they are much more likely to agree with you when you ask the closing question, that is, when you make the formal request for their business. You want to be careful not to talk past the sale. Close when the prospect wants to buy.

Many salespeople think of closing as the last phase of a sales call. If they do, they may not get all the sales that they should. During every sales call there will be a number of opportunities to close the sale. How do you know the proper time? When in doubt, test the prospect with trial closes such as:

1. "Is this what you're looking for?"

2. "Can you imagine how this will boost your productivity?"

3. "Do you have the necessary budget for this?"

4. "What else do you need to make a decision?"

5. "Does this sound like something you would like to do?"

Although it resembles a definite attempt to close, the trial close is used to probe and to reveal how far along the prospect has gone in the decision-making process. You do not need to ask a closing question if you know the prospect is not ready to buy. The time to ask for the order is when the prospect is fully ready to buy. You can, however, ask for an *opinion* at any time.

A Closing Question

A *closing question*, in contrast to the trial close, is designed to produce an answer that confirms the fact that the prospect has bought. Look at these two examples:

1. *Would it be better for you to receive shipment of a full month's supply immediately, or would you prefer to receive half at the end of this week and the other half in about ten days?*

2. *We can have the product on your dock next Monday. Is Monday a convenient delivery day for you?*

When you ask a closing question, say nothing else until the prospect gives an answer. The pressure of silence is enormous. Silence is golden because of what it brings you in terms of the information you need. Never miss the opportunity not to say something. If you can remain silent after asking the closing question, only two outcomes are possible: 1) the prospect says yes or 2) the prospect gives a reason for not wanting to buy. In either instance, you are better off than you were before you asked the question. If the answer is yes, you have a sale. If the prospect gives you a reason for not buying, a concern has surfaced that you can convert into another opportunity to close.

TYPES OF CLOSES

Become familiar with as many types of closing techniques as possible. One or two standard closes are not enough in the competitive selling arena that is filled with many different kinds of buyers, all with varying needs and personalities. You need a specific close for every occasion and for every type of prospect. If you attempt to use the same close for every prospect, you will walk away from much of the business that should be yours. The sales plan for each interview calls for a specific type of presentation strategy; your plan should also extend to the type of close you use. Just as circumstances often dictate some changes in your presentation, however, they also point up the need for shifts in your closing plans. Your *sales call plan* should provide the preferred closing routine to fit with the presentation you expect to deliver. Be sure to plan some alternative closing routines you can use in the event you find it is necessary to modify your presentation.

For example, you had prepared a comprehensive insurance program to present to a client. Upon arrival you find an excited prospect who shares information that he and his wife are actually expecting triplets. This prospect's needs have changed dramatically in just 24 hours. Your presentation now becomes a work session to devise a new program, and the close you anticipated may not be appropriate.

A master salesperson with a full repertoire of closing techniques merely chooses one that fits the revised situation and moves on as though nothing unusual is occurring. The various closing methods shown in Exhibit 13.3 and described here are not the only methods available. Most of them are subject to combination with other methods to fit your unique personality, your product, and your market. Learn the principles upon which these techniques rest and adapt them to your needs.

Exhibit 13.3

Successful Closing Techniques

Assumptive closes

Throughout the entire presentation, assuming that the prospect will buy allows the prospect to make the decision more easily by presenting opportunities to make smaller or easier choices. Common assumptive closes include the *continuous-yes* close, the *physical-action close*, the *order-blank close*, and the *alternate of choice* close.

Impending-event close

Stress the urgency to make a decision because something is about to happen that means the opportunity to buy with the present advantages may be lost.

Direct close

Make a straightforward request for the order. Many buyers appreciate a no-nonsense approach, but be mindful of each prospect's behavioral style and use this approach only with those who welcome such tactics.

Summary close

Review the features and benefits of the offering with particular emphasis on selling points that generated the most prospect interest earlier in the presentation.

Call-back close

Most sales are not closed on the first attempt. Offer to call back on a prospect with a specific purpose in mind and with new information.

Trial-order close

Either guarantee the prospect's money back or offer to absorb all expenses if the prospect tries the product or service and decides not to keep it.

Balance-sheet close

You take an active part in the decision-making process to help the prospect understand that the reasons for buying heavily outweigh the reasons opposed to buying.

Assumptive Closes

In a sense, every close is assumptive. You do not attempt to close until you have received one or more buying signals from the prospect and have reason to believe you have a better than even chance of success. When you enter every sales interview with a positive expectation of success, you are assuming that the prospect will buy at the close. Your attitude throughout the interview is assumptive. Say, "When you use this product" and "As your program progresses." Avoid words like *if* and *should* because they are conditional and block closing action.

The assumptive approach to closing establishes a positive environment in which the prospect can more easily say yes. These closes work well with indecisive buyers who tend to be nervous about making a final decision. Present them with minor decisions that give them the opportunity to appear decisive in a small matter while they are actually painlessly making the big decision at the same time. The closes described below are common assumptive closes.

Continuous-Yes Close. By asking a series of questions throughout the sales presentation, all of which are designed to be answered in the affirmative, it becomes more difficult for buyers to say no when they've already said yes a number of times. That is why you must get agreement on minor points before you ask for the order.

These questions begin in need discovery. For example: "I'd like to ask you a few questions that help me understand your particular needs. Would that be okay with you?" Yes. Continue them during the presentation: "Do you like the idea of our billing in six-second increments on all your long distance calls?" Yes. During the closing phase you may ask: "Are you satisfied with the comprehensive service contract that we offer?" Yes. "Does the financing of this telecommunications system seem fair to you?" Yes. "Then it seems we can go ahead with our plans to begin the installation process." Yes. These are all closed-end type questions, so you must be confident that you will receive an affirmative response before you ask them. When the final closing question is asked, the prospect is inclined to keep on agreeing with you. You have a sale.

Physical-Action Close. The physical-action close is quite simple, but can be most effective. Without directly asking for the prospect's order, begin taking some action that assumes the sale is completed. For example, you can begin filling out paperwork and ask the prospect for a signature when you finish. A retail salesperson may simply begin wrapping the merchandise or move to the cash register to ring up the order. If the prospect does not object or stop your action, the sale is made.

Order-Blank Close. Begin to ask the prospect a series of questions and write the answers on the contract or agreement form. You might ask, "Do you use your complete middle name or just an initial?" Continue to fill out the information and then ask for a signature. "Now that we have reached agreement, I know you will want to expedite delivery. Just indicate your approval by placing your name right here."

Alternate of Choice Close. In general, people like to exercise their freedom of choice and salespeople like to lead their buyers toward an easy agreement. This well-known close consists of giving the prospect a choice between two positive alternatives. Here are some suggestions:

1. *Would delivery be convenient on Thursday, or would you prefer Friday?*

2. *Do you prefer to pay cash or is our monthly payment plan more convenient for you?*

3. *Where would you like the order sent — directly to your warehouse or to the main office?*

The idea behind the alternate of choice close is to offer the prospect a choice between buying *A* and buying *B* instead of a choice between buying or not buying. The question is not "Will you buy?" but "When?" or "Which one?"

Impending Event Close

This close uses the sense of urgency that is suggested by some impending event that will affect the terms or the effectiveness of the buying decision. Use this close with discretion. It must be based on truth and must not seem manipulative. The most common inducements are concerns that prices are going up or that resources will be in short supply.

> *My company has announced that prices on this product will go up about five percent next month because of an increase in supplier costs. If I can call your order in now, you can stock up before the price increase becomes effective.*

Never use this close deceptively! Whatever the impending event is, it must be real and in the prospect's best interests to take advantage of an order placed now. Because this close is often abused by unscrupulous salespeople, prospects are likely to be skeptical of it. When you have good information to work with, you can prevent a customer from running short of inventory or from facing an unexpected price increase, and this gains the appreciation and the loyalty of the customer. Properly applied, this close can work wonders for your long-term credibility.

The Direct Close

The direct close is a straightforward request for an order. Once you have covered all the necessary features and benefits of your product and matched them with the buyer's dominant buying motives, you can ask with confidence, "May I have your business?" This type of close is quite common when selling to industrial buyers. Many buyers appreciate a no-nonsense approach. Of course, be mindful of the buyer's behavioral style. Amiables, for example, could find this approach threatening.

Be sure to keep the direct close positive. *Avoid the word don't.* "Why don't we begin next week?" and "Why don't you try the product for a while and see what happens?" are open invitations to additional objections. Insertion of a negative into the close may implant doubt where none existed, and the prospect may try to tell you why not. Use positive statements like these:

1. *May I schedule delivery for next Tuesday?*

2. *It comes in five-pound, ten-pound, and twenty-pound bags. I suggest you take five of each to begin.*

3. *Let's run your first ad beginning Friday of this week.*

When you use this type of closing statement, then you and your customer can make positive plans together.

The Summary Close

One of the best closing tactics is to summarize the major selling points made during the presentation. This method is especially good when the prospect must defend a purchase to someone else. The repetition of benefits at this point overcomes the prospect's tendency to forget or overlook points previously identified as important to satisfying existing needs. Review the benefits and ask the prospect to confirm again that they are important. Avoid mentioning any new benefits during this close. Bring up additional points only if the summary fails and you need additional ammunition to answer new objections.

Concentrate in the summary close on those items that were of most interest to the prospect and that related directly to the dominant buying motives. For example, the sales representative selling advertising space in a consumer magazine might use the summary close like this:

Mr. Hardwick, let's review the major points on which we have agreed:

1. *An ad in our magazine will give you maximum effective circulation coverage.*
2. *Your ads will enjoy high readership.*
3. *We saw that businesses similar to yours have had a great deal of success advertising with us (indicate testimonials or case histories used during presentation).*
4. *Our marketing staff will help you develop ads for all the media you use, not just our magazine.*
5. *You'll receive free artwork and layout help. These services are included in our basic price.*

This summary puts into capsule form the highlights of your sales story. It gives both you and the prospect an opportunity to reconsider what was covered throughout the sales interview.

Give the prospect an opportunity to agree that the summary is correct. Once agreement has been expressed, the prospect is in a positive frame of mind, and the time is ripe to get some sort of formal commitment. The summary close must be combined with some other closing technique to complete the sale. For example, you might use the alternate of choice close like this:

Mr. Hardwick, with all of these major benefits available, you can see that advertising with us is a sound investment. Do you want to run your first ad on October fifteenth, or would November first be better for you?

Call-Back Close

Many sales opportunities are lost every day because salespeople take the prospect's decision not to buy as permanent. Studies show that many accounts are won by salespeople who call five or more times on the same prospect. Each time you return, you must present new information or ideas that will stimulate the prospect to buy. If you have the same old story told in the same old way, you probably will not make a new impression. If you walk into the prospect's office and say, "Well, have you thought it over?" the prospect's natural tendency is to restate the original objection: "Yes, and I still feel it is not a good time to spend that much money." In other words, "No deal." Here is an effective plan for a call-back situation:

1. **Approach**. Begin by giving a reason for calling back: "Coach Blevins, after I left the other day, I realized that there is some information I did not give you that has real bearing on your situation." Be sure you do have something different to present — new data, additional proof material in the form of testimonials, or whatever. Be sure it is pertinent and logical.

2. **Review**. Next, review the whole presentation. Begin with, "Let me review briefly the items we talked about last time." The last meeting may be fresh in your mind, but the prospect will not remember ten percent of what you presented. Throughout the review, use phrases like *as you remember*, *you will recall*, and *we said that* to suggest points of agreement from the previous meeting.

This approach may not always work, but you know that you cannot sell to someone without face-to-face contact. Being there gives you the only opportunity you will ever have to sell this prospect.

The Trial Order Close

This technique involves asking the prospect for a trial order with no obligation. You either guarantee the money back if not completely satisfied or absorb all expenses and make the offer free. Prospects like it because they can simply refuse to pay for any unsatisfactory merchandise. Their risk is low and yours is minimal because only a small quantity is shipped with the possible result of establishing a satisfied customer who will give you repeat orders. Sometimes salespeople call this the puppy dog close. How could you ever return a puppy to the pet store and get your money back after the children have played with it for a week? By then, everyone is in love with it.

Suppose you are selling personal leadership training materials to a career counselor, and the prospect says something like this: "I have never used material like this in my teaching or counseling activities. Let me think about it before I decide." Respond with this trial order close:

> *"I can certainly appreciate that. One thing we do that might be helpful to you is to make the program available on a fifteen-day, satisfaction-guaranteed basis. This enables you to work with the material firsthand and see if it is something that would be useful in your career counseling and training. We encourage you to listen to some of the tapes, go through the manual, and try it out in some actual counseling situations. After you have done that, if you find that you can use it in your library, then just hang on to it and we will bill you next month. In fact,*

you can even spread the payments out over six months; that would mean just $43 per payment. But if you find that you can't use the material or that it's not suitable for your situation, we'll understand. All we ask is that you return it to us. Is that fair enough?

Follow this statement with one of the assumptive closes to get the prospect to take action that will allow you to actually enter the order.

The Balance-Sheet Close

This practical, decision-making format is familiar to most prospects, and they will feel comfortable as you use it. The procedure involves using a blank sheet of paper with a line drawn down the center to form two columns. In the first column, list all the reasons for making an affirmative decision in favor of your buying recommendation. These are the assets. In the second column, list all the questions or concerns about a buying decision — the liabilities involved in saying yes. The closing process is an analysis of the two columns to show the prospect that the reasons for buying heavily outweigh the reasons for not buying. Give the prospect the opportunity to express agreement with your conclusions. The prospect must take an active part in the decision-making process.

As you build the balance sheet, resist the temptation to hurry. As you list each advantage for buying, pause and allow time for the prospect to absorb the idea. Be sure that you have many more ideas in favor of buying than opposed to it so that the number of reasons will be so impressive that you won't have to deal with the relative weights of individual reasons. To use the balance-sheet method, you can begin like this:

Mrs. Hillman, the decision you are about to make is important. I know you want to be sure you are making a sensible choice. So that we will be sure to make the decision that is best for you, let's look at all the reasons in favor of buying this product and any questions or concerns about it. We can then determine which side weighs more and make your decision accordingly. Let's begin with the ideas that favor a positive decision today. Is that fair enough?

Take out a sheet of paper and begin to list the reasons for buying. Be sure to avoid the word objection. Instead of talking about the prospect's objections to buying, state them as concerns or questions to be answered: "You expressed concern about delivery schedules." When you use the word objection out loud, you are setting up the prospect and yourself as adversaries; if you are adversaries, one of you must win and the other must lose. You are looking for a win-win solution to the buying decision. Table 13.1 shows a partial balance sheet for selling a mutual fund.

Table 13.1

The Mutual Fund Decision

Reasons for buying

1. This fund has grown faster than savings accounts.

2. Diversification lowers risk.

3. Professional management lowers risk.

4. Blue chip portfolio lowers risk.

5. Stocks are a hedge against inflation.

6. You can quickly redeem or borrow on shares.

Questions or concerns

1. Higher risk than a savings account.

2. Less liquidity than a savings account.

After the Close

Once you have closed the sale and have completed any necessary paperwork, you have no further business with the prospect at this time. Learn to leave gracefully. Don't become afflicted with "lingeritis." You may be tempted to stay and enjoy the company of a new customer you especially like. You feel like celebrating a successful sale. However, the customer has other work to do, and so do you! If you linger, you invite second thoughts and perhaps even regret. Leave while the client still has good thoughts about you and your efficient, professional manner. Thank the client for the order, say you are looking forward to meeting again, and leave.

Confidence is contagious; it infects prospects and draws them to your side.

Closing the Sale

- Closing the sale is a natural conclusion to a carefully prepared and well-conducted presentation to a qualified prospect. Successful closing is often a matter of attitude.

- Learn to recognize buying signals. These enable you to close at the earliest possible point in the presentation. Learn the CHEF technique.

- The most threatening element in the sale for many salespeople is the fear of rejection. Develop a plan for dealing with rejection.

- Both verbal and nonverbal clues point to the prospect's readiness to buy. The buying signals often suggest the type of close that would be appropriate.

- Close when the prospect is ready to buy.

- One effective tactic is a trial close that asks for an opinion rather than a commitment; this allows the salesperson to determine just how ready the prospect is to say yes!

- Use words like when or as during the close. Avoid words such as if and should because they are conditional and block closing action.

- The summary close consists of restating the major selling points made during the presentation. This repetition of benefits overcomes the prospect's tendency to forget or neglect main points.

- The balance sheet close works well because it also allows you to present a summary of the main selling points, but in a pro and con format. Many of us tend to think this way and this close is well received by the analytical and amiable social styles.

Part V

Management Aspects: Personal and Organizational

Keeping customers happy and coming back takes more than smiles and thank-yous; it takes outrageous service.

THE HANDBOK FOR RELATIONSHIP SELLING

Chapter 14
Service After the Sale

FOCAL POINTS

- **Total customer service**
- **What constitutes service quality**
- **When and how to service**
- **Upgrade and cross-sell current customers**
- **Winning back angry customers**
- **A systematic plan for follow-up activities**

BUILDING PARTNERSHIPS WITH TOTAL CUSTOMER SERVICE

Increased Expectations

How do you sell your products or services and keep them sold when there are so many others fighting to do the same thing? Total customer service is the answer. More and more companies are turning to *service quality* as a strategy to acquire and maintain customers.

The value of customer service is not lost on Luis Martinez, manager of Daimler-Chrysler's Five Star program, a multimillion-dollar process to change the *sales culture* within the company's 4,500 dealerships. His job is to make the salespeople and support personnel look at their jobs differently. That is, not just get people in the door and sell them a car, but *to do what is best for the customer no matter what.* The customer absolutely defines quality in every transaction. Don't *talk* customer service — *live* perfect service.

Because meeting and exceeding customer expectations is so vital to success, companies must develop customer service strategies. This usually involves segmenting customers because they generally have different service needs. You can go out of business if you provide too much service to the wrong people, or if you fail to deliver adequate service to the right people. So you must inform specific customers what kind of service they can expect, and the key to success is exceeding what you promise. Keeping customers happy, and coming back, takes more than smiles and thank-yous. It takes *outrageous service*. Allen Endres of the Juran Institute explains that "customers have an increasing rate of expectation for services and a decreasing tolerance for poor service, and as a result are more likely to migrate to the vendors who provide the highest-quality service." To effectively use service as a competitive weapon, you must surpass customers' expectations.

> "A lot of people have fancy things to say about customer service, including me, but it's just a day-in, day-out, ongoing, never-ending, unremitting, persevering, compassionate type of activity."
>
> — Leon Gorman, L.L. Bean

Second-mile Action

Be willing to give your customers more than they demand, more than they expect, even more than they deserve. Exhibit 14.1 depicts a salesperson with such an attitude. Act from the desire to serve — not the desire to gain. When this is your policy, you will do whatever you must to be of service to your client. That means you sometimes deliver an order in your own car to get it to the customer sooner than the company truck could deliver it.

Going the second mile may involve a service for the customer that is unrelated to the business. "Big Jack" Frazier, who sells industrial chemicals, had a regular client in Waco, Texas, whose son was a student at San Angelo State University. The student's mother had typed a term paper for the son. Because Jack was leaving Waco for his regular trip through West Texas, he offered to take the paper to the student so it would be sure to arrive on time. Going through San Angelo was a bit out of his way, but he was happy to do it.

Paul J. Meyer, founder of SMI International, once had a client who made a hobby of collecting rocks containing fossils. When Meyer was on a vacation trip one year, he found a rock with a particularly interesting fossil on it. He packed the rock carefully and mailed it to his client. That kind of extra service, when given from sincere interest, pays rich dividends.

Exhibit 14.1

Second-Mile Service

Here are a few additional ideas that could be seen as going the extra mile in the eyes of the customer:

- **Offer to pick up or deliver goods to be replaced or repaired.**

- **Give a gift of merchandise to repay for the inconvenience.** The gift may be small but the thought will be appreciated.

- **Reimburse for costs of returning merchandise such as parking fees or gas.**

- **Acknowledge the customer's inconvenience** and thank him for giving you the opportunity to make it right. Make the wording of the apology sincere and personal.

- **Follow up to see that the problem was taken care of.** Don't assume the problem has been fixed unless you handled it yourself.

Moments of Truth

Awareness of quality service by your customers and prospects can be a great advantage. Salespeople are far more likely to make a sale when they can truthfully say, "If you buy from me, I

will never let you down. Servicing your account is my top priority." Jan Carlzon, president of Scandinavian Airlines (SAS), writes in his book *Moments of Truth*, "Each of our 10 million customers come in contact with five SAS employees. Each contact lasts about 15 seconds. Thus, SAS is created in the minds of our customers 50 million times per year, 15 seconds at a time."

Those 50 million "moments of truth," when customers are made aware of service quality, are the moments that ultimately determine the success of SAS. All employees must realize and care that their work effects customers' perception of service quality and even product quality, no matter how far they are removed from the "front line" or from direct communication with customers. Customer satisfaction is measured as moments in time. Plenty of customers do not come back unless the service you provide is consistently better than service provided by competitors. You must create a trust-bond relationship. Sixty-five percent of a typical firm's sales volume is done by loyal customers who return to buy again and again because of the service quality provided.

CUSTOMER SERVICE TECHNIQUES THAT SUPPORT THE RELATIONSHIP

Value Added

Jim Jewett, author of *Discovering Fast Track Success* and founder of Telco Research, an international telecommunications company, attributes much of his company's success to the ability of his salespeople to engage in value-added thinking. He defines this concept as "seeking out every possible opportunity to add customer value." Recognizing value added is much easier than defining it. When you are in the position of the customer, you recognize value added when you receive it — and you remember it!

Another way to consider the importance of customers' loyalty is to take a long-term view of their value. Instead of considering customers' worth in terms of single transactions, you should factor in all of the possible purchases over their lifetime. The automobile industry estimates that a brand-loyal customer represents a lifetime average revenue of $140,000 to the manufacturer. Carl Sewell estimates the lifetime value to his Cadillac dealership in Dallas of one satisfied buyer at well over $300,000. Home improvement retailer Home Depot determined its typical shopper's lifetime value to the store to be $25,000. The professional salesperson has numerous opportunities for follow-up activities that determine whether particular customers will reorder as well as whether they will tell others of their satisfaction or provide referrals to other prospects. The relationship sales rep is sincerely and unselfishly helpful to clients and prospects alike. Sometimes value-added service costs nothing except thoughtfulness and a few minutes of time.

Herb Kelleher founded Southwest Airlines to set itself apart from other airlines. Since inception the company has been known for its low fares and attention to customer service. Southwest has maintained an extremely high level of customer satisfaction not just because of its flight schedules, but also because of its value-added service. Exhibit 14.2 shows how Southwest Airlines adds value to its service and developing a loyal customer base.

Exhibit 14.2

A Friend in Need

At 9:00 p.m. one Christmas Eve, customer service agent Rachel Dyer was working the ticket counter at Southwest Airlines when a man with a cane approached her. In a faint voice he told her that he had to go to New Orleans. It seems that his sister-in-law had dropped him off with some cash and a plastic bag full of clothes, and told him to go to New Orleans where he had some relatives. Confused and worried, the man explained that he'd also recently undergone bypass surgery.

Dyer responded by reassuring him that they would work everything out. She booked him on the earliest flight to New Orleans the next morning, got him a hotel and a meal ticket for dinner and breakfast, and tipped a World Services employee to take the man to the airport shuttle. Dyer bent down to explain his itinerary to him and told him everything would be okay. He told her, "Thank you," then bowed his head and started to cry.

In Southwest's monthly employee newsletter, Dyer wrote, "I am so proud to work for a company that not only allows but encourages me to help people who really are in need. I truly believe the success of this company has to do with the fact that it was founded and is run by kind, honest and loving people."

Get More From Current Customers

Managers are increasingly telling their sales forces to get out of the office and start building personal relationships with their customers. As vice president of sales and marketing for Phillips Inc., a midsize steel manufacturer in Boise, David Schumacher has instructed his salespeople to focus on solidifying their current customer base. Just a short time ago he was telling them to go after new business and try to shift purchasers to do e-commerce. Schumacher says, "Now I have to quickly reverse my course, because there aren't as many new customers out there. We have to do our best to nail down our short-and long-term revenues by getting closer to current customers."

Sell current customers more of what you're already selling to them. Other departments may have a need. Sell them upgrades, enhancements, or additional products. Needs change over time. Sell your current clients something new. Keep them up-to-date on new products. Sell customers on you. Strive to become a trusted member of their team and opportunities will present themselves.

Upgrading or Up-selling. Upgrading, also known as up-selling, is the process of persuading the customer to purchase a better-quality product or, perhaps, a newer product. Upgrading is largely a matter of selling your company and pushing the quality factors of your product and customer image. You ask for the upgrade because the newer or higher-quality product will serve the needs of the client better than the less expensive version of the same product. Most firms have products that vary in quality and price. And most buyers like to have choices when making a purchase. The only way you can succeed in upgrading is to believe one hundred percent in what you're doing, think ahead, service your clients, and create win-win relationships.

The cornerstone of selling — especially when trying to upgrade a client — relies on continuously qualifying the prospect throughout the buying process. It's ultimately the customer's choice and you don't want to oversell, but giving them options is just logical. You want to sell to the real needs of the prospect. Salespeople need to remember they don't sell products — they sell results.

Cross-selling. Cross-selling is the process of selling products that are not directly connected to the primary products being sold to new and/or established clients. For example, cross-selling occurs when in a conversation with your bank's loan officer *about a loan* for expanding your business, you casually mention how expensive it is to keep your two elementary school children in a private school. Several days later, you receive a note in the mail from that same loan officer with materials describing how a *limited trust fund* could be used to help pay college expenses and *offering* the bank's services to help set it up.

Cross-selling and upgrading have become increasingly important to many companies in this information age. Customers have to be convinced that what you have available is going to solve a problem or save them money before they're even willing to talk. "To be truly customer-focused you have to make as many channels available as your customers are demanding," says Ann Vezina, vice-president of customer relationship management at systems integrator EDS. To do the best job of fostering lifetime loyalty, you need to know exactly what your customers are thinking.

The ideal scenario goes like this: When a customer contacts our customer service hotline via email or telephone, the agents in our call center can call up a comprehensive record of every interaction, no matter how, why, or when. And the most profitable callers are identified and directed to the most knowledgeable agents right away. Our agents get a view of our customers that is so granular they can *cross-sell* and *up-sell* products to our customer base.

RETAIN OR WIN BACK UNHAPPY CUSTOMERS

A customer calls and launches into a tirade, complaining and whining about everything. Who needs an account like this? But then you stop, catch your breath, and think — "When clients are rude it's usually because they are having a problem with some aspect of our product or service." No matter how badly clients behave, avoid responding angrily. You must learn not to take their rudeness personally. Maintain a positive attitude and an even tone of voice. This serves to disarm them and they will generally follow your lead.

Restate the client's concerns to demonstrate that you were listening. Employ empathy by putting yourself in their shoes and seeing it from their perspective. Remember that this customer is reacting to a real or perceived problem with your product or service that they feel has let them down.

Thank the customer for bringing the issue to your attention and then recommend a plan to solve it while the client is still on the phone. Make sure your proposed solution meets with the customer's approval. Lastly, follow up with a personal visit to ensure the issue has been resolved and the client is completely satisfied. This tends to build a stronger relationship and greater loyalty with clients.

Service in Response to Needs

When you are practicing ongoing service, you can anticipate complaints and handle them promptly before they become serious sources of customer dissatisfaction. A customer who is dissatisfied with a product or service tells an estimated nine or ten other people. Always respond immediately to the possibility of a complaint or to one that is actually expressed.

The salesperson who assumes that a customer must be satisfied because he has voiced no gripes over an extended period, is living in an unreal world. "Unless those dream customers called me to order goods or praise my products or service, I wouldn't let too much time go by without visiting them. Complaints can be customer-saving opportunities," says Ray Dreyfack.

Technical Assistance Research Programs Inc. (TARP), based in Washington, D.C., conducted research among manufacturing concerns that produced overwhelming evidence of the value not only of "handling" complaints but also of going out of the way to encourage and then remedy complaints. TARP's key findings include these:

- Of unhappy customers, only four percent complain to company headquarters. For every complaint received, the average company has 26 customers with problems, six of which are "serious," who do not complain.

- Among customers with problems, complainers are more likely than non-complainers to do business with the company again, even if the problem isn't satisfactorily resolved.

- Between 54 and 70 percent of complainers will give repeat business if their complaint is resolved, but a staggering 95 percent are repeat customers if they feel the complaint was resolved quickly.

- Dissatisfied complainants tell 9 or 10 people about their experience. 13 percent recount the incident to more than 20 people.

- Customers who have their complaints satisfactorily resolved tell an average of five people about the treatment they received.

Retaining Existing Customers

Service after the sale is critical to retaining existing customers, particularly in technical selling. In many technical sales, up to fifty percent of the sale involves the follow-through stage of the selling cycle. More technical sales are lost through inadequate follow-up than from any other cause. When so much time is invested in making a sale, attempting to save time by neglecting follow-up is a costly mistake.

All the efforts to retain customers is certainly not without benefits. Customer retention results from customer satisfaction. The average business loses about 15-20 percent of its customer base a year, forcing them to put money and effort into attracting new customers. It has been estimated that reducing customer defections by as little as five percent can double a firm's profits. A bad buying experience can be a bitter and enduring memory. There is no substitute for salespeople asking their customer base how they feel about the service the company is providing.

> "Those who enter to buy support me. Those who come to flatter please me. Those who complain teach me how I may please others so that more will come. Those only hurt me who are displeased but do not complain. They refuse me permission to correct my errors and thus improve my service."
>
> — Marshall Field

Win Back Those Angry Customers

No one enjoys losing a customer. Winning back a customer who has turned to a competitor helps your feelings as well as your sales records. The first step in regaining a customer is to discover why you lost the account. Almost 80 percent of former customers leave because they feel they've been badly treated. It is your responsibility to mend this relationship. Exhibit 14.3 gives some of the most common "excuses" given by salespeople for losing accounts. If you put aside such excuse-making, then some real delving into reality can show you why the account was lost.

Exhibit 14.3

"Excuses" Salespeople Give for Losing Accounts
It's not my fault I lost that customer . . .

- If it isn't price, then it's because the competition uses unfair or unethical tactics.

- My company fails to back me up; delivery is late, or quality deteriorates.

- That customer is just too difficult for anyone to get along with.

- The customer never cares about anything but price, so I was helpless.

- I just don't have time to make all the service calls I'd like to make.

- There can't be anything wrong with my sales techniques. I'm doing exactly what I've been doing for years.

You will find other questions to ask that relate directly to the product or service you sell. Listen carefully to what the customer tells you in answer to each question. Do not contradict what the customer has told you, argue, or become angry yourself, no matter how angry or unreasonable the customer may seem to you. When faced with an angry customer, you have two choices. One — you can walk away and consider the account lost; or two — you can resolve the conflict and further reinforce the relationship. If you listen politely, ask additional questions, and probe for hidden feelings, the mere act of telling you what is wrong often defuses the negative feelings of the customer. The former satisfaction experienced in doing business with you surfaces and the customer may be quite happy to consider reestablishing your relationship.

Do your best to glean every bit of current information you can regarding this angry customer, along with what you know of your past relationship with the customer, in order to decide what went wrong. Here are some possible reasons that you might lose an account.

1. **Something you have done**
No one is at top effectiveness all the time. Without intending to do so, you may have said or done something that offended the customer or damaged your credibility in some way. Exhibit 14.4 illustrates a sure-fire way to offend a customer and destroy a relationship. The old slogan for Arpege perfume began, "Promise her anything, but . . ." For you, the "but" must be followed by "don't promise what you can't deliver."

Exhibit 14.4

Destroying Credibility with the Customer

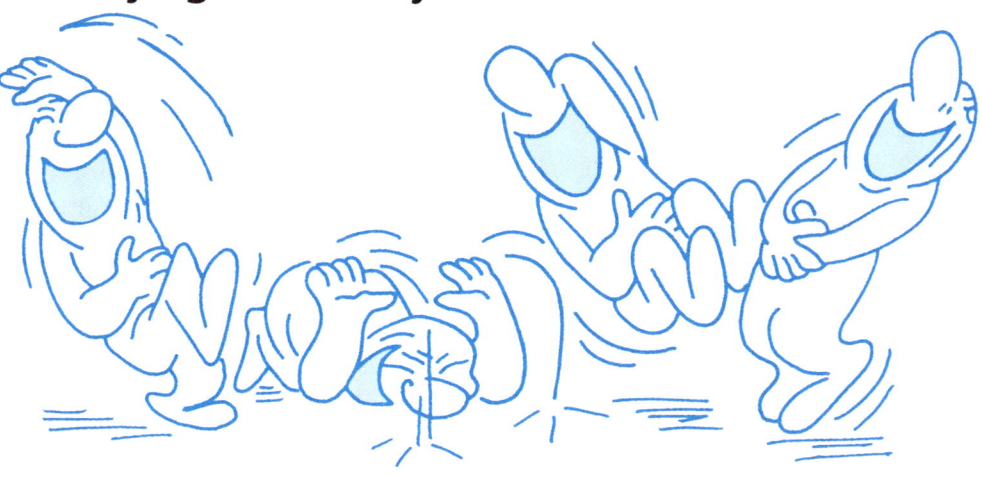

You want it *when?*

THE HANDBOOK FOR RELATIONSHIP SELLING

2. Something you fail to do

Failing to tell the full story about what the product can or cannot do, failure to keep the customer informed about product or delivery changes, failure to meet promises, failing to follow up or waiting too long to follow up — all these omissions destroy the customer's faith in you, your product, and your company.

3. Something the company does

If the company delivers only a portion of an order, substitutes some items in the order without telling the customer or makes errors in billing, the customer may become dissatisfied enough to change suppliers.

4. Something the company fails to do

The company may fail to meet the promised delivery schedule without warning, fail to provide necessary training and technical backup as promised, or fail to meet maintenance agreements.

Take some time for problem solving. Until you discover and acknowledge the real problem, you cannot solve it. Sometimes the answer is unpleasant. If the problem lies in your actions or attitudes, you must accept responsibility so that you are free to solve the problem and regain the account. If you deny your obvious responsibility, you escape into excuse making and are blinded to the options available for regaining the customer's goodwill. When you know what the problem is, you can plan strategies for rebuilding the account.

SYSTEMATIC PLAN FOR FOLLOW-UP ACTIVITIES

Your tracking system for servicing should be as well-organized as your prospecting system. Set up a rotating tickler file by dates of expected contact for each account. Use a card file or computer program. The file method chosen should list the customer's name (company and individual with whom you deal), the date of each service contact, and the form it took (telephone call, letter, visit). Whatever organizing system you choose, be sure to have a specific, written plan for servicing. Your plan should include these four elements:

1. Stay Informed

The process of buying and selling does not end with the purchase — unless you intend for the current purchase to be the only possible transaction you will ever have with this customer or with anyone this customer can influence. Service is the activities you do to keep customers sold permanently. The sale is not complete until the customer is satisfied.

Frequent service calls on existing customers help you keep up with personnel changes in their company. If you meet new personnel, a relationship can be developed and your credibility established before you ask for a new order. Make sure you do not continue to send mail addressed to a buyer's predecessor. Keeping up with personnel changes not only helps you solidify your presence with the existing company client but also gives you an ally in the company to which the former employee has moved.

Gaining a New Customer Costs Five Times More than Keeping a Current One.

2. Make Phone Calls

The telephone is one of your best service tools. It allows you to give the customer personalized attention with less investment of time for both you and the customer than would be required by a personal visit. Customers respond positively to the fact that you are interested in them and how the product is meeting their needs, and they are also pleased that they did not need to spend half an hour in a personal visit with you. Here are some of the items of service you can handle through phone calls:

- Verify delivery
- Check for problems
- Inform the customer of price changes or possible shortages
- Check customer's inventory level

A variety of communication devices. "Make it possible for your customers to reach a live person–even when you aren't available," advises Eric Harris, sales manager at Benefit Partners in Roseville, California. His job is to offer independent insurance agents or brokers and their customers access to a wide selection of health insurance plans. The brokers need fast, accurate information when they call, and for that reason Harris' phone does not have voice mail so that callers can always talk to a live person. If their specific rep is not available, brokers talk to another member of the sales team who can also answer their questions.

The telephone isn't always enough. Use a variety of communication media to make sure you reach your customer and that your customer can reach you. When you secure a new client, learn the person's schedule, best times to call, e-mail address, fax number, cell phone number, other office telephone numbers, and even his home telephone number. Exhibit 14.5 illustrates the value of having the necessary information and the trust of your client.

Exhibit 14.5

Telephoning a Client on a Sunday Afternoon

Robert Lowcher, national account manager of Time Distribution Services, called a customer at home on a Sunday, and it paid off for both of them. Lowcher said, "When John F. Kennedy Jr.'s plane went down, most people were uncertain if he was dead." However, Time magazine assumed he had died and planned a memorial issue in his honor. The buyer he called usually ordered 5,000 copies for his stores, but that would not be nearly enough because this issue would be a big seller if indeed their assumption proved correct. Lowcher talked to his buyer on Sunday afternoon and told him about the special issue and that the deadline for ordering extra issues was that evening. The customer ordered 25,000 copies and sold 90 percent of them that next week. Lowcher says, "If I hadn't been looking out for my customer and built a relationship based on trust, both of us would have lost out."

3. Determine Call Frequency

Decide how often you will call on each customer. Base this on your experience with each customer and with customers in general in your business. Consider account penetration (current and potential volume) and customer need. Rate your accounts as A, B, and C, much as you rate prospects, according to how much business you can expect to develop with each one and how many referrals that customer can generate for you that will produce business in addition to what that account provides. Also consider the personality and needs of the customer and determine what care is needed to maintain goodwill and a solid relationship. Decide also whether calls will be by telephone, in person, or a combination.

4. Send Mail (Letter or Card)

When your customer has no specific problems or need to reorder, keep your name before the customer with direct-mail items like these:

- New promotional material your company produces that will help the customer use the product more successfully.

- Information about new products from your company that might interest your customer.

- Your company in-house newsletter that includes trade information, promotional articles, and stories that might interest your customer (Be sure to write a few words of greeting.)

- A letter with a self-addressed business reply card on which the customer can check the level of satisfaction (excellent, good, fair, poor) with your product.

Give close attention to the effectiveness of each type of service contact you offer to your customers or clients. Discard methods that do not work, and repeat methods that do. Keep your service records as meticulously as you do your data on prospecting. Know what you have done for each customer, what you plan to do next, and when. Exhibit 14.6 illustrates how a thank-you card and a follow-up phone call paid off for a creative salesperson.

Exhibit 14.6

A Prompt Thank-You and a Follow-Up Telephone Call

Thank each client you visit promptly! This is what Julie Puckett, a sales rep with Home Buyer Publications in Fairfax, Virginia, does. And it is something worth emulating. Before Julie travels on business she addresses an envelope to each customer she plans to visit. After each appointment, and while the details are still fresh in her mind, she immediately creates a handwritten card thanking them for their time and expressing how much she enjoyed the meeting. The note is mailed that day in their city!

By the time she returns home to make follow-up phone calls, the clients have received the "thank you" cards. Puckett says, "It's surprising how often my customers refer to my note and express appreciation for its timeliness." It doesn't surprise me! It may seem like a no-brainer, but it certainly is effective for her.

THE OFFICIAL HANDBOOK FOR RELATIONSHIP SELLING

Service After the Sale

- The right kind of customer service brings you repeat business over time. A buying decision is a one-time action unless you turn it into a habit with effective follow-up and follow through procedures.

- Service after the sale adds value to what you sell by showing the customer that you are willing to take care of any problems. Service after the sale can be more important to your client than the actual sale itself.

- After sale service gives you an opportunity to keep up with personnel and other company changes so you will know who to contact for reorders and what additional opportunities you have for supplying this customer.

- Service is an ongoing activity. It is never too soon or too long after the sale to provide service.

- Plan, execute, and track any personal visits, telephone calls and mailings to your customers and measure how effective they were.

- Service is the key to winning back lost accounts. No matter what causes the loss of an account, that loss is a signal for renewed service activity. Contact the former client with sincere concern and interest.

Manage your time and choices - and you'll manage your life.

Time, Territory, and Personal Management

DEVELOPING A TIME MANAGEMENT ATTITUDE

Time is perhaps your most precious commodity. Although a continuous supply of time is available, it cannot be stored for future use, and it cannot be reclaimed if it is wasted. When you realize that life itself consists of time, the value of time becomes clear. We loudly denounce attitudes or practices that show a lack of respect for human life, but we seem not to notice when we throw away priceless hours — the fabric of life — in useless activity or idleness. Begin your program of managing time by asking yourself a question posed by Alan Lakein in his book *How to Get Control of Your Time and Your Life:* "What is the best use of my time right now?"

The term *time management* is a misnomer. Because every minute has sixty seconds and every hour has sixty minutes, time itself cannot be managed. It can only be used. What can be managed, however, are you and your activities. Time management, then, is actually personal organization as well as self-management. It involves three areas:

- Self-management (self-discipline)
- Planning and organizing
- Systems and techniques to automate routine

Use your time instead of simply spending it. Time is made up of a series of events. The key to managing time is controlling these events to your advantage. Time control and self-management can be learned. You have the ability to control your present thoughts and actions and to decide how to use your time.

> **Dost thou love life? Then do not squander time, for that's the stuff life is made of.**
> — Benjamin Franklin

Get a firm grip on the reality of the worth of time. Pretend that the president of your bank informs you that you have been chosen to receive a special prize: Every day for the rest of your life $86,400 will be deposited into your account. The only stipulation is that it must all be spent every day. Anything left at the end of the business day goes back to the bank. You can't hold anything over from one day to the next. Those first weeks are exhilarating. By the end of the first month, you have received over $2 million. After a while, however, you begin to have trouble spending that much every day. Think how you would feel the first time $20,000 slipped away from you and went back to the bank because you failed to spend it all. You would quickly realize that using this much money every day calls for some serious planning.

This imaginary scenario is not entirely fantasy. The old adage is true: Time is money. Every day 86,400 seconds are deposited in your account and in that of everyone else. You cannot save any unused time for another day. How many — or how few — of your 86,400 seconds go back to the "bank" unused depends on your skill in planning and managing your time. The important questions are these:

1. How will you spend your time?
2. How will you invest your time?
3. How much time will go to business, to service for others, to family, to leisure?
4. How much time will be reserved just for yourself — for the things you want to do?

Your most important asset is time, and how you use it is crucial to your success. Noted speaker Ira Hayes says,

> **"The inability or lack of desire to become organized is responsible for the vast majority of failures. It is why otherwise bright people turn out to be only mediocre performers and achieve only a small degree of the success that they rightfully could achieve. A disorganized desk, car, or way of life leads to rushing around and confusion and generally results in a poor attitude which makes people around you question the advisability of doing business with you."**

Everybody has the ability to manage time. The desire is the variable that makes the difference, and taking charge of your life depends on your personal choice.

Nearly everything that we think, say or do is governed by patterns of behavior that we have developed over the years. We develop most of them early in life and rarely change them. The only way to lose a habit is to stop practicing it. Stop practicing negative habits and start practicing positive ones, and your life will improve automatically. If you want to achieve good results in professional sales, establish good habit patterns.

In sales, more than in many other professions, the management of time is a matter of personal choice and responsibility. Here's an idea for you to try: Get to work by 5 a.m. three times a week, and you'll gain an extra day. You will realize a great feeling of satisfaction at 8 a.m. when you've already finished what would have taken you six hours to do after 8 a.m. because of the interruptions.

Attitudes Toward Time

Mental preparation is necessary to win the race against time. Developing a time management attitude helps to overcome life's obstacles. Just as Olympic champions practice diligently and relentlessly to perfect their athletic techniques, you can practice time management techniques and maximize the benefits to be enjoyed from both professional and personal pursuits.

You can let the whole subject of time management assume such proportions that the mere thought of attempting to master it becomes frustrating. You might even feel trapped and manipulated by the demands others make on your time. When you feel time pressures and believe you are working to your full capacity, you would probably be surprised to learn that a significant portion of each day is being wasted.

According to a number of top sales experts, the typical salesperson spends an average of only two hours a day in productive selling. However, just increasing the time spent with a customer doesn't do very much for you, it's what you do with the time that's important. As a salesperson focus your time so that it matches opportunity. Perhaps it is a better strategy to target five large accounts, rather than target 50 accounts and divide your time trying to get each one of them. You don't have enough time or enough protection, and competitors swoop in and take them away.

Keep a positive perspective toward time and your use of it. Here are four suggestions for establishing the kind of time attitudes that will bring you success:

1. Make a list of the activities you want to complete during the next week to achieve the results you desire.

2. For an entire week, keep an hour-by-hour record of exactly what you do with your time. Summarize your record and compare what you actually do to the list you made of what you want to do to achieve your goals. (Exhibit 15.1 illustrates a form you can draw to use for this purpose.)

3. At the end of each day and at the end of each week, take a personal accounting of what you have accomplished compared to what you set out to do.

4. List the five habits or attitudes that were the biggest obstacles to the achievement of the results you wanted. Write out a plan for changing these habits or attitudes. Conduct another time analysis study three months from now and compare the two. Determine whether you are making progress in replacing these habits or attitudes with new ones.

Conducting a detailed personal time-analysis study at least twice a year is a good habit to establish. Just as you schedule a regular medical checkup, plan for a time management checkup to keep you aware of how well you are using your time resources.

> **Put a dollar value on what you have to do; if it doesn't add up in dollars and cents, don't do it.**
>
> **- Edward J. Feeney**

Exhibit 15.1

Daily Time Summary

Record time every hour or more frequently to ensure an accurate record. Keep the record for an entire week. Activities listed are typical for salespeople.

	Prospecting	Telephone for Appointments	Sales Interviews	Travel	Reports and Paperwork	Meetings	Sales Training	Servicing Accounts	Preparing for Interviews	Studying Product Info.		
6 am												
7 am												
8 am												
9 am												
10 am												
11 am												
12 noon												
1 pm												
2 pm												
3 pm												
4 pm												
5 pm												
6 pm												
7 pm												
8 pm												
9 pm												
10 pm												

PROCEDURE FOR GETTING ORGANIZED

Before you can gain any measure of control over your time, you must address your need for laying the groundwork to handle the onslaught of information you encounter every day. Several techniques can help you.

Remove the Clutter

You can think more clearly and more creatively if you remove as much clutter as possible from your life and your living space. Remove unnecessary papers from your work area — your desk, your attaché case, your car. Even if the stacks of paper are neat and appear to be well organized, they promote a subconscious psychological tendency to review and think through the items in sight. In a very few seconds you can think through all of the tasks or incompletions that are represented by a sizable stack of paper. For all practical purposes, however, your mind does not differentiate between doing a task physically and doing it mentally. If you mentally review a big stack of paper a dozen times a day in the process of deciding which one to tackle next, or which one to avoid, you are exhausted long before the day is over. Once you decide to dispense with the clutter, tackle the job at once. Follow this plan:

Collect the Clutter. Gather up all the clutter that affects you and take it to one convenient work area. Empty your car, bedside table, pockets, and any other cubbyhole where you stick things that are waiting to be done. Dump all the clutter into one container.

Sort the Clutter. Divide the clutter into two categories: Time-critical material (that is, items with a specific due date) and "someday" material.

Deal With Priorities. Deal first with the time-critical items. Provide a series of thirty-one folders to represent the days of the month. (This is commonly called a 1-31 file.) Examine each of the items you have identified as time critical. If it involves a meeting or a specific hour of the day, write it on your calendar. Then put each item in the folder for the day that the first action must be taken to meet the due date. Each day check the appropriate folder as you make your daily to do list.

Set Up Working Categories for the Rest. Now begin to organize the someday material. Set up two convenient files — the stacked "in-out file boxes" are handy. Label these files reading and projects. Go through your someday items and sort them in the two files according to their nature.

Handle Interruptions

To handle them properly, you must first determine whether an occurrence is truly an interruption or part of your job. Only when you understand this difference are you able to control your attitude toward the people and the circumstances that threaten to get in your way as you are doing your job. Once you determine that an interruption is part of your job, decide whether it is more important than what you are currently doing or whether it should be postponed. This determination helps you keep your priorities straight and reduces procrastination.

Interruptions typically fall into three categories, each of which you can handle with the right attitude. The following is a list of the three types of interruptions — people, paper, and environment — and examples of the most common ways that people experience them.

People	Paper	Environmental
• Superior	• Notes	• Telephone calls
• Associate	• Memos	• Visual distractions
• Subordinate	• Correspondence	• Comfort factors
• Client or customer	• Periodicals	– temperature
	• Messages	– light
	• Projects	– clothing

People Interruptions. People interruptions are the most frustrating because they are the most difficult to solve, and who the person is makes a difference in the way you respond. If you are interrupted by your superior, remember that that person probably has the right to interrupt you. If you are working on an item of extreme importance with a tight deadline or are due to leave for an appointment with a prospect, however, you can properly ask respectfully whether your superior might wait until your project or call is completed. As your work is presumably important to the success of the organization, and therefore to your superior as well, most bosses consider such a request to be a mark of both effectiveness and self-confidence on your part.

When a client interrupts you either by phone or in person, adopt the attitude that this contact is not an interruption. You do not automatically put your full day at the disposal of a client's whim, but you do give full attention while the client is talking and then do whatever is necessary to take care of the situation.

Paper Interruptions. People who work in a disorganized environment experience both confusion and frustration when confronted with necessary paperwork. They feel confused because they have no automatic method for handling the item; they spend too long thinking about how to handle it. Then, because they dislike feeling confused, they become frustrated with the repeated inroads made on their time by additional paperwork. Before very long, disorganized people decide they just hate all paperwork. Salespeople are often among those who say they hate paperwork because they feel that it is less important in producing their income than their direct selling activities.

Environmental Interruptions. Distractions in your work space can wreak havoc on your productivity if not properly addressed and controlled. Instead of feeling overwhelmed by environmental distractions such as frequent phone calls, schedule a specific telephone time each day to set up appointments for sales presentations and take care of other sales-related business. Then the remainder of the day is free for those vital selling contacts. When you have a particularly important piece of work to complete, take everything you need to do the job and go to a place where you can work without any kind of interruption.

AN ORGANIZING SYSTEM

Once you remove the clutter and the incompletions from your work area and get a firm grip on controlling interruptions, three simple tools will help you organize your activities.

The Master Calendar

Many salespeople prefer a pocket-sized book that is always available to note an appointment. Whatever its size, the calendar should list only specific time commitments such as appointments with clients and meetings to attend. All the information needed for those specific commitments is collected in the 1-31 file folders or recorded on the computer master calendar until it is needed for the appointment or other commitment.

Daily To-Do List

The second time-organizational tool you will need is a daily to-do list. Be sure to prioritize each item on your list. Highlight those activities completed, and carry forward the uncompleted items. A familiar story about Charles Schwab, former president of Bethlehem Steel, confirms the real impact of this simple tool. Schwab called in consultant Ivy Lee and proposed, "Show me a way to get more done with my time, and I'll pay you any fee within reason."

"Fine," said Lee, "I'll give you something in twenty minutes that will increase your output at least fifty percent." Lee then handed Schwab a blank sheet of paper and said, "Write down the six most important tasks that you have to do tomorrow and number them in order of their importance. Now put this paper in your pocket, and the first thing tomorrow morning look at item one. Work on it until you finish it. Then do item two, and so on. Do this until quitting time.

Don't be concerned if you have finished only one or two. You'll be working on the most important items. If you can't finish them all by this method, you couldn't have finished them by any other method either; and without some system, you'd probably not even decide which was the most important."

Lee continued, "Use this system every working day. After you've convinced yourself of the value of the system, have your men try it. Try it as long as you wish and then send me a check for what you think it's worth." Several weeks later, Lee received Schwab's check for $10,000 — a much more impressive sum around the turn of the 20th century than it sounds now.

Remember you can't alter time. The trick to managing your time is to manage not your time, but your activities. Keep a daily to-do list of what needs to be accomplished and use the list to make sure your moving the sale forward. The value of a to-do list is apparent, but it becomes even more valuable when you use it not only to identify needed tasks but to establish priorities for them. Putting top priorities first is the only way to be sure that your activities are making a direct impact on your goals. Sales success depends on establishing and steadfastly pursuing a series of goals.

When you develop specific and measurable growth goals, you gain the determination and drive it takes to succeed. Figure 15.1 is an example of a format you can use for your to-do list. If you are using a computerized master calendar, you can print out your daily to-do list. The form is not nearly as important as the practice!

The Integrated System

The 1-31 reminder file, the master calendar, and the to-do list together constitute a place your mind can trust and a place where you can store all the reminders that must surface at a given time in the future. You can safely forget about incompletions until they surface in your system. Together these organizing tools form a system that makes organization of your daily activities an automatic process. At the close of each day's work, transfer any left-over items from today's to-do list to the new list for tomorrow. Then consult your 1-31 file and your master calendar to find all the items you have scheduled for tomorrow. Note any specific times associated with those items, such as the time for an appointment or meeting. Now you are ready to begin work tomorrow without even thinking about what to do first. You are ready to begin your day with the task of highest importance.

Exhibit 15.1

A To-do List with a Daily Plan to List Appointments

Priority	Done	Date _____ IMPORTANT	Priority	Done	Date _____ IMPERATIVE

Courtesy of Success Motivation, Inc.

THE HANDBOOK FOR RELATIONSHIP SELLING

Identifying Priorities

An important concept for good time managers to understand is the Pareto principle. It states that 80 percent of the value (or the frustration) of any group of related items is generally concentrated in only 20 percent of them. In other words, "a minority of the input produces a majority of the results." The principle, named for the Italian economist who proposed it, holds true for many areas of today's experience. For example:

In Measuring Value, You Receive . . .

80% of:

- Sales
- Productivity
- Profit
- Referrals
- Commisson Income

from 20% of:

- Customers
- Activity
- Products
- Clients
- Orders

In Measuring Frustration, You Experience . . .

80% of:

- Absenteeism
- Errors
- Servicing Problems

from 20% of:

- Employees
- Workers
- Customers

Likewise, 80 percent of your success comes through the achievement of the top 20 percent of your goals. In managing your time effectively, you must recognize that which items you complete, not how many items you complete, determine your success.

To identify the special 20 percent of your activities that have the potential for producing the greatest success, practice establishing different categories of priorities.

> **"A" priorities** are the most pressing. They include the items that must be done by a specific date if you are to reach one of your major goals and items that would damage the reputation of your company or your personal credibility if you failed to accomplish them.

> **"B" priority** items are any items that can be done at any time within the next week or month without causing any repercussions.

> **"C" priority** items would be nice to do at some time when you have nothing else pressing to do, but you would suffer no real loss if you never got around to them.

Obviously, you want to give first attention to your "A" priorities and carefully number them in the order of their importance. Your goal is to complete as many "A" priorities as you possibly can each day and then supplement them with any "B" items you can.

Time Goals

Once you have established the habit of using a to-do list, begin to record next to each item your estimate of the amount of time you will need to complete it. Estimating the required time lets you judge whether you can complete everything. If you can't, you have the possibility of getting someone else to help before you fail to complete some vital item. Time studies have shown that even people who know which items are most important and set priorities still waste an average of fifteen minutes between items of work in simple procrastination or in trying to decide what to do next.

A second benefit of estimating completion times is to help in avoiding procrastination. A deadline — even an informal estimate of the time required — pushes you to complete the work in the allotted time. Northcote Parkinson is noted for his observation that *work expands to fill the time allowed for its completion.* Something about a stated time allotment seems to establish a mental set that causes you to use just that amount of time. If the time is short, you work efficiently and push for completion. If the time allowance is too generous, you procrastinate, spend extra time getting ready to work, and find a dozen small interruptions to make sure you don't finish too early. By estimating times for completion, you eliminate the tendency to procrastinate.

MAINTAINING A POSITIVE ATTITUDE TOWARD TIME

Anyone who expects sales success should also expect hard work and long hours. If you always seem to have more work than working hours, though, you may be due for a refresher course in time management. These techniques can't give you more time, but they can help you make the most of what you've got. Follow them to help you get — and keep — time on your side.

Set Deadlines — and Beat Them. When you've got a lot to do and not a lot of time to do it in, deadlines can help you to stay on schedule. Prioritize your tasks, then draw up a schedule for completing them.

Learn to Say "No". When it comes to time management, many of us are our own worst enemy. You'll never have enough time to finish your work if you're always biting off more than you can chew. When people ask you to take on extra projects, they are putting unneccesary burden and stress on your shoulders. If you agree to take on too many jobs for others, you are soon carrying an impossible load of monkeys on your back and accomplish nothing.

Take Advantage of Your Peak Time. To be most efficient at the jobs you like least, tackle them at the time of day when you feel most productive. Pay attention to your moods and work output throughout the day to find out when you're most productive, and save your worst jobs for when you're at your best.

Place a Time Limit on Meetings. If you or your salespeople tend to dread meetings, maybe it's because they drag on too much and accomplish too little. Knowing your meeting lasts only an hour should help keep things moving. Before each meeting, decide on a limited number of topics to discuss and a limited time period for discussing them.

Don't Overload on Overtime. If your work week consistently exceeds a reasonable number of hours, ask yourself why. Identify the tasks that take up the most time and look for ways to complete them more efficiently. Also, compare the number of hours you're working to what you're actually getting done. A too-small return on your time investment indicates a problem.

Decide to Delegate. Don't feel guilty about delegating responsibility — if you take on a job that someone else could handle more effectively, you're not making the best use of your company's resources.

Put It in Writing. To remember phone numbers, important dates or anything else, write them down. Freeing your mind of clutter helps you think more clearly, and concentration is key to productivity.

MANAGING TRAVEL TIME IN YOUR SALES TERRITORY

One of the most important considerations for field salespeople is protecting their time for making those vital sales presentations. Travel through a territory — small or large — is, in a sense, nonproductive although necessary time. Linda Meyer, sales director for Oakstone Publishing Company in Maineville, Ohio, says, "Organize your time before you hit the road, not while on the road." She plans for time blocks — how long it will take her to write letters, do reports or recap a meeting. Look at your time as a 24-hour cycle of fragments. Travel time must be kept to a minimum.

The Pareto principle says that 80 percent of your business will come from 20 percent of your customers. Thus, you must determine how much time and energy each account receives. Scott Gander, a sales rep for Geneal, a company selling restaurant supplies, divides all accounts into A, B, C and D accounts. He tries to spend 40 percent of his time helping A's, 30 percent with B's, 20 percent with C's, and 10 percent with the D's — the D accounts are only interested in price. Be sure to categorize your accounts in a priority ranking such as:

"A" — High-volume, repeat customers.
"B" — Moderate sales volume, but reliable customers.
"C" — Lower-volume accounts.

"**D**" — Accounts that presently cost you more time and energy to service than you receive in sales and profits.

Field salespeople travel through time and space, so it will help if they set themselves in motion on the most efficient route between customers and prospects. Sales professionals pay close attention to the routing and scheduling of their calls. They take into consideration the proper mix of accounts on each trip. Prioritizing is useful for determining a profitable mix of account visitation and servicing. A common mistake is to call on "**D**" accounts simply because they are located near "**A**" accounts, and require little travel. These customers do not need to be called on with the same regularity as the "**A**" accounts. Instead use your time to prospect for new high volume, repeat customers.

COMPUTER MAPPING SYSTEMS

It's probably a safe bet that most sales managers have spent time with magic markers and paper maps to plot their sales reps' positions. Mapping systems, or Geographic Information Systems (GIS), is a rapidly growing market of sophisticated products which put numeric data into visual form, making the data easier to understand. These products create computer-generated maps of geographic areas of interest to both sales managers and their salespeople. This software is used to balance sales territories, optimize driving time, and target new markets and accounts. This desktop mapping software lets managers do in minutes what used to take hours, or even days to complete.

Unless you have intimate knowledge of all the ZIP codes in every sales territory, it's impossible to know which areas border one another, and which don't. "You can look at a spreadsheet, but there's no substitute for looking at them nicely mapped," says Richard Bohn, president of Denali Group. Spreadsheets and databases tell you how much and what kind, while mapping software tells you where.

Have Personal Data Assistance, Will Travel

Wherever your travels take you it helps to know where to eat, where to stay and what to see. Now all of this information is available in a handheld computer. Use the AvantGo Internet Information Service (www.avantgo.com) and download the information to your Personal Data Assistant. Avantgo choices include a mapping program for getting you from point A to point B and RestaurantRow.com that organizes restaurants based on ZIP code. The maps that are generated are so precise that large buildings, tunnels, bridges, and even historic landmarks are indicated. And it will even phone or e-mail a hotel reservation on your behalf through the channel's concierge service.

Dave Delmonte, sales engineer for Steel Heddle, uses a product called TripMaker that simplifies his trip planning. Delmonte types in his point of origin, his final destination, and any stopover points. In seconds, the digital atlas generates the appropriate map and compares alternate routes side-by-side. The program can help track expenses and budget costs for hotel, gas, meals, and also includes information on 2,800 restaurants and 12,000 hotels.

Strategize Your Prospect Calls

Like a leaf in the wind, many salespeople leave home in the morning with no idea where they're going. They go where the wind blows and when the wind changes direction, so do they. The solution is a good contact management system coupled with a good mapping system. The goal of all the various mapping programs is to minimize your travel time and maximize your selling time.

For example, Thom Frame, photo processing equipment salesman for Noritsu, uses a mapping system called *BusinessMap* to plan his road trips more efficiently. He covers a midwestern territory that spans seven states, requiring him to spend 70 percent of his time on the road. Frame says, "If I know that I will be visiting a customer in Milwaukee, I can map out my route so that I can call on customers on the drive out there as well as on the way back."

The uses of computer mapping systems are limited only by your creative imagination. For example, when prospects ask for referrals, really impress them by trying this: Use your mapping system to place the prospect on a map, and then use the system to draw a circle that identifies every one of your customers in a 25-mile radius. By doing this, you provide your prospect with a comprehensive and organized list of referrals who are within their proximity, which is important when providing referrals to potential customers.

This mapping technology also enables a sales rep to get a list of every potential customer in a geographic area and map it against a display of the company's existing accounts. The result is an up-to-date analysis of how well you have penetrated your territory and the potential that remains. Maximizing travel time is an obvious and critical competitive advantage for today's *Road Warriors*.

Time is like talent — you can't create more of it, you just have to make the most of what you've got. You need self-discipline from the time you wake up in the morning until you go to bed that night. Spending your time more wisely starts with paying attention to how you spend it. Once you decide to take control of your time, you'll have the power to stop squandering it.

Time, Territory, and
Personal Management

- The ability to manage time efficiently and effectively is largely a matter of attitude. Time is money. If you seek advancement and a comfortable income, managing time properly is one of the best skills you can develop.

- Interruptions are time wasters, so handle them with planning and control. Interruptions arise from people, paper, and environmental factors.

- A workable system for time management includes at least three elements:
  - A master calendar for scheduling commitments
  - A daily to-do list to record activities to be done each day to reach your goals and
  - A reminder file to hold items that will become important at a specific later date.

- Use mapping systems to balance sales territories, optimize driving time, and target new markets and accounts.

- PDAs allow you to download mapping software onto your handheld to make getting around and tracking appointments more convenient.